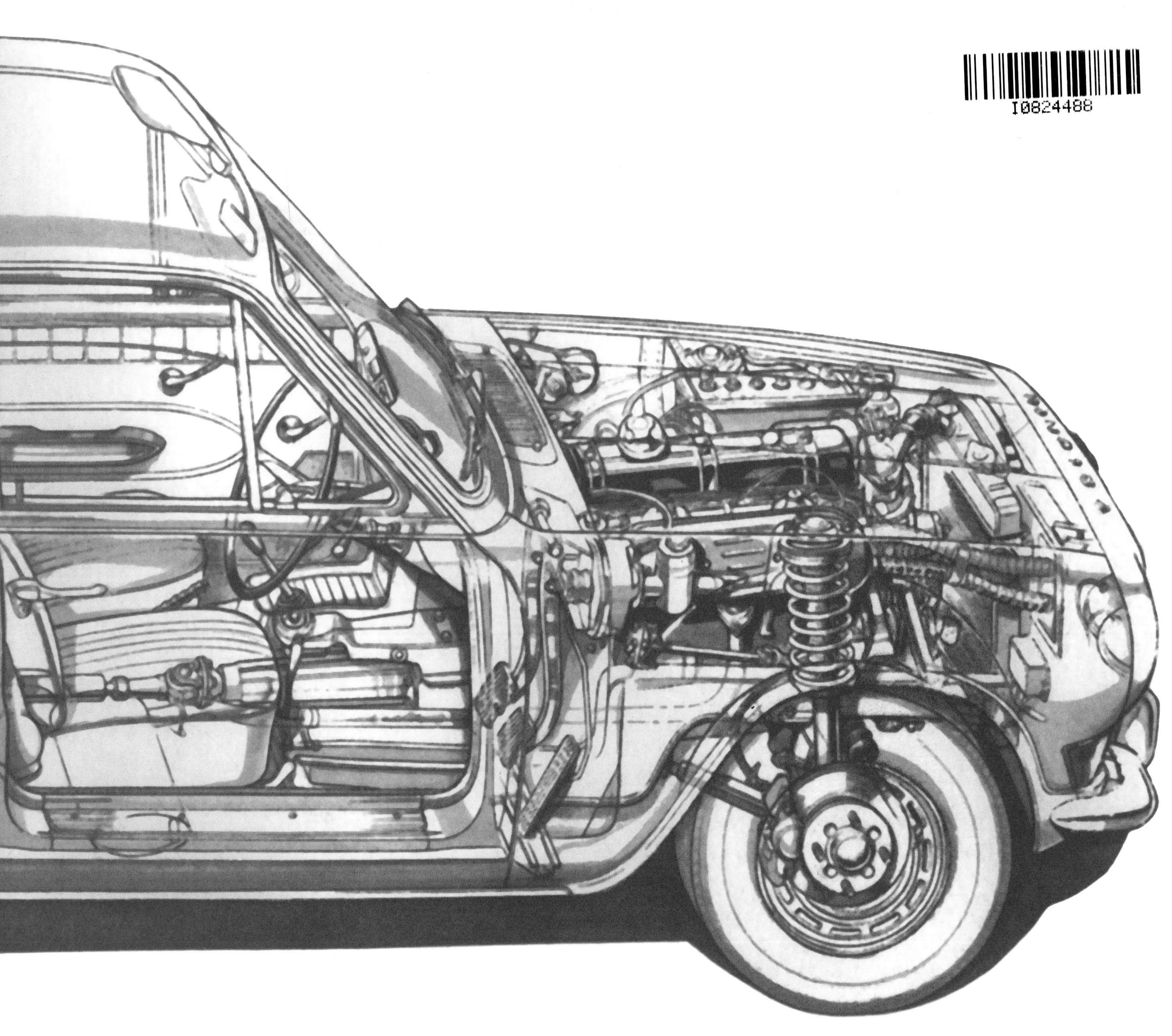

THE CARS OF THE 60s

A HISTORY OF CARS MANUFACTURED AND ASSEMBLED IN AUSTRALIA DURING THE 1960S
NH
NEW HOLLAND

THE CARS OF THE 60S

GAVIN FARMER

DODGE

CONTENTS

ACKNOWLEDGEMENTS

This book would not have been possible without the assistance of a great many people, all enthusiasts for their particular marque or model. Included in this illustrious group were Paul Hickman from the Chevrolet Club, the late Laurie Cousins from the Triumph Owners Club, Jonathan and Dianne Pyle who coordinated various members of the Vauxhall Club to have their cars photographed, John Roberts, David Robinson and Monica Kruger from the Humber Car Club, from the Chrysler world I had assistance from Chris Cowan, Brenton Hamilton, Ian Webber and Steve Tyler (librarian for the CRCSA), Peter Tavener, Fraser Ludlow, Matthew Lambert and Leighton Passant from the Hillman Car Clubs, Vin Youngman, (Ms) Lesley Bourman, Margaret Chapman and Bill Watson from the Morris Car Club, Ralph Drage and Ron Burchett from the Austin Car Club, Ross Kerslake and Henri Redman from the Standard Car Club

From the Ford enthusiasts I received assistance from Graham Tonkin, Bob Kennaway, Neil Phillips, Peter North, Peter Fry, Don Henley, Michele Cook and Doug Wallace; from the Holden world I had help from Stuart Underwood, Geoff Francis and Robin Camen; John Whittaker from the Mercedes-Benz Club; David McDonough, Ted Mereweather and Simon Fitzpatrick from the Renault movement; Jim Quinn, John Brown and Ross Fleming from Simca; Rod Davies, Phil Matthews and Dean Hosking from the VW world; Marius Venz and Tim Kelly helped where the Lloyd Hartnett was concerned; Brenton Thomas, Jim Quigley, Darryl Jones and Michael Pink assisted where Studebaker was concerned ;not to mention Matthew McAuley, Peter Wilson, Gordon Miller and Mac Chapman for Peugeot; Bill Buckle regarding Goggomobils; and Bob Freeman and Colin Mann where the history of Rambler was needed.

I also had considerable help from Pedr Davis, Ted O'Brien, John Regan, Kenneth Wright Jnr, Robert Simpson, Richard Johns, Max Gregory as well as people from the Sporting Car Club in Adelaide and the National Motor Museum at Birdwood, South Australia.

INTRODUCTION

Following the boom times of the fifties, the sixties became a decade of consolidation on the one hand, and a series of challenges on the other, some economic and some political. It marked the beginning of a very real challenge from Ford on GM-Holden as well as from Chrysler and several Japanese manufacturers that had quietly entered the Australian market. The decade began with a federal government credit squeeze that created difficult times for the whole industry.

Holden with its FB range continued its dominance with a market share that rose to as high as 50 per cent. However, it was under siege from the XK Ford Falcon released in September 1960 and two years later Chrysler released the powerful and very stylish R series Valiant to enormous acclaim. The Valiant was to single-handedly change Australian car buying habits forever. Think about that: The two major British manufacturers operating here, BMCA and the Rootes Group, did not improve their position in the market as a whole and in fact began to slowly lose ground, their market share stagnating as the market itself grew substantially.

BMCA began the decade with its conventionally engineered Morris, Austin and Wolseley sedans and wagons plus the MG A sports car. However, it abandoned its well-trodden path and ventured into new territory that would ultimately lead to its demise. It began with the Mini 850 in 1962 (in Australia) followed by the Morris 1100 in 1963 and the Austin 1800 in 1965. Technically and conceptually they were fine cars but their manufacturing qualities left much to be desired and soon buyers departed BMC showrooms and migrated to the Japanese manufacturers who had established a reputation for supreme reliability even though their products were very conventionally and conservatively engineered. Goodies like a radio, heater/demister and a set of tools merely added spice to their offerings but all other makers looked down their noses at such frippery, to their cost.

Toyota had entered into an assembly agreement with AMI from the beginning (1963) with the Tiara, which was added to the Rambler, Mercedes-Benz and Standard-Triumph products already in its portfolio. As the decade unfolded AMI/Toyota added the Corona, Crown and Corolla models to the range and set the stage for massive expansion through the latter years of the millennium.

Meanwhile, Volkswagen had increased local content in its Beetle and Kombi and by 1963 had added the assembly of the new Type 3 VW 1500 sedan, wagon and (later) fastback to its range. Fiat dipped its toe into the water with limited assembly of its 600 and 1100 in collaboration with Pressed Metal Corporation in Sydney but the volume was not there and that program was soon closed. Prince Motors from Japan announced that assembly of Prince cars would begin in collaboration with Larke Consolidated Industries who owned PMC but nothing came of that because Prince was absorbed into the Nissan fold.

With the rise and rise of the Japanese there were some casualties among the more traditional makers. BMC, Rootes, Renault, Fiat and later Volkswagen all lost market share to the point where the businesses were no longer profitable and eventually led to the departure of all of them from the local market.

The sixties saw the beginnings of Australia's power wars with the likes of the Ford Falcon GT sedan, Holden Monaro GTS coupe, and the Chrysler Pacer sedan. In 1960 we had the first of the real production sedan races, the Armstrong 500 (miles), run at Phillip Island before being transferred to the Mount Panorama circuit near Bathurst and renamed the Hardie-Ferodo 1000 (kilometres). It has gone on to become one of the biggest sporting events in Australia and attracted the crème de la crème of the world's drivers.

The big story in Australia in the sixties was the emergence of the compact class of car epitomised by the Holden Torana that evolved out of the dreadfully dull Vauxhall Viva. By 1968 it had been developed by Australian engineers into a compact six-cylinder car that opened a new market segment missed by its rivals. Ford entered the small-car market with a dual attack: firstly the 105E Anglia followed two years later by the Consul Cortina that was a huge international success.

The other major story for the local motor industry was the rise of medium-sized luxury saloons derived from their plainer siblings. Ford initiated this market with the release of their ZA Fairlane in 1967 with Holden following some time later with their Brougham, which proved not to be a competitor, and Chrysler trailed along with their VIP by Chrysler that sold in minuscule numbers.

It was in the sixties when the Japanese manufacturers really established a foothold in Australia. Datsun arrived first with the quaint-but-outdated Bluebird sedan, wagon and utility followed by the impressively ugly Cedric, but by 1964 there was a new Pininfarina-styled Bluebird 1200, the six-cylinder Datsun 2000, and the Fairlady sports car. Later in the decade came the sensational Datsun 1600. Local assembly of Datsun sedans began in late 1966 at Pressed Metal in Sydney before transferring to Clayton in Victoria at the under-used VW factory.

In the sixties Australia lost its innocence and life changed in every way; the 'good ol' days' as they were remembered were gone. Established companies were floundering and failing as they were left behind in the dash to modernise and re-equip old factories – the Germans and the Japanese all had brand new factories full of the latest-technology equipment that meant parts could be made faster and cheaper – and so the old order rather quickly changed. Today began back then. Think about it.

Gavin Farmer
Bridgewater, 2023

Austin
NSW
EYB-374

Chapter 1

GENERAL MOTORS-HOLDEN

The first Australian car to be released for the new decade was the FB Holden that was announced on 12 January 1960. Although described as 'all new' by Holden's PR and advertising people, in reality it was little more than a minor upgrade of mechanical components under a new body design that was in so many ways old before it was new. The FB's styling was clearly based on the 1957 Chevrolet so it was already three years old in styling ideas when it was released.

For GM enthusiasts the cues were there for all to see – the vertical A-pillar, wraparound windscreen, rear fender fins with vertical light units (the difference being that the tail-lights at the base of the fin were round on the FB, semicircular on the Chev), while the curvature of the roof was almost identical. Inside was a glamorous new dashboard that was again based on themes from Chevrolet but still only told the driver how fast they were driving and how much fuel was in the tank. For the first time the old scuttle air flap was consigned to the bin and in its place was a wide air-inlet vent at the base of the windscreen that led air into a plenum chamber before being trunked into the interior, or through a heater when fitted. Critics complained that the FB's styling was too American but that never stopped the buyers who had supported Holden to market dominance since 1948. In its life it was easily Australia's best-selling car and GM-H enjoyed a remarkable 50 per cent market share with what was basically a one-model range consisting of sedan, wagon, utility and panel van.

It was longer, wider and more powerful than its predecessors. Mind you, the increases were marginal; although there were some significant mechanical improvements that Holden made a big deal about in 1960 but which today we would wonder why they bothered. The reason was simply that expectation levels were not in the stratosphere like they are today. For example, the engine's cylinder bore was increased from 76.2 to 77.5mm (the crank stroke was unaltered) taking the capacity up to 2262cc, its power output rose from 72bhp to 75bhp at 4200rpm. In addition, there were wider rear leaf springs, wider brake drums for greater lining area, stronger front wheel bearings, a bigger radiator and a stronger gearbox. All were part of the ongoing development program that Holden had set in play once the Lang Lang proving ground had been commissioned.

Australian Motor Manual carried out a comparison test between the FB Holden and XK Falcon and in the opening paragraph of the report said, "Stylewise the Falcon is the leader, its long, low and wide lines, like those of the Vauxhall Velox are more in concert with today's trends than the FB's shape and the simplicity of the exterior adornments will appeal to folk with conservative tastes." While the exterior styling of the FB was conservative (old-fashioned even) they liked the Holden's dashboard more than the Falcon's, which appeared to have been drawn in haste. And on the score of fit and finish the Holden won easily. As for power and performance it was lineball between the two cars with the lighter (and more fragile) Falcon having a 3.2 km/h (2mph) advantage top speed – 134km/h (84mph) versus 130.8km/h (82mph) – and a quicker 0–96km/h (0–60mph) acceleration time of 17.1 seconds against 20.7 seconds. To the then average motorist these small differences were insignificant and had little influence on the buying decision. Trade-in and discounts had a far bigger say.

The mildly facelifted EK model (note the new nomenclature) arrived in showrooms on 2 May 1961 and sported a new, much bolder grille, new badges and, importantly, the availability for the first time of the Hydramatic three-speed automatic transmission for an extra £119. Lost in the hype was the fact that the EK was the first Holden ever to have electric windscreen wipers, the dangerous old vacuum system being consigned to the rubbish bin where it should have been all along; and it had an internal bonnet release. The Falcon initially took sales away from the FB and EK but it was soon apparent that the Falcon was no match for the ruggedness of the Holden. From a performance point of view there was little between the Holden and Ford; although once Chrysler entered the market with the R Series Valiant both were left in its tyre smoke.

To some extent Holden made up ground on Ford with the much more modern looking EJ that arrived on 30 July 1962. It was lower by 88mm (3.5in) (1473mm compared with 1562mm, 58in compared with 61.5in), an inch wider at 1727mm (68in) and almost 127mm (5in) shorter at 4521mm (178in) on a 2667mm (105in) wheelbase, and still remained a comfortable six-seater that came as a saloon, station wagon, panel van and utility. Mechanically it was a carry-over from EK (and the FB in so many respects) although there was a new three-speed manual gearbox that had a separate clutch housing, and there were now reinforced seatbelt anchorage points in the body. Unlike the troublesome Falcon, the EJ came with a proven reputation for being able to cope with local conditions. Interestingly, the commercial models were held over and not released until February 1963.

Going with the neater but understated exterior with its Chevrolet-like panoramic windscreen was a completely new dashboard that had a prominent hooded instrument binnacle (that was sparsely instrumented in the Holden tradition) sited on top of a sloping upper section with a triangular-shaped foam padded section that stretched full width across the front of the panel; a metal section below (painted body colour) contained the switches and provision for the optional radio and heater/demister controls.

With the EJ, Holden introduced buyers to the more luxuriously equipped Premier sedan and wagon, available for the first time to those for whom status was important. Exterior clues were iridescent metallic paint, special bonnet and fender badges and nameplates, while its equipment list was impressively long including standard Hydramatic transmission, reversing lights, heater/demister with fan, individually contoured front seats with two-toned leather upholstery, floor carpet, front centre console, centre armrest in the rear seat and door armrests, as well as a host of smaller details.

While it was a huge step forward in style, the weightier Premier – 1196kg (2632lb) compared with 1132kg (2492lb) – was noticeably slower than the Special sedan when tested by *Modern Motor* in its September 1962 issue. Flat out on the Lang Lang high speed loop the Special recorded a speed of 131km/h (82mph) while the Premier could manage only 123km/h (77mph) and the 0–96km/h (0–60mph) acceleration run took 18.0 sec for the Special, 25.5 sec for the Premier. Nevertheless, the writer predicted that Holden would continue as market leader because of the EJ's style, excellent finish and proven ruggedness. At £1420 it was more expensive than the Ford Futura, which was priced at £1398 and had more power and performance, and the Wolseley 24/80 (the car that really started the trend) which cost a very reasonable £1340 as an automatic.

Holden announced its most significant new model since the 48-215 in the form of the EH range that appeared in August 1963 and with it reasserted its position in the market place. Chrysler had certainly set the cat amongst the pigeons with the 145bhp Valiant sedan. In response

Holden designed, developed and tooled the completely new 'red' motor that was described as totally new (but it did in all fairness share many aspects of its design with the American Chevy II six-cylinder engine). Cylinder block and head were made from cast-iron while the crank was a seven-bearing forging and the overhead valves featured hydraulic tappets, a first for an Australian-made engine. The 'red' engine was available in two capacities, 149 and 179 cubic inches, both sharing a 76.2mm (3in) stroke with slightly different bore widths – 82.55mm (3.25in) for the 149 and 90.5mm (3.563in) for the 179. On a compression ratio of 8.8:1 the 149 gave 75kW (100bhp) at 4400rpm (up 33 per cent on the old grey motor) while the 179 delivered 86kW (115bhp, up a whopping 53 per cent) at a slightly slower 4000rpm. Despite the huge power (and torque) increase Holden retained the 9in drum brakes all round and basic suspension system, as was the norm for the times.

Overnight the rules of the game had changed; Holden was on the offensive and would take no prisoners. Performance was now something openly talked about, and only Valiant could match or exceed it.

The EH was a facelifted EJ, most of the styling updating taking place at the rear of the body where the roofline was squared up with the so-called Thunderbird line (copied from the US Ford Thunderbird by Holden and others) and the boot was similarly squared up with a much flatter line and higher rear quarter panels that added significantly to luggage space. The tail-lights were now vertical – amber on top for indicators, red below for tail and stop light with a reflector between them – while at the front the grille had a new texture and the badges were repositioned. All EH Holdens powered by the 179cid six sported a 179 badge (with a chequered flag behind it) on the boot lid; if a 149 engine was ordered there was no badge of identity.

An interesting four-car comparison was published in *Wheels*, November 1963, in which the EH Holden 179 was pitted against the AP5 Valiant 225, XL Falcon 170 and Austin Freeway. The Holden leapt from the slowest (EJ) to be the quickest in this contest, nudging out the Valiant slightly in top speed (147km/h (91.9mph) compared with 145.7km/h (91.1mph)) and the 0–80km/h (0–50mph) sprint (10.1 sec versus 10.4 secs). The other two cars were left quite some way behind.

The Holden was considered to be the best made and the Freeway was by far the best equipped although it was noticeably smaller in size and therefore accommodations.

There was a special version of the EH made available in September 1963 for competition purposes (Holden had their eye on a victory at Bathurst but a Ford Cortina thwarted their plans) called the S4, although it was also referred to in-house as the 179M, with the legendary Norm Beechey being one of the first to race one along with Brian Muir. It was a limited production special of 120 units but GM-H later changed that to say they would build as many as the market demanded after an altercation with the race organisers. Because there was an international ban by General Motors on racing the S4 was entered by some GM-H dealers.

What was upgraded? Surprisingly GM-H never admitted to any power improvements to the engine (it still quoted 86kW (115bhp) and 237Nm (175lb-ft)) but the availability of the stronger manual gearbox suggested it was more powerful. Out of sight the brakes were improved with sintered-metallic brake linings (still 228mm (9in) drums!), 3.55:1 differential, heavy duty dampers, stronger clutch, gears and tail shaft, larger fuel tank (55 litres/12gal up from 43 litres/9.5gal), blue-printed engine and stronger wheels. It retailed for a modest £1160 with most of them being painted a fire engine red with a contrasting white roof. Later, from January 1964, GM-H offered the manual gearbox as an option behind the 179 engine for an extra £23. *Modern Motor* tested a 179 manual and was mightily impressed with the car except for the brakes which they said were 'overtaxed'. As for performance, it ran 0–96km/h (0–60mph) in 13.0 sec, 0–112km/h (0–70mph) in 18.8 sec and had a best top speed of 160.4km/h (100.3mph) with 64km/h (40mph) available in first gear and 115km/h (72mph) in second. It was a performance bargain. Although most critics would not have foreseen it, the arrival of the new 'red' engines was the beginning of a whole new era at Holden.

In keeping with Holden's policy of a new model almost every 18 months, the EH gave way in February 1965 to the much-anticipated HD (new series name) range. Mechanically the new models were simply carryover EH under a completely new US-designed body that was the first from Holden to feature curved side glass. When released the HD created quite a controversy with the media and public alike with its very rounded body proportions and unusual 'cheese cutter' leading edges to the front fenders. Former director of styling at GM-H, Leo Pruneau, worked on the HD's styling in Detroit and commented, "I hated those sharp fender ends so each night I'd smooth them off the clay model only to be told by Bill Mitchell, GM's Czar of styling, to put them back on in the morning! They were dreadful and the buyers thought so too."

Body length was now 4569mm (179.9in) (up 50.8mm/2in), wheelbase was an inch longer (now 2692mm/106in), width was 1778mm (70in, up 50.8mm/2in) and body height was 1498mm (59in, up 25.4mm, an inch) and there was an increase in weight (1183kg versus 1134kg (2603lb versus 2496lb)), with the result that they might have been roomier inside but their dynamics were the worst of any Holden so far. Part of the problem was the fact that the wheel tracks were too narrow for the much wider, more bulbous body and the engineers had softened the spring rates a little for a better ride thereby increasing body lean quite dramatically. The media was not kind to Holden or the HD, some unkind critics referring to it as "Holden's Disaster" or similar derogatory names.

A new more powerful engine option arrived with HD, the 179 X2 with dual Stromberg carburettors, cast exhaust headers, revised camshaft lift and valves plus a higher compression ratio to give 104kW (140bhp) at 4600rpm. As an option priced at £145 it was probably the high point of the HD's brief career!

What was intriguing was the replacement of the Hydramatic automatic with the cheaper Powerglide *two*-speed automatic transmission. Many saw this as a backward, cost-cutting, step. Listed for the first time as an option were vacuum-assisted disc front brakes.

To nobody's real surprise, the HD had a relatively short production life (14 months) to be replaced by the much better-looking HR in April 1966, several months ahead of schedule. Not only were the controversial cheese cutter front fender elements gone but the front was tidied up and looked much cleaner and more appealing while at the rear a similar job had been carried out with neat vertical tail-light units replacing the around-the-corner items from the HD. Importantly, the car's wheel tracks had been widened (only by an inch to 1397mm/55in front and rear) to fill out the wheel arches more fully and give the car's style better balance; it also helped the car's dynamics considerably.

New with the HR were two expanded capacity engines, the former 149 unit was taken out to 161cid and the 179 was out to 186cid. Cylinder dimensions were 85.7 x 76.2mm (3.375 x 3.00in) for the smaller unit and 92 x 76.2mm (3.625 x 3in) for the larger engine; power outputs were now 85kW (114bhp) at 4400rpm and 94kW (126bhp) at 4200rpm respectively and as an option buyers could specify the X2 version of the 186cid engine that featured dual Stromberg down draft carburettors and a dual exhaust manifold for more power (108kW/145bhp at 4600rpm) and performance. Torque outputs were 212Nm (157lb/ft) at 2000rpm, 245Nm (181lb/ft) at 1600rpm and 249Nm (184lb/ft) at 2200rpm respectively. In August 1967 the X2 designation was replaced by 186S and the carburettor was now a single twin-barrel Stromberg; output remained the same.

Several new options were made available in HR, items like an Opel-sourced four-speed all-synchromesh manual gearbox with a floor shift, limited slip differential (LSD), power steering and a vinyl roof.

Both *Australian Motor Manual* and *Modern Motor* published road tests of the HR X2 and both were impressed with its power and performance which saw it achieve a maximum speed of 153.2km/h (95.8mph – the car was a Premier X2 with Powerglide automatic) and a 0–96km/h (0–60mph) time of 12.6 seconds from *MM*. *AMM* achieved a time of 11.5 seconds and a slightly quicker top speed. The disc front brakes came in for praise and the X2's handling was described as "well-mannered and forgiving" even if body roll was most noticeable and understeer was of monumental proportions.

On 28 January 1968 Holden announced the new HK range of vehicles – sedans, wagons, vans and utilities – to great acclaim. Not only was the HK longer, wider and lower but it featured the then in vogue long-nose-and-short-tail styling theme that Ford had brought to Australia with their XR Falcon 18 months earlier. These cars were significantly larger than any previous Holden, the wheelbase having been increased to 2819mm (111in) taking the overall length to 4674mm (184in), width to 1814mm (71.4in) and height to 1460mm (57.5in) while weight had risen to more than 1280kg (2810lb) for the base six-cylinder sedan. HK brought new model names to the Australian motoring landscape – Belmont to replace the former Standard and Kingswood in place of Special, the Premier name continuing on from before.

Several new safety features were included in the HK due to the impact of the Australian Design Rules (ADR). These included dual brake circuits, double-sided safety wheel rims, energy absorbing collapsible steering column, front seatbelts, burst-proof door locks and recessed interior switches and door handles.

Significantly, the HK range could be ordered with an imported Chevrolet 307cid V8 developing 156kW (210bhp) at 4600rpm and 406Nm (300lb-ft) at 2400rpm while the previous 161, 186 and 186S six-cylinder engines were carried over. Holden's marketing people decreed that buyers should have the option of specifying their own individual Holden by simply ticking boxes on the dealer order form; this meant that a bewildering array of options were available, something that created a nightmare for the production and purchasing people. Not only was there a choice of three six-cylinder and two V8 engines, there were gearbox choices, brake and suspension choices plus a myriad of interior selections to be made.

HVN-443

HVN-441

Test reports soon appeared in newspapers and magazines around the country and all were positive in their tone. What was immediately obvious was the vast improvement in handling: "It is no longer the kneeling, mushy, swaying car that the HD-HR series had become," said *Wheels*, April 1968. Styling was liked by some, felt to be bland and uninteresting by others, while the roominess of the car's interior and boot was appreciated as was its ride and general quietness. Against the clock the V8 version with the Powerglide automatic took 12.2 seconds for the 0–96km/h (0–60mph) dash, ran to a 150km/h (94mph) top speed and returned 19–14 litres per 100km (15–20mpg) while the 186-engined Kingswood (also with the two-speed automatic) needed 15.5 seconds for 0–96km/h (0–60mph), ran an equal 150km/h (94mph) top speed and returned 11.8–10 litres per 100km (24–28mpg).

Six months later the Australian motoring public was stunned by a dual announcement from the company: the release of the luxury Holden Brougham together with the two-door hardtop Monaro range. Top of the Monaro range was the GTS 327 that packed a big imported (from Chevrolet in the US) 327cid V8 engine under the bonnet, Muncie four-speed manual gearbox, wide tyres and standard front disc brakes (they were a puny 254mm/10in diameter), radius rods on the rear axle plus the obligatory body stripes. Buyers could order from a wide range of options from a basic Monaro with the 161cid six and three-speed column shifter up to Premier levels of luxury. Monaro paralleled the sedans in its specifications and equipment. The range plus options was incredibly wide and this, combined with sporting successes, gave sales an enormous fillip.

From a styling perspective the Monaro had that 'something' that lured buyers to it even though certain cynics described it as a Kingswood with a fastback roofline! Here for the first time was a big, Aussie-designed and built coupe that could challenge the world. Interior roominess was on a par with the sedans with access to the rear seat being through longer doors and tip-forward bucket seats with a backrest lock. In a typically Holden cost-cutting measure the Monaro retained the rather ordinary looking Kingswood dashboard and as part of the sporty feeling the tachometer was plonked down on the centre console where it was almost impossible to read. Holden, however, was not disappointed with Monaro sales.

As Ford had done the previous year, Holden enjoyed a maiden-outing racing victory at Bathurst thereby guaranteeing the Monaro hero and legend status forever.

Prior to the race *Wheels* published a comparison test between the Monaro GTS 327 and a Falcon XT GT, much of the driving being carried out at the Mount Panorama circuit near Bathurst. Which would win? That was the question. With its bigger 110-litre (24gal) tank several thought the Monaro had a huge advantage provided of course that it was reliable enough to reach the finish line. What was obvious after driving the pair was that the Falcon was the most comfortable and easiest to control, the Monaro's ride being judged as harsh, its gearshift clunky and the steering was heavy. By way of comparison, the same testers described the Monaro 186S as a 'darling car', so easy was it to live with. Against the clock the Monaro GTS 327 was clearly faster at 195km/h (122mph) versus 187km/h (117mph) (there must have been a problem with the GT) and it took just 7.8 seconds for the 0–96km/h (0–60mph) dash compared with a comparatively slow 9.6 seconds.

The Brougham, however, has all but disappeared off the radar and been forgotten as a cynical low-cost attempt to compete with Ford's Fairlane in the luxury car stakes. All it was in reality was a Premier sedan with an extended (by 203mm/8in!) tail and little else that could not be had in the better value for money Premier. The only engine on offer was the 307cid V8 mated to the Powerglide two-speed automatic, power boosted front disc brakes were standard and the limited slip differential ratio was 2.73:1; kerb weight was a hefty 1475kg (3247lb)). Frigidaire air conditioning, 11 transistor push-button radio, reclining front seats and electric windows were offered as options on the Brougham, another first with the HK range. As several GM-H people involved at the time said, the Brougham was all rather late in the day and done in one hell of a hurry.

A comparison test between the Brougham and Ford Fairlane 500 was published in *Australian Motor Manual*, January 1969 and it soon became clear that the Fairlane was the superior car. It was the better handling car with less body roll and was more predictable at the limit but against that the Brougham was better on corrugated surfaces showing less of a tendency to skitter across the road; although the longer wheelbase on the Fairlane gave it a superior ride with less fore-aft pitching and it soaked up irregularities more effectively. But the killer comment as far as the Brougham was concerned read, "As prestige cars both the Fairlane and Brougham have a lot of appeal. In appearance the Brougham is a little flashier than the Ford, but the Ford is decidedly the larger car – and it doesn't look as much like a Falcon as the Brougham does a Premier."

There was not a lot in it where performance was concerned, the Fairlane 500 running to 168km/h (105mph) and taking 11.0 seconds to dash from 0–96km/h (0–60mph) where the Brougham managed 163km/h (102mph) and 11.6 seconds, the Ford taking 17.4 seconds for the standing quarter mile versus the Holden taking 18.4 seconds.

The remaining two years of the sixties saw minor updates on the HK body to bring buyers, the HT in May 1969, its claim to fame being that it was the first Holden to have a moulded plastic grille and to be powered by the optional Australian-designed-and-manufactured 253 and 308cid V8 engines. Cosmetically the HT was distinguished by the larger tail-light assemblies, revised badges and the articulated windscreen wiper arm for the driver's side wiper. Inside, the dash pressing remained the same but the instrument unit now had round dials in it – the Monaro now had proper round dials including a tachometer located where it should have been all along. A new all-synchromesh three-speed manual gearbox (M15) came with the HT while in the Brougham the Chev 307cid V8 was replaced in September 1969 by the Australian-built 308cid V8.

For the HT Monaro, released in August, the 327 V8 was replaced by the more powerful (and heavier) Chev 350cid V8 in two states of tune – 223kW (300bhp) for those equipped with a manual gearbox and 205kW (275bhp) for those with the automatic gearbox. Little else, badges apart, was changed. If it ain't broke don't fix it seemed to be the plan.

The Kingswood and Monaro story will be continued in *Australian Cars of the 70s*.

TORANA

With the influx of smaller and less expensive cars from Japan it became necessary for Holden to address their impact on the market. To this end the company assembled the Vauxhall Viva from March 1964 until early 1967. It was reasonably successful but certain attributes of the Viva counted against it, notably its bland, boxy styling and sparse interior fittings. Unusually, the Viva was a 'clean sheet' design from Vauxhall and featured a 1057cc OHV four-cylinder engine (74.6 x 60.9mm) that produced 37kW (50bhp) at 5200rpm and drove the rear wheels through a new four-speed all synchromesh gearbox with a remote floor shift; suspension was by leaf springs front and rear (transverse up front, longitudinal at the rear with a torque tube mounting) while steering was by rack and pinion (a first for Vauxhall) and braking was by small cast-iron drums all round. What the boxy shape did confer on the Viva was a very roomy interior and a cavernous boot.

Modern Motor published a full test (July 1964) and gave it a reasonable report but the reporter found many items that could have been better – boomy exhaust, doors that clanged when closed, very noisy engine and gearbox, poor equipment level and so on. However, the little car's on-road performance was praised with its top speed being 115km/h (72mph), its 0–80 and 96km/h (0–50 and 60mph) times being 13.9 and 21.6 seconds respectively and it returned more than 9.4 litres per 100km (30mpg) after all tests. That put it on a par with the Morris 1100, Hillman Imp, Triumph Herald and Ford Anglia. At £885 for the Deluxe model it was considered to be reasonably good value for money.

Back in England, Leo Pruneau was a key member of a team charged with spicing up the Viva's styling to make it more appealing to a wider audience. This new body came to Australia and was released on 21 May 1967. It was assembled from CKD components until September 1968 when full local manufacture began. The new car carried the name Torana, an Aboriginal word meaning 'to fly'.

The HB was almost an all-new design because apart from the engine and gearbox very little was carried over from the Viva. It was also quite a bit larger now standing on an 2197mm (86.5in) wheelbase, stretching 4115mm (162in) overall by 1600mm (63in) wide by 1320mm (52in) tall and weighed 795kg (1750lb).

Modern Motor carried out a full comparison test between the Torana SL and Toyota Corolla in its October 1967 issue and found it difficult to separate the two so close were they in specification and capabilities. The Torana was more expensive ($1951 compared with $1748) but was larger inside especially in the back seat and had a far more capacious boot. The Corolla was felt to be better finished; although neither car was quiet when driven hard, the Torana's handling on rough bitumen and dirt roads was rated as excellent whereas the Corolla was skittish. From a performance perspective both cars had top speeds of 138km/h (86mph) but the Corolla was slightly quicker from 0–96km/h (0–60mph) at 15.1 seconds versus 19.6 seconds.

In the same month *Wheels* carried a comparison test between the Torana, Hillman Imp, Toyota Corolla and Datsun 1000. It was 42kW, 41kW, 45kW and 46kW (56bhp versus 55bhp, 60bhp and 62bhp); $1795 versus $1799, $1758 and $1778 respectively; 772kg against 713, 702 and 646kg (1698lb against 1569, 1545 and 1422lb); 130km/h versus 135, 136 and 122km/h (81.8mph versus 84.3, 84.7 and 76.5mph). The Torana was by far the roomiest and best handling but its equipment levels and finish were not as good as the two Japanese rivals.

The most obvious difference between the UK Viva and Australian HB Torana was the use on the local car of round Lucas headlights in place of the rectangular units used in England. Initially it was available as a two-door sedan in S and SL trim (S was equivalent to a Belmont and SL was trimmed to Kingswood levels) but with local manufacture a four-door sedan variant was introduced some weeks later. From September 1968 specification changes were introduced that included a collapsible steering column, dual-circuit braking system and two-speed wipers while inside a new instrument nacelle housed round dials in place of the previously rectangular one. Engine capacity was raised to 1159cc by boring the cylinders from 74.6mm to 77.7mm.

While the base engine was essentially the Viva unit and the Torana carried over the rack and pinion steering (a first for Holden), the Torana now sported the then fashionable Coke-bottle styling along with a short nose and a long(ish) tail that housed a huge boot. Where Torana differed markedly from the original Viva was in its suspension; the Vauxhall engineers had developed a completely new double wishbone and coil spring front suspension and a four-link coil spring system to suspend the live rear axle. Tiny 12in slotted steel wheel rims shod with 6.20 x 12 cross-ply tyres were standard as were tiny 215mm (8.5in) disc front brakes without boost.

Even though sales were at a reasonable level, buyers complained about the relative lack of performance and in response Holden introduced the Torana SL70 in mid-1968. It had a higher compression ratio (9.0 instead of 8.5:1), a different camshaft and Stromberg carburettor which raised its output from 42kW (56bhp) at 5400rpm to 52kW (69bhp) at an excruciating 5800rpm. Maximum speed remained at 131–134km/h (82–84mph) while the 0–96km/h (0–60mph) time came down to 15.6 seconds with its economy staying at 30+mpg.

In a further attempt to garner some of the more overtly sporting market held by the Mini Cooper S and the Cortina GT, Holden introduced the Brabham-Torana in May 1967. The engine was worked over to include dual Stromberg CD carburettors, 9.0:1 compression, sports camshaft and extractor exhaust system, power rising to 60kW (79bhp) at 5600rpm. External clues to the model included Brabham badges and bonnet stripes while inside was a new instrument package with matching large speedo and tacho flanked by four smaller gauges (two each side), sports steering wheel and a mahogany gearshift knob. Intriguingly, the Brabham Torana was *slower* than the SL70 according to *Modern Motor* (0–96km/h (0–60mph) in 16.2 seconds) although its maximum speed was almost 145km/h (90mph), still no match for the Cooper S and barely faster than a standard Corolla.

In October 1969 Holden introduced the LC Torana and with it changed the face of the market. Not only did Torana have a svelte new body style but it was now available in two wheelbase lengths (2443mm and 2540mm (95.8 and 100in)) with four- and six-cylinder engine options as well as two- and four-door body options. Holden had discerned the need to return to a car more like the FB-through-EH in size and power and with the LC they created a forgotten market segment. While loosely based on the proportions of the outgoing HB Torana, the new model's styling was uniquely Australian, overseen by Leo Pruneau and a small team of local stylists. It featured smooth and unadorned body sides, a sweeping rear window line and the suggestion of hips around the C-pillar area plus two distinctive nose treatments, one very plain for the cheaper four-cylinder models and the other more pointed ('beaky'?) for the six-cylinder models that was much more stylish and distinctive. On the four-cylinder cars the grille was rectangular with a single headlight at each end, a prominent Holden badge in the centre and five chromed segments each of five vertical bars, all in a chromed surround. For the sixes it was different. Single headlights were retained but the grille was patterned and swept around the corners of the front fenders; it was divided by a broad horizontal bar on which the large Holden badge was positioned and in the lower left corner a model designation badge was placed. S or SL badges were placed on the C-pillar. Tail-lights were slim horizontal units that curved around the corner of the rear fender and there was a simple chromed blade-type bumper front and rear.

The interior was sufficiently roomy for four adult passengers on front bucket seats and a rear bench, and the dashboard was symmetrical insofar as it had two prominent sections under which the dials were housed on the right, glovebox on the left. A legacy of the English heritage remained with the steering column not exactly aligned parallel with the seat and foot pedals which meant that the driver sat at an ever-so-slight angle. Interestingly, there was no flow-through ventilation system incorporated

JXN-428

TORANA

in the interior.

Short wheelbase (and short nose) Toranas retained the 1159cc four-cylinder engine and the long wheelbase (and long nose) models were powered by 138 or 161cid (2.25 and 2.6 litres respectively) six-cylinder engines based on units from the HT model range. The smaller of the sixes had the cylinder dimensions of 79.4 x 76.2mm (3.125 x 3.00in) and produced 70kW (95bhp) at 4600rpm while the larger engine had a bore and stroke of 85.7 x 76.2mm (3.375 x 3in) and produced 84kW (114bhp) at 4400rpm; the smaller six-cylinder engine was unique to the Torana.

Both models offered a choice of gearbox (four-speed all-synchromesh with a floor shift for the four-cylinder models plus the Trimatic for the SL70) while the six-cylinder models offered either a three-speed manual with a column shift or a four-speed with floor shift plus again the Trimatic automatic. Rear axle ratios varied from 3.89 for manual four-cylinders to 4.125 for the automatics while manual sixes ran a 3.08 differential with a 3.36 ratio as an option and the autos ran a 2.78:1 differential with 3.08 as a performance option. As for tyres, the fours ran skinny 5.50 x 12 tubeless on 4.00J x 12 ventilated rims and the sixes ran A78L x 13 tubeless tyres on 4.5J x 13 slotted rims with the GTR using B70H x 13 tyres on 5.50J x 13 ventilated rims.

New to the range was the Holden Torana GTR, a car that was inspired by the need to go racing with a lighter and more athletic car than the heavy and at times cumbersome Monaro GTS 350. In fact, the development of the six-cylinder Toranas was apparently inspired by Harry Firth and the need to go racing and win at Bathurst. The GTR was based on the two-door body and was distinguishable from the outside by discreet body stripes (one wide, one narrow) along each side beginning on top of each front fender and ending with the letters GTR at the base of the C-pillar, 5.5 x 13in slotted sports wheels with chrome dress trims and B70H13 red band tyres, simulated air vents behind the front wheel arches, black painted lower door and sill panels and a blacked-out grille. Inside there was a GTR-only instrument cluster comprising matching speedometer (right) and tachometer (left) flanked either side by four smaller dials (two each side) registering fuel contents, amps, engine oil pressure and coolant temperature. A sports steering wheel and houndstooth cloth upholstery completed the picture.

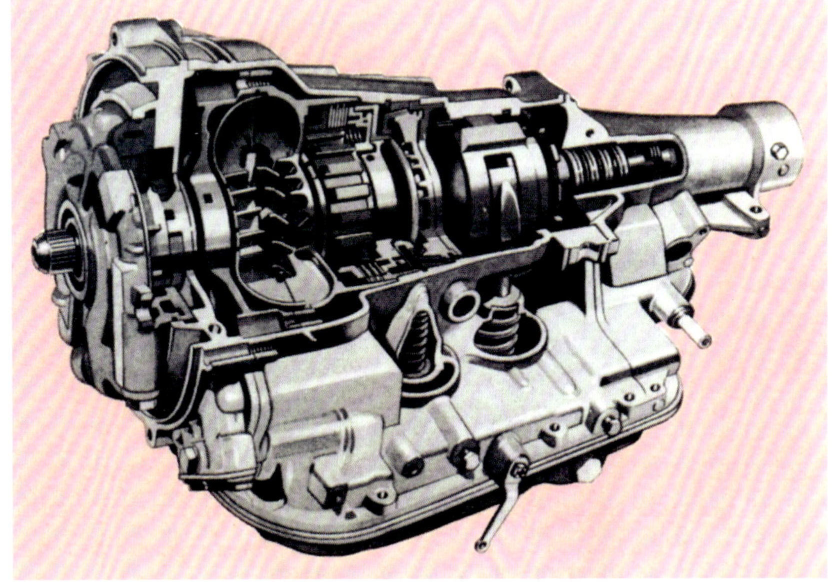

Under the bonnet was the 161S engine that had a higher compression cylinder head (9.2:1), dual Stromberg CD carburettors, performance camshaft, double valve springs and a dual-manifold exhaust system. Power output was 94kW (125bhp) at 4800rpm and 203Nm (150 lb-ft) of torque at 2800rpm. An Opel four-speed all-synchromesh manual gearbox transmitted the power to the rear wheels via a 3.08 rear axle.

In reviewing the LC range *Modern Motor* (December 1969) opined that GM-H was disappointed with the sales of the Torana through which they had hoped to wrest four-cylinder sales supremacy away from Ford but for much of the time it was running a distant third and competing with the Morris 1500 and Hillman Hunter. However, they predicted a better future for the six-cylinder cars. Available across the entire range (except for the GTR) was the locally-manufactured Trimatic (soon to be known as the Trau-matic) three-speed automatic gearbox.

Various examples were driven at Lang Lang by the media and generally they created a positive impression although they did write of the four-cylinder version, "Performance is not too strong, and is made to look worse by the relative ease with which the sixes get moving." On a brighter note they said, "The four-cylinder car is a very good handler. It points with precision, holds the road well but rides in a fairly dippy manner when the going gets really choppy."

No surprise that the GTR was their favourite car and when tested against the clock returned a time of 11.4 seconds from 0–96km/h (0–60mph) and ran out to 169km/h (106mph). They liked the sharp and responsive rack and pinion steering, the excellent brakes and the way it could be hustled quickly along winding roads under power. In-gear maximum speeds were 48, 80 and 128km/h (30, 50 and 80mph).

The sixties was a momentous decade for Holden, beginning with the ultra-conservative FB range that segued through EJ and EH into the unloved HD/HR range that brought the admired HK/HT range that embraced the Monaro sporting coupe and Brougham luxury saloon. In addition the company embarked on the Torana program to better compete with the burgeoning range of compact Japanese cars on the market, this program expanding to include Australia's first compact six since the original Holden. It certainly was a period of great change for the company.

The Holden story will be continued in *Australian Cars of the 70s.*

FORD FALCON
AUSTRALIAN –
WITH A WORLD
OF DIFFERENCE
FORD
Falcon

Chapter 2

FORD

Ford began the new decade with the release of the Falcon, an event that brought media hype and public interest to amazing new heights, borderline hysteria in fact. Such was the clamour to see and drive this completely new Ford that dealer showrooms were crammed with people from dawn until dusk; it was something that Ford dealers had never experienced before and probably never have since. The hysteria was akin to that which greeted the first Holden.

The company made much of the fact that it was the most tested car in all of Ford's history (Henry Ford II said that to the assembled journalists at the release), but somewhere between the copywriter and the engineer's reports the facts went missing! Almost all of the testing carried out was done on Ford's huge proving ground in Michigan, America and virtually none here under local conditions. That was a mistake of catastrophic proportions for Ford and very nearly brought the Australian subsidiary of the company down, it was touch and go for a while there.

Falcon was Ford's direct challenger to the supremacy of Holden and replaced the Zephyr that had originally been allotted that role but proved to be too expensive to manufacture to be price-competitive and that was the key issue. Based on a completely new 'clean sheet' design, the Falcon was light years ahead of Holden in styling terms. It was lighter in its construction (not a plus, as it turned out) with huge glass areas and was the right size package having a wheelbase of 2768mm (109in), overall length of 4597mm (181in), width and height of 1778mm and 1384mm (70 and 54.5in) respectively; kerb weight was 1107kg (2436lb). Virtually every media report commented on the Falcon's more modern styling, its roomier interior that was more comfortable because of the longer wheelbase and slightly softer suspension setting, and even though it had only 3.7kW (5bhp) more, it felt livelier on the road. The shallow boot with the spare dumped on the floor drew criticism as did the pathetic vacuum-operated wipers, skinny 6.00 x 13 cross-ply tyres, cheap bonnet stay and dreadful steering. On-road performance was the same as for the Holden, fractions of a second only separating them. The buying decision suddenly got a lot harder!

Power came from an entirely new six-cylinder engine of all cast-iron construction, the crank having four main bearings and the side camshaft was chain-driven, the overhead valves being opened by long pushrods and rockers mounted on studs, not a shaft. The cylinder dimensions were 88.9 x 63.5mm (3.5 x 2.5in) for a capacity of 2365cc (144cid); power was 67kW (90bhp) at 4200rpm while torque output was 185Nm (138 lb/ft) at 2000rpm. Interestingly, the intake manifold was cast integrally with the cylinder head, which severely limited any performance options by the trade. Like the Holden, it had a three-speed manual gearbox (non-synchro first gear) with column shift and for those who wanted an automatic there was the availability of the Fordomatic two-speed unit. Front suspension was by coil springs mounted on the upper wishbone (the Falcon was a Ford without the ubiquitous MacPherson strut front suspension but what the US engineers designed was for all intents and purposes similar) and there was a conventional live axle on leaf springs at the back. Braking was by tiny 228mm (9in) cast-iron drums with 114sq in lining area and the recirculating ball steering had more than six turns lock-to-lock!

The Falcon's interior was pretty much as buyers would have expected in 1960. The dash was a pressed steel affair with a dinky toy-looking binnacle plonked in front of the driver (it looked like a last-second addition, something the stylists had forgotten) that contained a speedometer, dial for fuel and temperature plus a few lights. Bench seats mounted very low were in front and rear with plastic mats on the floor. A deeply dished white plastic steering wheel was positioned close to the chest of the driver and required six turns to go from lock to lock. Under the dash was the pistol-grip handbrake. Rather basic but that's what you got at the time.

Australian Motor Manual conducted a comparison test (November 1960) and found it difficult to separate the XK Falcon and the FB Holden, especially where performance was concerned. The Holden's top speed was 131km/h (82mph) versus the Falcon's 134km/h (84mph), in-gear acceleration from 32–64km/h (20–40mph) took 8.4 seconds in the Falcon, 9.4 for the Holden, 0–80 and 0–96km/h (0–50 and 0–60mph) times were 10.9 and 17.1 seconds for the Falcon, 13.1 and 20.7 seconds for the Holden and fuel economy was 12.3 litres per 100km (23mpg) each on test. What the test did highlight was the glaring inadequacies of the Holden grey motor which was by then more than a decade old. The Ford had the better ride and handling, the Holden's being judged as too hard but the Holden had far better steering, neither had very good brakes, the seating posture in the Holden was thought to be better than the Falcon where the passengers sat very low in the seats and the Holden had by far the better boot – the Falcon's spare was simply dumped in the middle of the floor. As they said, you pays your money and you makes your choice!

The Geelong plant was enlarged and re-equipped with the latest foundry and machine tool technology to manufacture the Falcon six-cylinder engine and manual gearbox while the pressing of body panels and final assembly all took place in the new factory at Broadmeadows to the north of Melbourne.

Initially sales were brisk but very soon tales of woe began to filter back to the dealer network and the media who pressed Ford to do something other than sit on its hands and do nothing as was the way in those innocent days. The Australian engineers had fed the information back to their colleagues in Dearborn who simply did not believe them! Eventually, under enormous public pressure, Ford initiated a program to fix the weak front suspension problems, the bending of the spring towers, weak gearboxes and the dreadful dust and water sealing among a host of other issues.

After little more than a year in showrooms the XK Falcon gave way to the XL that was little more than a cosmetic touch up (new grille, mildly altered tail-lights, badges) and the availability of a larger capacity 170cid engine to cater for the demand for more oomph. The extra capacity came from a longer stroke of the crank, increased from 63.5mm to 74.6mm (2.5in to 2.94in) while the bore remained the same, capacity was now 2778cc; 75kW (101bhp) at 4400rpm and 211Nm (156 lb/ft) at 2400rpm was the result. Of styling interest was the arrival of the so-called Thunderbird roofline that squared-up and widened the C-pillar area; it was a styling feature that many rival manufacturers would soon adopt. With XL Ford introduced the Futura sedan and Squire station wagon that were the 'luxury' Falcons to compete with Holden's Premier and the Wolseley 24/80. The Futura's individual front seats were upholstered in pleated leather-lookalike vinyl with a console between them for extra storage, door armrests and ashtrays front and rear, padded dashtop, and floor carpets. Interestingly, a heater/demister was an *option* as were windscreen washers and a radio! Exterior adornment included a chrome airscoop on the bonnet, front fender ornaments, prominent chromed side spear, chromed wheel discs and whitewall tyres. The Squire wagon was identified by the garish fake 'wood' trim applied along each side of the body.

For those with long memories it will be remembered that an XL Falcon won the 1963 Armstrong 500 race at Phillip Island, the third time (and last) that the event had been held there. The winning car was number 21 in Class B and was driven by none other than Harry Firth and Bob Jane. Given the car's reputation for frailty one must wonder what 'fixes' Harry developed for the race!

Behind the scenes much was going on at Ford Australia and this was seen in the form of the vastly improved XM Falcon that arrived in February 1964. Another engine option was made available, a 200cid

FALCON

version of the six with dimensions of 93.4 x 79.4mm (3.68 x 3.125in) for a capacity of 3277cc; power was up to 90kW (121bhp) at 4400rpm and torque to 250Nm (185 lb-ft) at 2400rpm. Ford decreed that it could only be purchased with the two-speed Fordomatic automatic transmission, the existing manual not being able to take the torque. With XM the car's weak front suspension issues had been addressed using US Fairlane components but other issues would have to wait until XP.

XM had a new chrome laden grille that graced the front of the car with the letters F-O-R-D spelled out in the chromed piece at the top of the grille, while new rear-quarter panels were needed because of the repositioning of the spare wheel to an almost upright position in the left rear corner of the boot and the larger and higher mounted circular tail-lights; the one-piece bumpers front and rear were new. Interior style and appointments remained basically unchanged.

What was new with XM was the Falcon Hardtop that was available with all the options from the sedan and wagon bodies. The Hardtop body was an amalgam of Australian panels at the front and US-sourced panels for the roof and rear, on a locally-pressed floorpan.

The last iteration of this body, the XP, arrived with considerable fanfare in March 1965. In the eyes of many industry critics the XP Falcon was what the XK should have been had Ford not taken the soft (and less expensive) option on its development. Included in the hype with the new model was the announcement by Ford that it was going to conduct a 70,000 mile durability test with five production Falcons on part of the new You Yangs proving ground near Lara between Melbourne and Geelong. Knowing the fragility of the earlier Falcons this was received with some scepticism within the company but Marketing Director Bill Bourke went ahead with it anyway. To everybody's amazement, on Monday 3 May 1965 at 1.42am car number 3 crossed the line and a record was achieved. The monkey was at last off Ford's back.

New squared-up front styling combined with a far more robust structure was the big story with XP, the front panels coming from the Mercury Comet, a Falcon sibling in the US. Torque boxes were now incorporated into the body structure and these along with larger 6.50 x 13 tyres made the package so much more acceptable to Australian buyers and conditions. With the XP buyers had the choice of two automatic transmissions: the two-speed Fordomatic that was available only with the 170cid engine, and the three-speed Fordomatic 3S that was a Borg Warner Type 35 in reality and was only available with the 200cid engine. No automatic was offered with the 144cid engine.

Among the tiny details can be listed a speedometer that now read to 120mph, an alternator was an option(!), the spare wheel was repositioned to a semi-upright position in the left rear wing, which greatly improved luggage space and accessibility, the engine bonnet was self-supporting when open (the cheap prop rod was no more), vacuum-assisted disc front brakes became an option and a new model was introduced, the Fairmont, which replaced the Futura and was far better equipped to compete with the Premier.

Wheels carried out a comparison test between the XP Falcon fitted with the 200cid engine and three-speed automatic transmission and an HD Holden with the X2 engine and three-speed manual option (not exactly comparing apples with apples but ...) in its May 1965 issue and published figures of 148km/h (93mph) maximum for the Falcon and a 0–96km/h (0–60mph) time of 14.6 seconds compared with 158km/h (99mph) and 11.6 seconds for the Holden. Fuel consumption was poor for both cars at 15.8–13.5 litres per 100km (18–21mpg). All in all, the testers admired the efforts of Ford's engineers in correcting virtually all of the problems associated with the Falcon and opined that it was by far the best Falcon yet. Buyers thought so too with XP selling around 70,000 units compared with 45,000 of the XM.

So impressed were the journalists at *Wheels* magazine that they voted the XP Falcon as the 1965 Car of the Year.

The first major model change for Falcon came in September 1966 with the release of the 'Mustang-bred' XR series that was US-designed but Australian engineered to cope with the far more strenuous local conditions. Ford had learned its lesson. In keeping with the attitude of the times XR was longer, wider and heavier, as would have been expected. It now rode on a 2819mm (111in) wheelbase, was 4699mm (185in) long, almost 1879mm (74in) wide with 1473mm (58in) wheel tracks and stood 1422mm (56in) high; weight had risen by between 100 and 136kg (220lb and 300lb) depending on equipment. XR brought with it the option of the 289cid small block V8 engine that could be mated to a three-speed all-synchromesh manual gearbox or three-speed automatic with front disc brakes inside new 14in wheels. For the buyer, Ford provided a veritable smorgasbord of options to allow individual selection of 'their' Ford. As with Holden it was a great idea but a logistical nightmare for purchasing and production at the factory.

Along with the new exterior style came a revamped interior with a completely new dashboard featuring a thickly padded moulded top and a chromed binnacle in front of the driver containing two large round dials comprising the speedometer on the right with the left one containing the fuel and temperature gauges plus warning lights. This was in contrast with the US Falcon that had a bulky-looking dash with a slim, difficult-to-read horizontal instrument pod in front of the driver. Minor switches, six of them, were lined up along the lower edge and the dished steering wheel was a large diameter affair of white plastic with a horn ring in the lower half. The handbrake was relocated to the left of the steering column and on the right was an internal bonnet release. Ford was getting the message about its fittings!

With XR Ford no longer offered the 144cid engine (the 170cid unit was now the base engine) and both the Squire station wagon and the Hardtop had been deleted from the model range. Running a 9.2:1 compression power was boosted to 82kW (111bhp) and torque was up to 212Nm (158lb-ft) while for the 200cid engine power was 90kW (121bhp) and torque 257Nm (190lb-ft). The 289cid V8 with its 149kW (200bhp) was the same one seen in US Mustangs as well as the larger Galaxie. Interestingly, Ford offered two automatic gearboxes: the 3S carried over from the XP and the 'Cruise-O-Matic' that featured two driving ranges. The steering was slightly more direct than on XP (5.2 turns, down from 6.0 turns) and the suspension continued with the strengthening process begun for XM and XP. This was necessary because of the need to cope with the extra weight and performance of the V8 engine. The leaf springs at the rear were wider and longer with a higher weight capacity, while the standard braking system was by 254mm (10in) cast-iron drums (up from 228mm/9in) with 154.4sq in of lining area. Two slightly different front disc brakes were available: for six-cylinder Falcons they were 273mm (10.75in) diameter and 12mm (0.5in) thick solid rotors, while for the V8s they were 279mm (11in) in diameter and 17mm (0.675in) thick, also solid. Standard tyres were 6.45x14 cross-ply with 6.95x14 as an option along with radial tyres. A larger fuel tank (16.4 gal) for the sedans was the only other change.

Peter North, formerly in product planning at Ford before being appointed managing director at Leyland Australia, said, "In the development of the XR Falcon we dropped all the six-cylinder body and suspension components and substituted V8 components that allowed us to use the marketing phrase *'Ford V8 Engineering Throughout'*. It saved a lot of capital cost but made the car marginally heavier which we were prepared to accept."

Modern Motor published a comparison test between the new XR Falcon and the Holden HR its November 1966 issue. It really was a comparison of the new versus the old because the HR was the last of the old breed from Holden, the HK not arriving for more than a year. The Falcon was longer by 101.6mm (4in), wider by 88.9mm (3.5in) and 91mm (3.6in) lower and heavier by 105kg (230lb). Both topped out at 144km/h (90mph) with the lighter Holden having slightly quicker acceleration times, the 0–80 and 96km/h (0–50 and 60mph) times were 13.5 and 20.0 seconds for the Falcon 500 with 200cid engine, 10.3 and 15.3 seconds for the Holden Special with 186cid engine. Roominess inside was a clear win for the Falcon as was roadholding and general handling.

The *MM* people concluded by writing, "The XR range looks like being Ford's most exciting yet and with their range of options, one of the most confusing. But there's nothing confusing about the XR's cleaner handling, very quiet running and greater room inside. It is, I believe, the car that will help Australia's motor industry back from its knees."

So impressed were the people at *Wheels* magazine that they voted the XR Falcon as their 1966 Car of the Year making it consecutive awards for Ford, a feat that has never been repeated in the ensuing half century of the award.

Ford replaced the XR with the XT in March 1968 and to the

untrained eye it did not appear to have changed all that much. From the outside the grille had a new texture, there was a chrome strip running the full length of the car that was positioned on the corner edge of the fenders and the indicator lens in the tail-lights was now a horizontal unit in place of the round one in the centre.

Inside it was a case of applying more padding for safety reasons, the steering wheel boss having a rectangular pad across the centre, the window winders and dash switches were now made of a soft plastic and the door latches were recessed behind the armrests.

The big news for Falcon was, however, under the bonnet where the six-cylinder engines had been increased in capacity and relabelled to their metric capacities. The 170cid was enlarged to 188cid or 3.1 litres (93.47 x 74.67mm, 3080cc, 3.68 x 2.94in bore and stroke) and produced 85kW (114bhp) and 244Nm (180lb-ft), up very slightly from before while the 200cid engine became the 221cid six or 3.6 litres (93.47 x 87.88mm, 3622cc, 3.68 x 3.46in bore and stroke) and produced 100kW (135bhp) and 282Nm (208lb-ft). These engines were the work of the engineers at Ford in Geelong and were different in many details from their US cousins For example, they had a deeper crankcase skirt with a thicker oil pan rail to increase the rigidity of the block and the head had been modified with new valve seats, larger cross-section of the ports and better gas flow. Where the V8 was concerned Ford upgraded it from 289cid to 302cid (101.6 x 76.2mm, 4949cc) for 156kW (210bhp) at 4600rpm and 406Nm (300lb-ft) of torque at 2600rpm.

A full test of an XT Falcon fitted with the 3.6-litre engine and three-speed manual gearbox was carried out by *Modern Motor* (May 1968) and apart from some reservations about the suspension's ability to cope with the power on rough surfaces and the braking system's marginal capacity, the report was generally very favourable. Top speed was 157km/h (98mph) with 80, 96 and 112km/h (50, 60 and 70mph) coming up in 9.8, 12.9 and 20.1 seconds respectively while the standing quarter mile took 19.2 seconds; economy was 15 litres per 100km (19mpg) for the test so the 16.4Imp gal tank was necessary.

XT gave way to XW in July 1969 and this time more substantial styling changes appeared, it being the work of Australian stylists under the leadership of Jack Telnack, an American on secondment. The XW was a more aggressive design with a squared-up nose allied to a reworked rear that had rectangular tail-light units cut into the outer edges of the rear fenders; they retained the red lenses top and bottom with the amber indicator lens between them. The passenger compartment remained as was; only the front and rear sheet metal was changed.

Within the broad grille area which was outlined by a thin chromed strip was a plastic moulding with fine horizontal strips that surrounded single 7in round headlights each end with new vertical parking (lower)/blinker (upper) light units projecting slightly outside the headlights. A large, plain chromed steel bumper sat below with an indentation for the licence plate. On the Fairmont the grille strips were highlighted and the name F-O-R-D was spelled out in individual letters on the leading edge of the bonnet. Buyer options continued to be the marketing push along with the power of the Falcon engines. New with XW was the availability of the GS (Grand Sport) option package that allowed buyers to drive away in a car that had most of the features of the GT but without the huge insurance premium.

The XW remained in production until October 1970 when it was superseded by the XY, the fourth and last iteration of the body design and that will be covered in *Australian Cars of the 70s*.

SA
RGS·235

FALCON GT

In June 1967, in time for the 1967 Bathurst race, Ford announced the availability of the Falcon GT sedan ostensibly in any colour you wanted as long as it was GT Gold with an all-black interior. However, a few (said to be 13) GT Silver sedans escaped through to executives of the Gallaher cigarette company who were sponsors of the race. Another five escaped the factory in other colours to 'favoured' clients. In many ways the GT was an off-shoot of another program at Ford where they were developing a 'special' for the Victorian police that had more power, better gearing, better handling and (especially) braking. The police were looking for a replacement for the much-loved Studebaker Larks that they had been running for several years. When it was clear to marketing guru Bill Bourke that the company had achieved all it could in competition with the Cortina, he authorised the transfer of the police program into regular production so that a win at Bathurst could be achieved with Falcon. In this he was successful first time out, putting the Falcon GT into the history books and immortality forever.

From a specification point of view the GT could be cynically regarded as a minor upgrade on the regular Falcon family sedan. It was in the details that the changes dramatically altered the outcome. The 289cid Windsor V8 (sourced from the US Mustang) had a four-barrel carburettor sitting atop a new intake manifold, 9.8:1 compression, new camshaft with higher lift and a free-flow exhaust system that combined raised its output to 168kW (225bhp) at 4800rpm and torque to 413Nm (305lb-ft) at 3200rpm. In addition, the suspension was lowered by an inch, the spring rates increased, the front anti-roll bar increased in diameter and the car's overall height had been lowered. The front brakes were vacuum-assisted discs with 279mm (11in) rotors and single-piston callipers while the rear brakes were 254mm (10in) cast-iron drums. A Ford US four-speed all-synchromesh gearbox (ratios 2.78, 1.93, 1.36, 1.00 and 2.78 for reverse) with a 254mm (10in) dry plate clutch delivered the power to the heavy duty rear axle running a 2.93:1 gearset giving 40km/h (25mph) per 1000rpm. A quicker 16:1 ratio steering box could be installed with the availability of power assistance if desired.

Inside the GT was trimmed to Fairmont levels (which meant a heater/demister was a standard fitting) with the vinyl upholstery being any colour you wanted so long as it was black, the front bucket seats being of the reclining type. Where in the Falcon sedan there were only two round dials, in the GT there were two large round dials (speedometer graduated to 140mph and tachometer reading to 6000rpm but redlined at 5500rpm) with three minor dials (fuel, temperature, oil pressure) all located in a chromed bezel. The steering wheel was a mock wood piece that had three spokes with 'thumb touch' horn buttons on each and a huge, garish centre pad. Plus, there was a Hurst floor gearshift lever sitting atop the transmission tunnel, carpets were on the floor. Other distinguishing features of the GT were a blacked-out grille except for three bars across the centre, a discreet GT badge near the left headlight and another by the right-hand tail-light, wheel rims were widened to 5.5in and shod with 185x 14 radial tyres and full chromed dress trims on the wheels. All this for just $3890 when a Fairmont V8 cost $3320 – it was a bargain.

Ford's General Sales Manager, Keith Horner, issued a Dealer Bulletin dated 18 April 1967 advising them of the imminent release of a 'high performance' vehicle suitable for trial and stock car racing but flexible enough for normal car use. The bulletin went on to say that it would be powered by a high-performance, four-barrel, 289cu in V8 Windsor with 168kW (225bhp), a floor mounted manual transmission with synchromesh on all four speeds, special suspension, 16:1 steering with power assistance optional.

In testing the Falcon GT, the consensus seemed to be that its top speed was around 192km/h (120mph) with 0–96km/h (0–60mph) acceleration in 9.7 seconds and a standing quarter mile time of 15.8 seconds. By the standards of the day it was indeed a 'high performance' saloon!

And as we all know, in its maiden race at Mount Panorama the Falcon GT came home first driven by Harry Firth and Fred Gibson and became an instant legend.

In May 1968 the XR gave way to the XT that was a cosmetic touch-up accompanied by minor engineering upgrades where the regular range was concerned. For the GT the engine was enlarged to 302cid (still from Windsor), power raised marginally to 171kW (230bhp) at 4800rpm, torque was now 420Nm (310lb-ft) at 3800rpm and the compression ratio rose slightly to 10.0:1. The brakes remained the same but now the system ran dual circuits, the floor gearshift was a straight chromed lever and not curved as in XR and the wheels now had 6in rims with 185 x 14 radial tyres. The same dials fronted the driver but their graphics were slightly different, a three-speed automatic gearbox (ratios 2.46, 1.46 and 1.00, 2.20 for reverse) was now an option and the rear axle ratio was lowered slightly to 3.00:1 for improved responsiveness.

Several colours were now available (Zircon Green, Polar White, Candy Apple Red, GT Silver and GT Gold) and there was a discreet full body length side stripe that accompanied each. The grille was now fully blacked-out apart from chrome strips across the top and bottom, a vertical red badge adorned the centre of the grille and smaller long-range driving lights – very necessary – added better night-time visibility to the standard 7in headlights. At the rear circular tail-lights were retained but the indicator lens was now a horizontal orange one across the light unit. On the left corner of the bonnet was a GT badge, another was on the boot lid and on each front fender between the wheel arch and door shutline was a badge the told anyone who wanted to know that this Falcon was powered by a 230hp high performance engine.

After extensively testing a XT GT *Wheels* recorded performance figures such as a top speed of 187km/h (117mph, fastest one-way was 195.8km/h/122.4mph), 0–96, 112, 128 and 144km/h (0–60, 70, 80 and 90mph). Acceleration times of 9.6, 12.4, 15.5 and 21.0 seconds meant that the Falcon GT was one of the quickest production four-door sedans anywhere in the world. Maxima in-gear speeds were 67, 104 and 146km/h (42, 65 and 91mph). In summary they wrote, "Taking what we did see of the car, from its lusty but smooth V8 power to its taut suspension, from its precise gearbox to its big, cushy seats and black trim the GT Falcon struck us as being one of the best integrated present day cars to follow in the true Grand Turismo tradition." All this for the modest price of just $4200.

Racetrack success eluded the XT although it gained a fourth placing in the Datsun 3 Hour Trophy race at Sandown Park driven by Don Toffolon and Tom Roddy, but Bathurst was a disaster with the GTs experiencing overheating, tyre and brake problems. The Gibson/Seton XT GT was leading the race with 15 laps to go but then it succumbed to overheating and blew a piston giving victory to the McPhee/Mulholland Monaro. An XR GT came in 7th to be the best-placed Falcon.

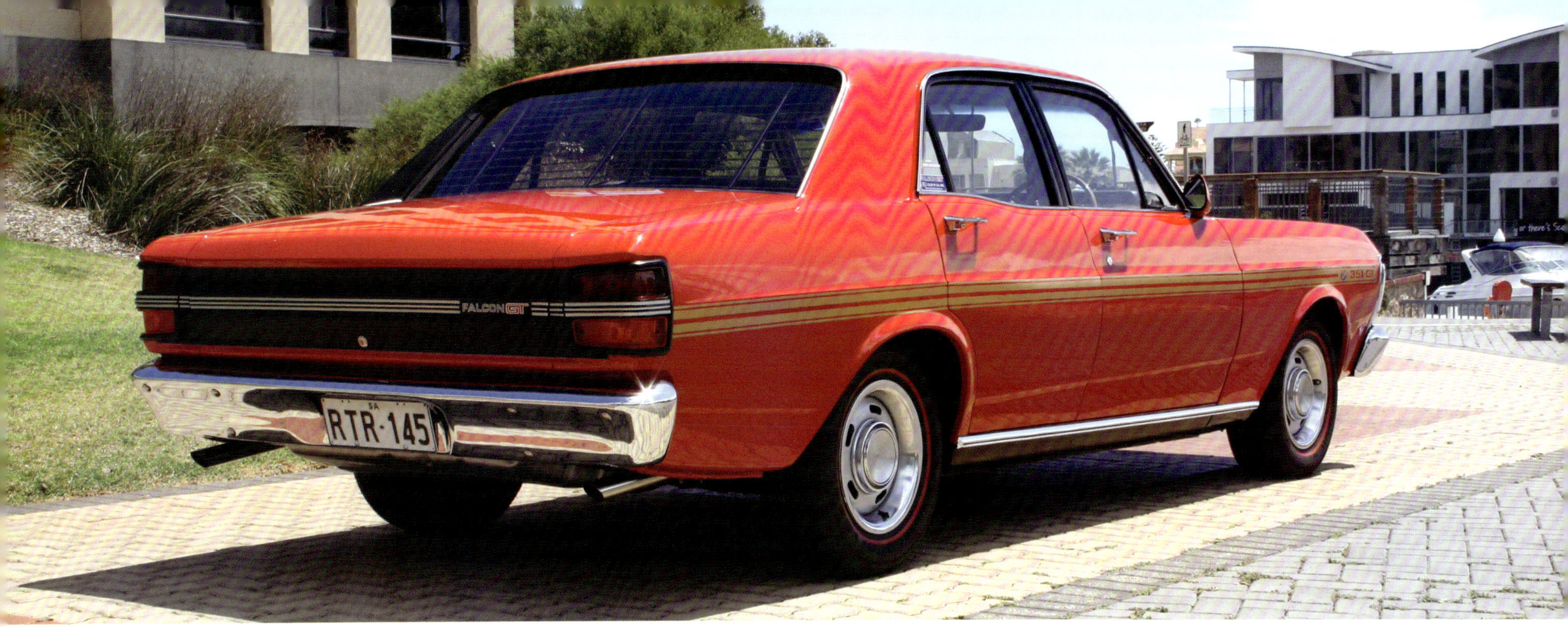

FALCON GT
RTR·145
GALLAHER 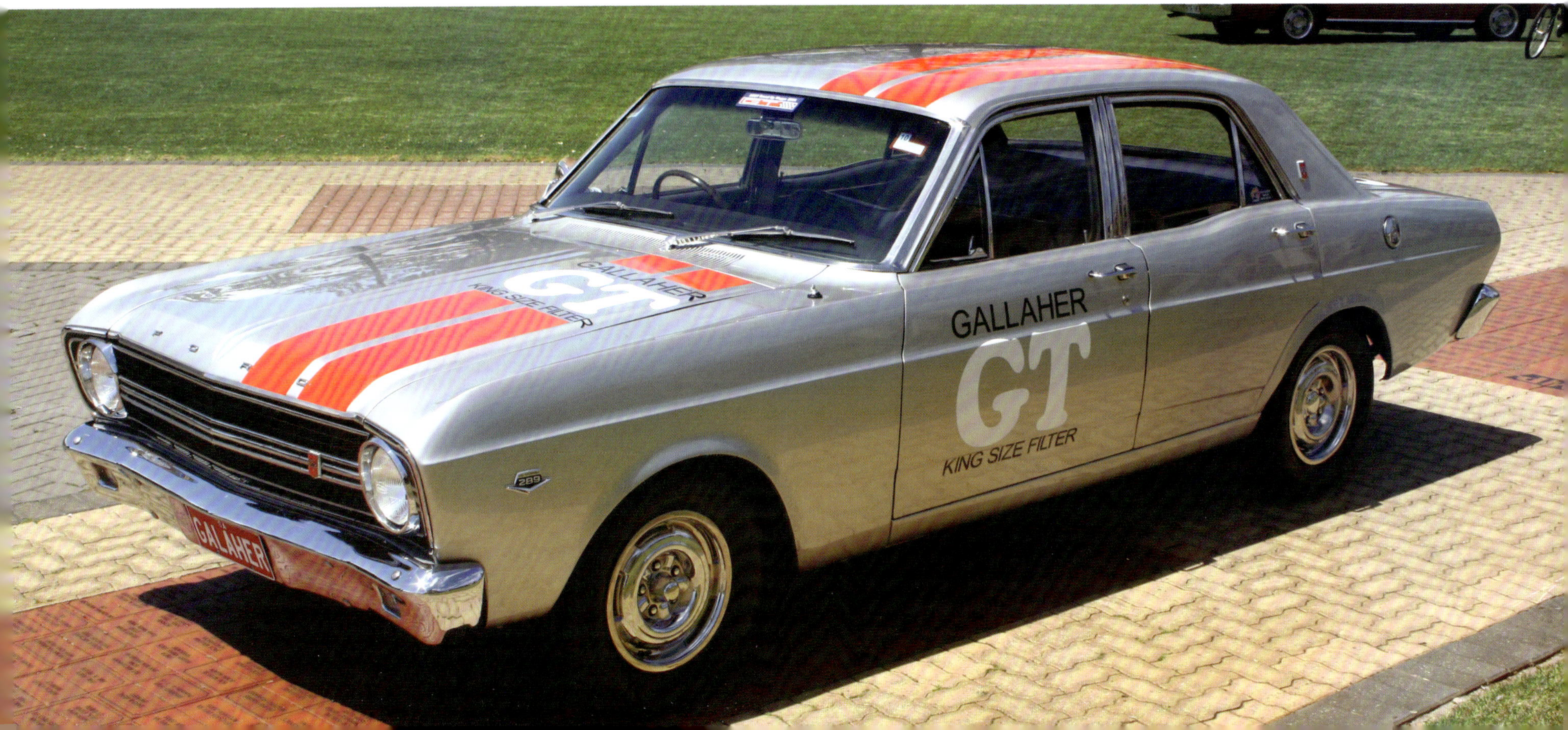
GT
KING SIZE FILTER
GALLAHER

Ford Australia entered a three-car team of XT GT Falcons in the inaugural London to Sydney Marathon, the cars being prepared by none other than Harry Firth. When the cars arrived in London the Australians found themselves on the end of some good-humoured banter about the sheer size of the cars. This was because the Poms and Germans had entered Cortina GTs, Lotus-Cortinas and their equivalent Taunus's from Cologne, cars that were high-revving and smaller and lighter than the big Aussies. In the event the three Falcons came home in the top ten finishers with the Ian Vaughan-driven car coming home third, Bruce Hodgson in sixth and Harry Firth in eighth place to win the Teams Prize, much to the chagrin of their English and German rivals. As with the 70,000 mile run at You Yangs with the XP, the marathon proved beyond doubt that the Falcon was more than strong enough to cope with driving conditions anywhere in the world.

With the release of the XW Falcon in May 1969 Ford raised the ante where the GT was concerned. GM-Holden had raced the Monaros at Bathurst with the big 350cid Chevrolet engine and won so it was no surprise when the XW GT appeared that it had the 351cid Windsor engine under the bonnet. In addition to the Falcon GT, Ford announced the GT HO two months later, the latter two letters standing for Handling Option. Many suggested they stood for High Output and given the nature of the improvements it was hard to disagree: 600cfm Holley four-barrel carburettor, aluminium inlet manifold, different camshaft and hydraulic lifters that raised power to 224kW (300bhp), but also included a heavy duty alternator, 3in diameter tail shaft, beefed-up coil springs and dampers plus a heavier sway bar at the front and one at the rear. In fact, the GT and GT HO looked identical from the outside with only a GT HO decal on the glovebox and the 'Super Roo' kangaroo on the front fenders giving the game away. The HO was designed and built for success on the race track, Bathurst in particular.

Wheels tested a GT HO manual in November 1969 and was startled by the rate of acceleration generated by the 351cid engine. In-gear maxima were 64, 99 and 144km/h (40, 62 and 90mph) in the indirect gears, and it ran to 204.8km/h (128mph) (5500rpm) in fourth. Against the clock it recorded the amazing figures of 4.9, 6.7, 9.2, 11.2, 14.4 and 16.7 seconds for the runs from 0–80km/h through to 160km/h (0–50 through to 0–100mph). 16.7 seconds from a standstill to 160km/h (100mph) … that was bloody quick then and it is still damn quick today!

Under the bonnet of a regular GT was a 216kW (290bhp) version of the 351cid engine that, when bolted to an automatic transmission, still ran to 192km/h (120mph) and accelerated from 0–112km/h (0–80mph) in 12.0 seconds and on to 160km/h (100mph) in 20.9 seconds – still damn quick.

As part of the upgrade to XW and the inclusion of the 351cid engine Ford upgraded the front brakes to Kelsey-Hayse 'turbo-cooled' ventilated rotors of 286mm (11.25in) in diameter. A dual-plate clutch was standard with the 351 (like the Chrysler Charger E49 R/T) as was a limited slip differential, wide oval high-performance tyres and boot space was compromised by the fitting of a 36gal fuel tank. New also were 12-slot steel wheels with a brushed aluminium hubcap that looked great and provided much-needed cooling for the brakes.

Inside there was still the fully instrumented dashboard, this year divided 60:40 towards the driver, the recessed dials having new graphics and soft padding for safety reasons plus the steering column was now collapsible.

The showroom price for a regular GT with a manual gearbox was $4250, barely changed from the XT, while a GT automatic retailed for $4510 which was still a bargain price. The GT HO sold for $4495.

As with the regular Falcon models, the GT would have one more iteration in this body, the XY, and that will be covered in *Australian Cars of the 70s*.

ENGLISH FORDS

ANGLIA

Ford continued to look to its English colleagues for product to compete in the small-car end of the market. The Anglia had been released in November 1959 (as a 1960 model) and was to revolutionise that end of the market in competition mainly with the innovative Triumph Herald, revolutionary Morris Mini and the ubiquitous VW Beetle. The Anglia, however, was a veritable breath of fresh air for the Ford dealers and a 'clean sheet' design with its distinctive styling epitomised by the very low bonnet that hinged at the front, raked windscreen and unusual reverse-slope flat rear window under an overhanging roof that allowed remarkable rear-seat headroom in such a small car.

The English branch of the family had been busy creating a series of cars under the direction of Sir Patrick Hennessey, a hard-driving managing director who shared a common mantra devoted to the accountants at Dagenham. These cars emerged from their rigorous development program beginning with the 105E Anglia. This seemingly ordinary car was the harbinger of change from Dagenham that would have far-reaching effects. The formula from Anglia to Classic to Cortina to Capri and to Escort would be consistent: MacPherson strut front suspension, disc front brakes/drums at the rear, live rear axle with semi-elliptic leaf springs, an all-steel monocoque body optimised for weight and strength and an interior that was sparsely equipped but could be improved by selecting options from an extensive list. It was also an important car in Ford's history because it was the first to feature a four-speed manual gearbox, electric wipers and an over-square engine design.

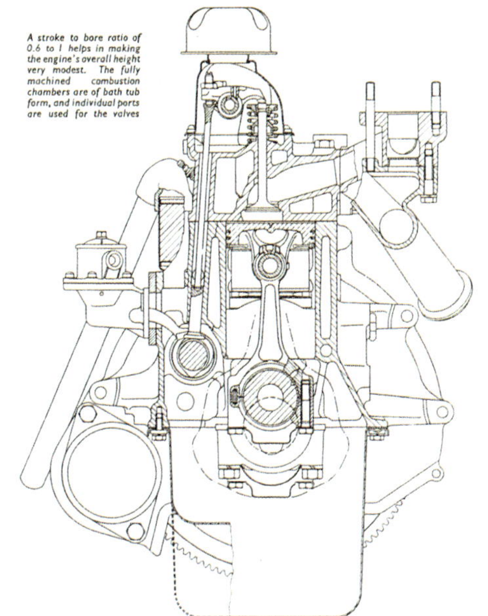

A stroke to bore ratio of 0.6 to 1 helps in making the engine's overall height very modest. The fully machined combustion chambers are of bath tub form, and individual ports are used for the valves

Built on a wheelbase of 2298mm (90.5in) and stretching 3890mm (153.5in) overall, by 1455mm (57.3in) wide and 1437mm (56.6in) tall, the two-door only Anglia was a neat two-plus-two-seater sedan ideally suited to commuter duties. Its weight was now 738kg (1624lb), around 45kg (100lb) lighter than the old Anglia. As was the custom then, the 32-litre (7gal) fuel tank was located under the floor of the 10cu ft boot that had the spare wheel mounted in a well at the very front where it was difficult to get out. Inside was a symmetrical dash with rhombus-shaped panels either side to easily accommodate right- or left-hand drive. Instrumentation was sparse comprising a speedometer and fuel gauge plus warning lights in a dial that was shaped to parallel the lines of the main panel. In the middle of the pressed steel dash panel was provision for the optional heater and radio, glove box to the left and an open cubby underneath. Seating was on basic and rather thin bucket seats in front that tipped forward to allow entry and exit to the rear bench, upholstery was washable vinyl and there were no locks on the front seats to prevent them inadvertently tipping forward during emergency braking. Ford used column stalks for high/low beam and indicators/horn, which was most unusual for the time. For the first time on a Ford the driver had electric windscreen wipers and the sturdy floor gearshift lever now gave access to *four* forward gears – almost a revolution!

What really set the Anglia apart from all other small cars was the new Kent engine, a completely new design overseen by chief engineer Allan Worters (who lived in Kent) and the first in a family of four-cylinder engines from Ford UK that would become available in 1.1, 1.2, 1.3, 1.5 and ultimately 1.6-litre forms and made in the millions. The cylinder dimensions for the Anglia were 80.9 x 48.4mm for 997cc. On a compression of 8.9:1 the engine developed 30kW (39bhp) at

THE ENTIRELY NEW
Anglia
the world's
most exciting
light car
ANGLIA

5000rpm and 71Nm (52.5 lb/ft) of torque at 2700rpm and delivered this to the rear wheels. The suspension was basically carried over from the 100E Prefect and utilised MacPherson struts and coil springs up front, live axle and leaf springs at the rear. Braking was by small cast-iron drums all round and the recirculating ball steering system was carried over as well. Interestingly, the Prefect name continued in the 107E, which was basically the old 100E body with the new Anglia mechanicals.

Performance was good without being spectacular, *Wheels* and *Modern Motor* both testing it and returning figures of 123km/h (77mph) for a top speed (*MM*) and a 0–80km/h (0–50mph) time of 15.9 seconds. Its performance was in line with buyers' expectations given that the leading four-cylinder car on the market was the ubiquitous VW Beetle that was no paragon of performance but excelled in other areas that were obviously important to buyers, areas like the superb paint and finish of the body, the absolute reliability and the after-sales backup. These were areas of the buying and ownership experience that Ford was not good at addressing; although in their defence neither was anybody else at the time, not that that should be an excuse.

Although the Anglia was really quite orthodox in its technical specification it was carried out well with few glitches to mar the ownership experience. On the road it felt eager to go and was able to post some astounding point-to-point times because of its balance and disarming roadholding. The media of the time loved it and said so, which in turn had buyers forsaking some of the other marques for the small Ford. Ford offered comparisons with the ubiquitous VW Beetle at the release event and many in the media continued that line. In so many ways the little Anglia was theoretically superior but VW sales continued unabated for now. The Anglia was assembled by Ford here until late in 1964 when it was quietly discontinued and not immediately replaced.

CORTINA

In October 1962 Ford introduced the Consul Cortina, a car that had been released in England six months previously and was dominating its market segment there, primarily against the Morris 1100. Like the Anglia that had been designed by the same team at Dagenham, the Cortina eschewed technical cleverness for manufacturing cleverness. It was utterly conventional in every way but every process in its design and manufacture had been examined to minimise materials and costs. Unlike the BMC cars, the Anglia and Cortina generated millions in profits for Ford.

Styling for the Cortina was perhaps what you would expect for the period – three boxes with accent lines to distinguish it from other cars on the market. The lines were slightly wedge-like in profile with an accent line running full body length at waist level starting behind the headlight; from the same point a second line followed it but sloped down so that at the tail-light it was perhaps three inches lower. Round headlights were at the head of the front fenders and round tail-lights graced either side at the rear, their lens being in three pieces for indicator (orange), tail and stop (red) and a reflector; oval-shaped parking/indicator lights sat below the headlights. Because of the body's profile the luggage compartment was huge – 21 cubic feet! It was by far the biggest in its class. A simple piece of pressed aluminium shaped like a rhombus comprised the grille and there were thin (and useless) blade-like chromed 'bumpers' front and rear. The stylist was Roy Brown who had previously designed the infamous Edsel and had a hand in finalising the design of the Mark III Zephyr.

Ford offered the Cortina initially as a two-door sedan built on a 2489mm (98in) wheelbase, the car being 4267mm (168in) overall by 1587mm (62.5in) wide and 1437mm (56.6in) high, its kerb weight being a light 802kg (1764lb). A tiny 36-litre (8gal) fuel tank resided under the boot floor and the spare was located upright in a deep well on the left rear corner out of the way of luggage and reasonably accessible.

Under the bonnet was an expanded version of the Anglia's engine, the bore and stroke now being 80.9 x 58.2mm for a capacity of 1198cc; power was 40kW (53.5bhp) at 5000rpm and torque 90Nm (66.5 lb/ft) at 2700rpm. Like the Anglia, the rear wheels were driven and the suspension was by MacPherson struts up front with the stabiliser bar doubling as a drag link. At the rear was a live axle and leaf springs with drum brakes all round and a recirculating ball steering box. All were similar to those same components used in the Anglia. Much the same applied to the all-steel body that had been optimised in panel count and weight for minimal-cost manufacturing.

Inside was room for five people, two on skimpy bucket seats in the front and a thinly padded bench in the rear. The dashboard was simple in the extreme comprising a flat sheet of pressed metal with a thin padded layer on top and an oblong plastic binnacle in front of the driver that housed the instruments, such as they were. Ford's brochure described it as "instrument reading at its easiest!" This was because there was virtually nothing to read – a simple fan-shaped speedometer and fuel gauge with lights for all other functions. The horn, lights and indicator switches were grouped on a steering column lever at the driver's finger tips.

When released the two-door retailed at £920 and the Cortina quickly became a bestseller in Australia and, as in England, the main loser was the Morris 1100.

The media were quick to drive the 'in-betweener' (rhymed with Cortina!) as they dubbed it and were generally pleased with what Ford was offering although there were many assembly quality glitches and items that they felt required attention. Items like the windscreen wipers (electric!) that had only the single speed that was too slow in anything but a light shower, a steering wheel that was set too close to the driver, door armrests that only an orangutan could reach, no heater, no windscreen washers, no self-supporting bonnet (like the boot lid), a poorly located dip switch and a glove box catch that would not actually catch. None of these were a big deal and could have been easily fixed, although quite why and how these issues got through to production was a mystery.

However, from a dynamic point of view, the Cortina was judged to be excellent. Bryan Hanrahan writing in *Modern Motor* said, "Pressed hard

CORTINA

TRIAL 1964 FINIS
PROVISIONAL
WINNER
CONSUL

AMPOL TRIAL
50c
HZW-365

Berger PAINTS
AMPOL TRIAL
45c

JAD-858

on a dry, smooth corner, the Cortina slides sideways in perfect balance without any sawing at the steering wheel." He did say that in the wet care needed to be taken because "the tail breaks fairly swiftly and you need to concentrate." Heavy braking from high speed could induce rear axle wind-up and some instability but you really had to be trying hard to make it happen. The Cortina would cruise happily at 104km/h (65mph) at which speed it was mechanically quiet, although there was quite a deal of road roar from the tyres. Against the clock the car ran a top speed of 125km/h (78mph), times of 13.8 and 23.1 seconds for the 0–80 and 96km/h (0–50 and 0–60mph) sprints while giving more than 9.5 litres per 100km (30mpg) on test.

In April 1963 Ford introduced the four-door body option together with a larger 1.5-litre engine that had the cylinder dimensions of 80.9 x 72.6mm for 1498cc. The significant difference was that the new engine had a five-bearing crankshaft while the 1.2 litre retained its three-bearing crank. Power for the 1.5-litre engine was 48kW (64bhp) at 4600rpm while torque was 116Nm (85.5 lb-ft) at 2300rpm. The four-door was not simply a bigger engined 1200; there were numerous differences that went with the more powerful version. Items like 5.60 x 13 tubeless tyres rather than the skinny 5.20 x 13s, the front brake drums were increased in size from 203 x 44.4mm (8 x 1.75in) to 228 x 44.4mm (9 x 1.75in) (the rear drums on both were 203 x 38mm/8 x 1.5in) which gave an increase in lining area from 81.68sq in to 95.3sq in, the sump held 6.5 pints compared with only 4.5 pints, the 1200 had a 4.125:1 differential ratio where the 1500 ran a 3.9:1 ratio, and the 1500 came only with a bench front seat and column gearchange. Intriguingly, in the Cortina sales catalogue the only options listed were two-tone paint and white sidewall tyres, no mention of a heater/demister even though under the general equipment section it talked about "provision for a fresh air heater and radio!"

Modern Motor tested a Cortina 1500 four-door sedan and felt it was a far better car than its two-door sibling. The larger engine was less stressed and seemed to cope better with crowded traffic conditions. Its top speed was only slightly faster at 131km/h (82mph) and 13.1 and 19.0 seconds for the 0–80 and 96km/h (0–50 and 0–60mph) dashes while fuel consumption was down to 10.9 litres per 100km (26mpg) over the duration of the test.

An additional model arrived in Ford Australia showrooms in September 1963, the Cortina GT. It could be bought in either the two- or four-door body and added some features inside. These included a huge tachometer (redlined at 5000rpm) perched on the left of the steering column, a centre console that had ammeter and engine oil pressure dials to go with the fuel and temperature dials, alongside the speedometer which remained the dreadful hard-to-read fan-shaped affair. The floor shifter was now remote and incorporated in the console. From an enthusiast driver's perspective, the gauges were too spread out to be read quickly.

Under the bonnet was a thoroughly reworked more powerful version of the new 1.5-litre engine. Rather than use the usual Zenith carburettor, Ford UK engineers opted for a Weber twin-choke downdraft unit on a new water-heated manifold, the compression was raised to 9.0:1 and a four-branch exhaust manifold fitted. These fiddles resulted in an output of 58kW (78bhp) at 5200rpm (a 20 per cent increase) and a torque reading of 131Nm (97lb-ft) at 3600rpm. The four-speed all-synchromesh gearbox from the 1500 was retained, remote shifter apart, as was the 3.9:1 rear axle ratio. The suspension was fitted with slightly firmer and shorter springs that lowered the ride height by about an inch.

Modern Motor tested a GT in its December 1963 issue and found it a most enjoyable fast family car; they recorded a top speed of 161.9km/h (101.2mph), 0–80 and 96km/h (0–50 and 0–60mph) times of 8.9 and 12.9 seconds and returned 10.5 litres per 100km (27mpg), which meant a cruising figure of well over 9.5 litres per 100km (30mpg). Ford immediately set out on a competition program with the Cortina GT and was to be very successful in rallying and circuit racing.

During late 1963 Ford quietly introduced a revised dashboard into the Cortina to counter continued criticism of the original; they basically put a raised binnacle in the same place with neat round Smiths instruments.

The next development with the Cortina came in April 1965 and with it came new model names – 220, 240, 440 and GT. External identifiers were easy because the 220 was the base 1200 two-door with a cheap painted slat grille, the 240 was the two-door body fitted with the 1500 engine, and the 440 was the four-door body with the 1500 engine, the 240 and 440 having a revised chromed grille that now embraced the parking and indicator lights. A redesigned dashboard appeared that featured two fully cowled round dials in front of the driver, provision for heater and radio in the centre, glovebox off to the left and adjustable air vents each end. Also new was the availability of front bucket seats and a floor gearshift as an option in the 440.

Front disc brakes (240mm/9.5in diameter solid rotor Girling units with no boost) were now standard across the range, the engines had slightly more power (41kW/54bhp) for the 1200 and 52kW/65bhp for the 1500) and windscreen washers were standard on the 240 and 440. Provision was now made for installing three-point safety belts as an option.

By far the biggest innovation of the time came with the introduction of flow-through fresh air ventilation that went by the marketing name of 'Aeroflow'. At either end of the dash were round eyeball air vents that could be adjusted to vary the direction of air flow and by turning a centre knob the air flow could be varied in quantity or closed altogether. On the C-pillar were chromed plastic air extractor vents. This initiative by Ford would set off a veritable revolution in interior ventilation for car occupants that would spread to every manufacturer sooner or later.

On the GT the dials were now more professionally integrated into the dashboard. In front of the driver were matching speedometer (on the right) and tachometer and off to the left on the upper centre were four smaller dials covering fuel, temperature, amps and oil pressure.

Having won the 1963 and 1964 Bathurst races with the Cortina GT (drivers were Harry Firth and Bob Jane in '63, Bob Jane and George Reynolds in '64) Ford wanted to go one better for 1965 and so the company engaged Harry Firth to 'improve' the GT. A batch of 120 cars was sanctioned although with the outcry in the media it modified its position to say it would build as many as the market required. The GT500 as it was badged, was based on the two-door Cortina 240 and was distinguished externally by 'GT500' script on each rear flank, twin fuel fillers behind the rear window with snap-lock caps and two aluminium alloy air scoops under the front bumper to guide cooling air over the front disc brakes.

Under the skin, however, myriad details had been changed: the cylinder head had been gasflowed, valves increased in size, compression raised (from 9.2 to 9.5:1), a special Wade camshaft and the Weber carburettor re-jetted so that it produced 74kW (98bhp) at 6000rpm, up from 58kW (78bhp) at 5200rpm; the flywheel and clutch assembly was lightened and dynamically balanced and the conrods were new forgings with special bolts and lock tabs. A close ratio four-speed manual gearbox (its ratios: 2.50, 1.64, 1.23 and 1.00 came from the Lotus Elan) delivered the power to a standard Cortina 3.9:1 rear axle. Other changes included lowering the car's suspension by 70mm (2.8in) and fitting a 39-litre (8.5gal) auxiliary fuel tank that gravity-fed the main 37-litre (8.25gal) tank.

A full road test was carried out by *Wheels* magazine that loved the GT500's dynamic qualities and forgave it for being a little rough around the edges. They recorded a top speed of 149km/h (93mph) but it was the acceleration that beguiled them, running the 0–80, 96 and 112km/h (0–50, 60 and 70mph) times in 8.6, 12.3 and 15.2 seconds respectively making it one very quick 1.5-litre sedan. Needless to say, it won the 1965 Armstrong 500 race at Bathurst driven by Bo Seton and Midge Bosworth with another driven by Bruce McPhee and Barry Mulholland finishing second. Ten GT500s had been entered, only four not going the race distance. Ford had achieved a hat-trick with Cortina!

Where the standard GT cost £1203, Ford priced the GT500 at £1498 and still had a sell-out on its hands.

After five years of success Ford introduced the Mark II Cortina in August 1967 that was little more than a completely new, more modern-looking body over the existing mechanical components. It now had a horizontal full body-width grille with single headlights at each end and small vertical indicator/parking lens squeezed in at the ends; the body sides were plain with two barely visible creases, one just below the door handles and other lower down on the doors. The roof was almost flat and culminated in an almost flat rear window, and there was the commodious boot behind with tail-light units on each rear corner that curved around

the sides like on the HD Holden. The glass in the doors was now curved which softened the car's look compared with the old model. The C-pillar continued with the Thunderbird look and the air vents for the flow-through ventilation system were positioned horizontally at the base of the pillar.

The interior was again roomy given the car's size and again offered buyers the choice of bench or bucket seats in the front depending on whether the buyer selected a floor gearshift lever or column gearshift. The dashboard was now a flat panel with a full-width padded top, the instruments being a speedometer on the right and combination dial on the left with switches placed symmetrically either side; at either end were the vents for the 'Aeroflow' ventilation system. For the GT version there were the two main dials in front of the driver (speedo and tacho) with the four minor gauges in a line across the top centre of the padded dash.

Mechanically it now had a base engine of 1300cc capacity to cope with the slight increase in weight. The 1300 and 1500 engines shared the same cylinder block and, where the old 1200 had a three-bearing crank, the new 1300 had a five-bearing crankshaft. It was only the stroke of the crank that was different and in the case of the 1300 it was 62.99mm. Power was now 43kW (57bhp) at 5000rpm, torque 95Nm (70lb-ft) at 2700rpm. The only other mechanical change of importance was the widening of the wheel tracks by 63mm (2.5in) up front and 38mm (1.5in) at the rear.

From February 1968 Ford introduced the new cross-flow cylinder head on the 1600cc block. Dimensions were now 80.97 x 70.62mm for 1599cc, power rose slightly to 52kW (75bhp) at 5000rpm and torque was up to 131Nm (97lb-ft) at 2500rpm. Both the 1300 and 1600 engines featured the cross-flow cylinder head but it was not an overhead camshaft design as many had hoped. It retained the side camshaft and pushrod operated overhead valves that were in a line along the cylinder block's axis, the actual combustion chamber being in the top of the piston. The carburettor was on the right-hand side of the engine viewed from the driver's seat and the four-branch exhaust manifold was on the other side; the spark plugs were angled into the combustion chamber from the exhaust side.

Modern Motor April 1968 carried a full test of the new Mk II 1600 (a 440 with four-speed manual and column shift) and came away well impressed with the revitalised performance, publishing a top speed of 144km/h (90mph) with 0–80 and 96km/h (0–50 and 0–60mph) times of 9.9 and 15.8 seconds and getting more than 9.4 litres per 100km (30mpg) on test. The showroom price was $2260, the same as for the old Mk II 1500.

Where the Mk II GT was concerned, the early cars had the 62kW (83bhp) 1500cc engine but once the 1600 engine became available the power rose to 70kW (93bhp) at 5400rpm. The GT now sported new stripes that began above the front wheels, dropped at an angle by about a foot and then went horizontally to the rear and comprised a thick upper and thin lower stripe. On the bonnet were two blackout patches, the front 'bumper' was now in two parts (there was a gap of about a foot in the centre) and twin long-range QI lights were a standard fitting. Inside, the dash had been revised by repositioning the four minor gauges within the centre section and not raised as they were previously; a less dished steering wheel gave the driver more arm room, and the hand brake was moved from under the dash to between the front seats. The GT now wore 165 x 13 radial tyres as standard on wider rims.

Australian Motor Manual tested a GT in its July 1969 issue and recorded a top speed of 158km/h (98.9mph), 0–80 and 96km/h (0–50 and 0–60mph) times of 8.2 and 11.7 seconds, ran the standing quarter mile in 18.1 seconds and returned 10 litres per 100km (28mpg) for the test period.

The car's ride and handling came in for praise: "All-in-all, the GT's handling is of a high standard and on sealed surfaces it is entirely predictable, the pleasant steering giving the driver that feeling of being well in control in all situations."

The Mark II Cortina continued with minimal change through until it was replaced by the TC in 1972 and that will be the subject of some discussion in *Australian Cars of the 70s*.

CAPRI

The Americans had derived the Mustang out of the Falcon and not to be left out the English designers designed and developed their own version using largely Cortina parts and called it Capri after the island in the Mediterranean Sea. Like the Mustang it featured the long nose–short rear deck styling and two plus two seating but was built around in-line four-cylinder engines and a V6 engine as the power option that came later. Assembly of the Capri took place from CKD kits at Ford's Homebush factory.

Introduced in Australia on 3 May 1969 at Amaroo Park with the by-line 'The Car You've Always Promised Yourself', it came in two versions each with its own engine option. Both were 1600cc cross-flow fours. The first was the Deluxe that had the 52kW (75bhp) engine and the other was the GT that had the 70kW (93bhp) engine out of the Cortina GT. The GT not only had more power, it had a tachometer on the dashboard, 'racing' exterior mirrors, bonnet lock pins, black-painted bonnet panels and delete option three-quarter length body stripes that swept up on the C-pillar with a round GT decal almost at the end. As with the Cortina, the Capri had a full-width grille comprising six thin horizontal bars and rectangular lighting units each end (square headlight and combination indicator/parking at the extremities) with a thin (and almost useless) chromed steel blade for a bumper. Out back was a near flat rear window with small sail panes either side, air extractor vents under the window and a truncated rear with small horizontal tail-light units in a slightly concave valance panel that was painted black and edged with a chromed strip. Again there was a useless piece of chromed steel masquerading as a bumper.

The Capri sat on a modified Cortina floor pan that had a wheelbase of 2560mm (100.8in) for an overall length of 4267mm (168in) by 1646mm (64.8in) wide and 1288mm (50.7in) high and weighed 918kg (2020lb). The Cortina was around 14kg (30lb) lighter and was taller by 152mm (6in), both had 40-litre (10gal) fuel tanks and the only other major difference between them (doors apart) was in the capacities of their boots – the Capri's was tight compared with the commodious Cortina.

In a road test published in *Wheels* (July 1969) they described the Capri GT thus: "Performance is in the pleasant bracket. It is lively and sufficient to stay with Fiat 125 and Renault 16TS-type machinery." And followed that with "The Capri is a driver's car and a lot of fun", to comments like "the rack and pinion steering is light and precise" to "the cockpit ergonomics are excellent except for the rocker-style switches which are hard to find and operate" and "the lights are disappointing and certainly not up to the 128km/h (80mph) cruising gait of the Capri." The report was mostly complimentary but there were obvious shortcomings with the car where corners had been cut. In terms of style and charisma the Capri tapped into the psyche of young Australians at the time and sold well.

From a performance point of view the GT returned a top speed of 159km/h (99.3mph), 0–96 and 112km/h (0–60 and 70mph) times of 12.5 and 17.5 seconds, a standing quarter mile time of 18.7 seconds at 115km/h (72mph) and it consumed fuel at the rate of 10 litres per 100km (28mpg) overall on test, 9.5–8.4 litres per 100km (30–34mpg) cruising. Those figures were fractions of a second different from big brother Cortina GT. Recommended retail on the Capri 1600GT was $2950 while for the Cortina it was $2530 so there was a big enough price gap for them not to be serious showroom floor competitors.

The 1600GT was replaced by the 3000 V6 GT in February 1970 and that will be discussed in *Australian Cars of the 70s*.

CONSUL

Apart from slightly different tail-lights and a full-length chrome side strip the Mark II Consul was continued into the new decade unchanged. Ford in Australia had lost interest in it because in the UK it had been surrounded by in-house competition in the form of the Consul Classic and Corsair and just over the horizon was the Consul Cortina. All three were far more modern designs that cost significantly less to manufacture and had far greater profit potential for the company.

By October 1961 the last Mark II Consuls had been sold and that chapter in local assembly history was closed.

ZEPHYR SIX

The Zephyr was not forgotten, or at least not yet. The last of the Mark IIs had been released towards the end of 1959 with restyled tail-lights, a straight chrome side strip that extended the full body length, a flatter roof line plus a new dash with a horizontal speedometer. A completely new body arrived in July 1962 in CKD packs that were assembled at the new Broadmeadows factory. Compared with the Mark II, the new Mark III had very international styling that had traces of American influences (the discreet rear fins and Thunderbird roofline) combined with Italian touches (the windscreen rake) and was unusual insofar as the body was distinctively wedge-shaped when viewed from above and the side glass was noticeably curved, a first for Ford in England and Australia.

Rugged 4- speed gearbox. Fully synchromesh on all forward gears it makes gear changing smoothly effortless — you move in and out of bottom gear as easily as top. Hydraulically operated, centrifugally assisted clutch adds even further ease for the driver.

3-speed automatic drive. As an optional extra, fully automatic transmission is available. With fluid coupling on its three forward gear ranges, all changes are scarcely detectable. The addition of a free wheel, operating through planetary gear train, gives efficient engine braking.

Underneath the stylish new body, however, it was very much as before with the exception of the new four-speed all-synchromesh manual gearbox with a column shift, a three-speed Borg Warner Type 35 automatic being an option. Power came from a mildly uprated edition of the same 2553cc OHV in-line six that now delivered 72kW (98bhp) at 4750rpm, up from 64kW (85bhp). New with Mark III were disc front brakes 240mm (9.5in) in diameter with solid rotors and a vacuum boost to lower pedal pressures, the rear drums being a carry-over. Physically the Mark III appeared to be larger but in fact that was mostly an illusion of the styling. It sat on the same floorpan with a 2718mm (107in) wheelbase but its length grew by just 76.2mm (3in), while it was 1460mm (57.5in) in height and 1753mm (69in) wide; kerb weight was 1250kg (2745lb). As with the Cortina, the Zephyr had a huge 21.75 cubic foot luggage compartment.

Where the Falcon was obviously trimmed to a price, the Zephyr was by comparison quite luxurious in its interior style and appointments for the era. Its interior ambience was quite different from the Falcon, the doors for example having full height trimming and long armrests that concealed the door handles, and there was full floor carpeting and substantial sound deadening. Like the last of the Mark II Zephyrs, the Mark III had a fan-shaped horizontal speedometer flanked by round temperature and fuel gauges in a slightly raised binnacle, the various switches for lights, choke, wipers and ignition being in a line in a flat walnut-veneered panel below the instruments; within the same panel was provision for the heater that was rather surprisingly an option. Below that again was another flat veneered panel that was to house the radio when fitted and then the T-handle hand brake. Over to the left was the large glove box and oddments tray under that. The colour-coordinated steering wheel had a full-circle horn ring.

The bench seats front and rear were upholstered with pleated brocade where the passengers would sit, the edges being in a colour-matched vinyl. Armrests were fitted to both seats and on each door, and the Zephyr was the first local Ford to use so-called zero-torque door locks that allowed the doors to be closed quietly and with little pressure (unlike Falcon!).

Ian Fraser, writing in *Wheels* October 1962, gave the Mark III Zephyr a full test and wrote a glowing article under the heading "Is this Ford's best car?" He continued by writing, "The least heralded but the most exciting of the new Ford range, the Zephyr, has the best specification and the smartest point to point performance of them all." Fraser liked

the styling and the roominess and quiet comfort of the interior as well as the capacity of the boot to swallow luggage. The padded dash was pleasing although the mock wood jarred and for the times he found the various switches were easy to reach and use. As for its performance, he wrote, "Out on the open road the Zephyr will steam along at its steady 128km/h (80mph) with still plenty in hand for overtaking." The power-assisted front disc brakes, were, he said, "remarkably effective and well able to bring the car to a grinding halt from high speed time after time without fade." Were there any grouches? Yes, the most obvious of all: there was no heater (as standard) and no windscreen washers to go with the new electric wipers. The test car produced a top speed of 157.9km/h (98.7mph), so tantalisingly close to the magic 160km/h (100mph), and ran from a standstill to 96km/h (60mph) in 14.9 seconds; these figures were way better than those for a 170cid Falcon. Perhaps with reclining bucket front seats, floor gearshift for the four-speed all-synchromesh gearbox (both available as options in the UK), electric windscreen washers and a good heater/demister the Zephyr Six or, better, badged as a Zodiac, might have been a better proposition for luxury car buyers than the Falcon Futura that came later?

Unfortunately for Zephyr enthusiasts, Ford Australia made the decision to concentrate on the Falcon range and so the last of the Mark IIIs left the showroom floors late in 1966. No requiem was held.

THE AMERICANS

Through the fifties Ford Australia had addressed the large-car market with their Customline V8 series that had proven to be popular. These were replaced in August 1959 by the huge 'tank' Fairlanes that were assembled from CKD kits (sent from Windsor, Canada) at the Homebush plant in Sydney. It was available in three versions – Custom 300, Fairlane 500 and the gargantuan Ranch Wagon. An updated model was released in July 1960 but picking the differences was difficult (slightly different grille texture is the most obvious) and these behemoths were discontinued in late 1961, although it took well into 1962 to clear all dealer stock.

These cars were huge, sitting on a 2997mm (118in) wheelbase and s-t-r-e-t-c-h-i-n-g 5283mm (208in) overall by 1956mm (77in) wide by 1422mm (56in) high and weighing in at 1630kg (3584lb) at the kerb, the Ranch Wagon being another 91kg (200lb) heavier. Shrinking violets they were definitely not! And as if their sheer size was not enough they possessed what was for the time quite outlandish styling. Up front was a full-width grille that was quite narrow and was surrounded by a deep chromed adage with the substantial chromed steel bumper below that had large parking light lenses at each end; above the grille were dual headlights each side. From there the huge forward-hinged bonnet (most unusual for the time) swept back to a similarly huge panoramic windscreen that curved around to make the A-pillars lean back and up into the roof.

The rear window swept around into the C-pillar and was followed by a huge boot lid. A Harrier jump-jet could have landed on either the bonnet or boot! At the rear were huge round tail-lights each side in huge chromed bezels with smaller indicator lenses above, the front and rear being joined stylistically by lashings of chrome along both sides of the body.

Inside were w-i-d-e bench seats front and rear to accommodate six passengers with ease while the driver looked at a plain dashboard that had a raised binnacle in front containing a horizontal speedometer plus small fuel and temperature gauges and some warning lights. The huge white plastic steering wheel had a three-quarter horn ring and needed more than six turns of the wheel from lock to lock!

Mechanically they were typical of all US cars from the era with the exception of Chrysler products. The all-steel body was mounted onto a substantial chassis that was described in the Fairlane brochure as 'all new' which seems to be a stretch of the copywriter's imagination. Large upper and lower wishbones with coil springs, telescopic dampers and stabiliser bar were fitted up front, 'Even Keel' semi-elliptic leaf springs and live axle at the rear, 'Magic Circle' recirculating ball steering sans power assist and braking was by four-wheel drums of 279mm (11in) diameter with 180sq in of lining area.

Under the bonnet was Ford's latest OHV V8 engine displacing 332cid (bore and stroke 4.00 x 3.30in, 101.6 x 83.3mm, 5424cc) that developed 152kW (204bhp) at 4400rpm and 406Nm (300lb-ft) at 2200rpm. Two gearboxes were available: three-speed manual with non-synchro first gear and a column change, or a Fordomatic two-speed automatic.

A full test was carried in *Wheels* January 1961 and while they generally liked the car they felt that Ford was a bit cheeky asking £2463 for it and not including a heater/demister or windscreen washers! Top speed was recorded at 157.6km/h (98.5mph) with 122km/h (76mph) available in low range. Acceleration was good for the time and the weight of the car at 9.5 seconds to 80km/h (50mph), 12.9 seconds to 96km/h (60mph) and 19.1 seconds to 128km/h (70mph) while fuel 'economy' worked out at 20 litres per 100km (14mpg) on test.

The 'tank' Fairlanes were popular mainly with the primary producer crowd but even they baulked at towing horses and other equipment because of the vast overhang at the rear. Today these cars are valued by a small group of enthusiastic individuals.

FAIRLANE

In America Ford introduced a new family of compact sedans badged as Fairlane that were much more in tune with local motoring needs. Ford's share of the large-car segment (where it was competing with Chevrolet, Pontiac and Dodge) diminished during the brief reign of the 'tank' Fairlane even though both the GM products had body styling that was considered extreme, vulgar to many. The beneficiary was Chrysler, which settled on the single model, the Dodge Phoenix, from 1960. Ford Australia made the decision to bring in the more pleasantly styled and compact Fairlane and assemble it at Homebush. It was released in April 1962.

Described as a super compact by many, the Fairlane represented a breath of fresh air in many ways for Ford US. Not only was it smaller in the physical sense it was virtually as roomy as their larger cars when it came to useable passenger accommodation. For Ford Australia it made sense to downsize to a car that was remarkably similar in size and concept to the Australian Fairlanes that would follow later.

Built on a new platform with a wheelbase of 2934mm (115.5in), it stretched 5004mm (197in) overall, was 1803mm (71in) wide, 1397mm (55in) high and weighed only 1300kg (2860lb), 295kg (650lb) less than previously! Its mechanical configuration could only have been Ford US: under the bonnet was a new V8 engine of 221cid capacity from a bore and stroke of 3.5 x 2.87in (3611cc, 88.9 x 72.9mm); it was an all cast-iron engine but used new foundry techniques to make the castings thinner and lighter. On a mild 8.7:1 compression and using a twin-choke carburettor the engine produced 108kW (145bhp) at 4400rpm and 293Nm (216lb-ft) of torque at 2200rpm. Two gearboxes were offered: three-speed manual or two-speed automatic.

From a styling perspective the Fairlane was up with the latest trends having a broad grille that wrapped around into the front fenders, four headlights, a plain chromed bumper that housed the park/indicator lights, a bright and airy cabin with a big glass area, the so-called Thunderbird C-pillar, and at the rear were typically Ford round tail-lights. Down the side were small fins that began almost from the front and were highlighted by a chromed moulding, and by the time they

TEMP
FUEL
0 10 20 30 40 50 60 70 80 90 100 110 120

RBJ · 894
SOUTH AUSTRALIA

RBJ · 894
SOUTH AUSTRALIA

TEMP H 0 10 20 30 40 50 60 70 80 90 100 110 120 E FUEL F

Fairlane 500

reached the tail-light units the stylists leaned them outwards by around 30 degrees.

Inside was ample room for six passengers on bench seats, there was carpet on the floor and in the three large instrument pods were only three gauges (speedometer with no trip meter, fuel and temperature), the rest of the car's functions were taken care of by warning lights. Lined up along the lower edge of the dash were the switches for lights, wipers and ignition.

Mechanically it was a Ford insofar as the front suspension used coil springs mounted on the upper wishbone with towers in the engine compartment onto which the springs pressed (the original Falcons used a similar system); at the rear it was the usual live axle on semi-elliptic leaf springs The braking system comprised four-wheel cast-iron drums and the recirculating ball steering required five turns from lock to lock.

While the media were generally complimentary about the new Fairlane's performance – 162.1km/h (101.3mph) maximum speed, 0–80 and 96km/h (0–50 and 60mph) times of 9.8 and 14.0 seconds, and a return of 14 litres per 100km (20mpg) for the whole test (13–10.9 litres per 100km/22–26mpg in normal driving) – they were very critical of the car's retail price of £2069 for the manual version and £2193 for the automatic. It was £800 more expensive than a Falcon!

Almost without exception the press was critical of the paucity of equipment included in the price – (no heater/demister, no windscreen washers, no armrests) – and the dreadful finish of the car. *Modern Motor* wrote in September 1962, "Finish generally on the test car was poor. Rippled duco testified to hasty painting, upholstery was wrinkled in places, and odd bits of inside trim obviously would remain incompatible with their surroundings." And the spare wheel was still on the boot floor above the rear axle hump where it was almost impossible to reach … dumb thinking!

For the 1963 model year the Fairlane received the usual annual updates for the sake of doing something, as was the way with the Americans then. For '63 there was a new bonnet pressing, re-profiled front fenders, the obligatory grille change and slightly different (but still round) tail-lights.

Mechanically the most significant upgrade was to the Windsor V8 which was enlarged to 260cid (4250cc) by a simple increase in the cylinder bores from 88.9 to 96.5mm (3.5 to 3.8in). Power rose to 122kW (164bhp) at 4400rpm and torque was up to 350Nm (258lb-ft) at 2200rpm. Performance was little changed at 162km/h (101mph) top speed and 11.5 seconds for the 0–96km/h (0–60mph) sprint. Equipment levels, too, were unchanged but prices had risen slightly to £2233 for the Fairlane 500 automatic.

The third and final variation of the compact Fairlane theme arrived at the end of 1963 for the '64 model year. Again, there was some fiddling with the sheet metal. The fins, small as they were, were gone and there were dummy air scoops on the rear door skins. And of course there was a new grille. Again, the engine was increased in capacity to 289cid, a Ford engine size that has a long history. The bore and stroke were out to 4.00 x 2.85in (101.6 x 72.4mm for 4722cc) and the power was raised to 145kW (195bhp) at 4400rpm, torque was up to 382Nm (282lb-ft) at 2400rpm. The 260cid unit was listed as an option, one that few would have taken. If a buyer opted for the 260cid V8 the gearbox was the two-speed Ford-O-Matic but the more powerful 289cid unit was only available with the Cruise-O-Matic three-speed automatic gearbox.

There was a minor gain in top speed (up to 163.3 km/h (102.1mph) according to *Modern Motor*) and the 0–96km/h (0–60mph) time was down to 10.8 seconds, while fuel consumption had increased to 17.5 litres per 100km (16.2mpg) for the test, say 15 litres per 100km (19mpg) for around town commuting. *Australian Motor Manual* achieved a 168km/h (105mph) top speed, a time of 10.4 seconds for the 0–96km/h (0–60mph) dash and 15 litres per 100km (19mpg) on test with a touring range of 400km (256 miles), not enough in their opinion. As they said, "The Fairlane cruises effortlessly at 128km/h (80mph) and is quiet and comfortable. The suspension is quite taut giving a stable ride over bad roads and enhancing handling qualities." They further commented, "brake pedal pressure is fractionally heavier than expected but the drum brakes are most efficient and suffer little fade."

Local assembly of the Fairlane ended in early 1965.

GALAXIE

GALAXIE

Towards the end of 1964 Ford began assembling the even larger GE Galaxie at its Homebush factory as a replacement for the Fairlane 500. Small numbers had been fully imported during 1963 from Windsor, Canada, and found favour with our politicians and so for the 1965 model year they were assembled from CKD kits. Apart from paint, glass, some interior fittings, plus probably battery and tyres, the rest was ex-Windsor.

While some motorists thought the Fairlane was big, the Galaxie was even larger. It sat on a 3022mm (119in) wheelbase and stretched 5334mm (210in) overall by 2006mm (79in) wide and 1412mm (55.6in) high and weighed in excess of 1730kg (3800lb)! Under the bonnet buyers had the choice of either the 'Challenger' 289cid V8 producing 145kW (195bhp) or the 'Thunderbird' 390cid V8 that produced 208kW (280bhp) and 540Nm (398lb-ft) of torque. The 'Thunderbird' V8's cylinder dimensions were 4.05 x 3.50in bore and stroke, or 102.87 x 88.9mm, for a capacity of 6373cc. The only gearbox offered was the Cruise-O-Matic three-speed unit, the suspension was by wishbones and coil springs at the front and a live axle, coil springs and links at the rear while the braking system was by 279mm (11in) diameter drums with 208sq in of lining area inside 15in wheels shod with 8.15 x 15 tyres, and the steering was a power-assisted recirculating ball system with four turns lock-to-lock.

From a styling perspective the Galaxie was bold and beautiful with its four headlights stacked in vertical pairs either end of the broad horizontal grille, the parking/indicator lights were hidden in the grille alongside the headlights, the overall lines were very square in concept with no consideration given to aerodynamics at all. Out the back were huge square tail-light units. There was a little of the successful Lincoln Continental about the Galaxie's styling. At the time Ford advertised it as the car that "rides quieter than a Rolls-Royce".

Unusually for a large American car, the Galaxie featured an all-steel unit construction body rather than the traditional body-on-frame arrangement that the US industry had used since Noah's day. Also unusual for a Ford were the equipment levels, remembering that the media gave Ford a panning for the lack of fittings in the earlier Fairlanes; the Galaxie had as standard reversing lights, wall-to-wall carpets, fully padded instrument panel, electric clock, automatic choke, windscreen washers and padded sun visors. Note that neither a heater/demister nor an air-conditioning unit was listed nor a sound system. This in a car that cost £2610!

Inside was ample room for six people, three on each bench seat. The interior had a sombre look about it as it was mostly all black, fashionable at the time but dated now. The dash was thickly padded with the instruments, such as they were, under a deep, hooded binnacle, and a glovebox was in front of the passenger. Despite the bulk of the binnacle, actual instrumentation was limited to a small horizontal speedometer with fuel and temperature gauges in a vertically position, separate dial to the right and a clock on the opposite side. Space was available for a sound system and the heater/demister slides were in the centre.

Tested in October 1966 the Galaxie with the 390cid V8 and three-speed automatic gearbox stormed to a maximum speed of 160.6km/h (100.4mph), dashed off the 0–80, 96 and 112km/h (0–50, 60 and 70mph) marks in 7.8, 11.2 and 14.0 seconds while returning 17.8 litres

per 100km (16mpg) on test. Not too bad for a car of its bulk and costing $5810.

For the 1967 model year the sheet metal front and rear was new, although the vertically stacked quad headlights continued and the tail-lights were recessed into the rear panel with a chromed strip around the hole. All new styling arrived for the 1968 model year that in some ways carried over from 1967 – the prominent side ridge in particular – although now the headlights were disposed conventionally in a wide grille that had a vertical divider bar in the centre. Mechanically the '67 and '68 Galaxies continued the same components. In a comparison test by *Australian Motor Manual* where the Galaxie was compared with the Dodge Phoenix and Pontiac Parisienne, the Galaxie was considered to be the least stylish of the trio and the dash was thought to be wasteful of space having five round dials (although only three actual instruments) spread over a span of 38mm (15in) – and "looked something like a throwback to a '36 model". As far as ride comfort and interior silence the Galaxie won easily, "it covered rough surfaced roads with an almost uncanny silence," they said. And as far as acceleration was concerned the Galaxie was the quickest racing from a standstill to 80, 96, 112 and 128km/h (50, 60, 70 and 80mph) in 6.8, 9.2, 12.1 and 17.4 seconds ahead of the Pontiac and Dodge that took 19.2 and 19.6 seconds to reach 128km/h (80mph), a margin of almost two seconds! Only the Galaxie had disc front brakes, incidentally.

Assembly continued at Homebush through to late 1968 before reverting to full import status until sometime in 1972 with the conversion to right-hand drive then being carried out at Broadmeadows.

AUSTRALIAN FAIRLANE

In the large-car segment Ford initially imported the American compact Fairlane but when it became obvious that competitive pricing could not be maintained Ford Australia engineers and designers developed the Australia-only Fairlane that was in essence a long wheelbase XR Falcon and shared almost all mechanical components plus most body panels, at least in the beginning. It was an immediate sales success and established a new market niche that has continued for much of the ensuing forty years.

Sales of the compact US Fairlane rolled along at a steady 1000-to-1200 units a year. Ford knew the market segment that the Fairlane was servicing was far larger than it was achieving but price, however, had become a problem. Currency fluctuations were continually pushing the price up into a segment where it was not competitive. Added to those woes was the fact that in the US it was about to undergo a full model restyle and preliminary pricing indicated quite clearly that it would be uneconomic for Ford to continue with it. What Ford desperately needed was a locally-produced alternative that would satisfy profit concerns expressed by management and meet the forthcoming federal government's local content requirements under Plan A, to which Ford had committed.

Ford began studies based on the forthcoming XR Falcon and a spin-off from that was a project coded XRL. In product planning they had identified a market niche that they labelled Upper Medium. In broad general terms it was between the Falcon and Mercedes-Benz. At the time it was occupied by cars like the Rover 2000, Triumph 2000 and later 2.5 PI, Volvo 144 and one or two others. It was thought by Ford that following their experience with the compact, imported Fairlane they were on the right track. They were also looking for ways to expand the Falcon body unit upmarket with incremental sales volume and greater profits.

XRL became the XRA under Bill Bourke and was integrated into the overall XR Falcon development program. Essentially the first local Fairlane was an amalgam of Australian-produced body parts and imported US Fairlane parts – the extended wheelbase floorpan and exterior rear body panels and one or two others. Within 18 months the imported Fairlane panels were replaced by locally pressed panels and Ford suffered no government penalty by not complying immediately with the 95 per cent requirements of Plan A.

From a mechanical perspective the ZA Fairlane shared all of its major components with the XR Falcon. Under the bonnet were two tried-and-true engines: the 200cuc in 'Super Pursuit' six-cylinder that was a direct descendant of the original 144cid Falcon six; and the 289cid small block V8 that had gained fame under the bonnet of the Mustang. The six had a bore and stroke of 3.68in by 3.12in (93.47 x 79.25mm, capacity 3280cc) and produced 90kW (121bhp) at 4400rpm together with 257Nm (190lb-ft) of torque at 2400rpm. It ran a 9.2:1 compression ratio and a single barrel downdraft carburettor.

The 289 V8 had the familiar cylinder dimensions of 4.00in by 2.87in (101.6 x 72.9mm, 4732cc) and produced 149kW (200bhp) at 4400rpm and 382Nm (282lb-ft) of torque at 2400rpm on a 9.3:1 compression and used a single twin-barrel carburettor.

Power from the six-cylinder engine went to the rear wheels through either a three-speed manual gearbox with a column shift lever or a three-speed automatic gearbox, the manual being synchronised on second and top gears only. The rear axle ratio was 3.23:1. Two automatic gearboxes were available, the Borg Warner-sourced Type 35 that was used with the six-cylinder versions, and the Cruise-O-Matic that was imported from America and mated to the V8.

The general running gear for the Fairlane was taken straight from the Falcon parts bin so that meant a double wishbone system that had the coil spring and damper acting on the upper wishbone, a system that had been thoroughly re-engineered and strengthened to withstand the rigours of local conditions. At the rear was a live axle assembly with semi-elliptic leaf springs and double-acting tubular dampers.

Braking was by 254mm (10in) cast-iron drums all round unless buyers ticked the disc front brakes box on the order form (although Fairlane 500 buyers did get front discs as standard). A vacuum boost, however, was optional. The disc rotors were solid, 254mm (10in) in diameter, with a single piston floating head calliper and made locally by Girling.

From the Falcon came the recirculating ball steering that boasted 5.2 turns from lock to lock. Despite severe criticism from the motoring press, minimal change was made to the steering ratio for XR/ZA. In fact, for the power steering system that was optional on ZA, the *same* ratio was used for both assisted and non-assisted steering systems.

As far as body dimensions were concerned the Fairlane sat on a wheelbase of 2946mm (116in), it stretched to 4978mm (196in) overall, was 1897mm (74.7in) wide and stood 1397mm (55in) high. With the 221cid six-cylinder engine kerb weight was 1386kg (3050lb), 136kg (300lb) more if the V8 engine was specified. Physically it was a close match for the superseded US compact Fairlane, which was intentional on Ford Australia's part.

The ZA Fairlane was introduced onto the Australian market on 27 February 1967 and was an immediate sales success. Model differentiation was clear and simple between Falcon and Fairlane. All Falcons regardless of trim level had single 7in round headlights positioned at the extremities of the wide grille opening where the Fairlane had four 5in units grouped horizontally as pairs at either end of the grille. A broad, central chromed bar stylistically joined the four headlights together. Left of centre, above the bar, was a simple rectangular Fairlane badge.

At the rear the round Falcon light units were replaced by vertically positioned rectangular tail-lights with a central amber lens that extended the general theme found on the Falcon. As was usual at the time, the tail and stoplights used the red lens and the amber served as direction indicators and reversing lights when fitted.

The stretched wheelbase was obvious to car spotters, the giveaway being the added distance between the rear door lower shutline and the wheel arch. While the wheelbase had been extended the rear door pressings were from the Falcon.

Inside the differences were again significant enough to warrant the higher positioning of the Fairlane in the market. The dashboard was similar with a moulded and padded dash top but was trimmed with better materials and had a completely different three-piece instrument cluster that was unique but was clearly based on that of the Galaxie – a broad, rectangular centre unit that housed the horizontal speedometer, and vertically mounted smaller rectangular units each side. The one on the left contained the fuel and temperature gauges while the other contained the engine oil pressure and volts gauges. Within the Ford range of cars, only the Falcon GT carried a similarly complete set of gauges.

The entry level Fairlane was equipped to Falcon 500 standards and had a bench seat front and back with fold-away armrests, carpet on the floor, courtesy lights in the boot and glovebox, while power came from the 200cid six mated to the three-speed manual gearbox with a column change. The V8 and automatic were options many took, as were power steering and power-assisted front disc brakes. The Fairlane 500 came standard with the 289cid V8 and SelectShift three-speed automatic gearbox, power boosted front disc brakes, power steering, reclining front bucket seats, centre console, heater/demister, clock, door courtesy lights and a driver's side exterior door mirror.

With the ZA Fairlane Ford filled a yawning gap in its range and tapped into a niche that neither GM-Holden nor Chrysler apparently had identified. The Fairlane slotted between the upper Falcon models (the Fairmont in particular) and the gargantuan Galaxie 500, and in many ways took cues from both.

The top of the range Fairlane 500 retailed off the showroom floor for $3885, the base Fairlane for a mere $3080. Despite the cost, the Fairlane 500 was by far the biggest seller taking more than 70 per cent of Fairlane sales.

Barry Cooke, writing in *Modern Motor* magazine's May 1967 issue said of the Fairlane 500, "Ford's new prestige car is great, except for just one thing … the steering."

He was referring to the fact that the Fairlane was fitted with power-assisted steering that required an amazing five turns lock-to-lock. It was light in its action but was unnecessarily cumbersome if pressing on. Interestingly, he made the comment, "The car doesn't fall into any particular category. It's bigger than the Valiant and both Ramblers, smaller than the Galaxie and (Dodge) Phoenix."

On the road, Cooke described the Fairlane as "a rapid and comfortable point-to-pointer" so long as the road was smooth and straight. He added, "There is surprisingly little body roll, the suspension is fairly quiet on all but the roughest surfaces, and performance is such that very few cars would have the legs to get past on the straight." He liked the brakes – "nicely modulated and with a progressive pedal action" – and found the amount of power to be 'embarrassing' on gravel roads.

On test the Fairlane 500 with the 289cid V8 achieved a maximum speed of 167.2km/h (104.5 miles) per hour, 0–96km/h (0–60 mph) in 12.15 seconds and ran the quarter mile in 18.3 seconds. Fuel economy worked out at 16.4 litres per 100km (17.3mpg) on average, which gave a cruising range from the 75-litre (16.4Imp gal) tank at less than 480km (300mi), hardly sufficient for a country with the vast distances of Australia.

Cooke concluded by writing, "The Fairlane, odd man out on the market at the moment, is likely to cause some concern among the big cars with which it competes."

Wheels tested the very same car and published its report in the June 1967 issue. In general, they concurred with Cooke and added some comments of their own. For example, they were critical of the fact that the Fairlane (and by extension the Falcon) had not adopted the English Ford Cortina's 'Aeroflow' interior ventilation system; and they felt that the headlights on high beam were not in any way up to the car's cruising capabilities.

They concluded by writing, "We have a funny feeling that the 116 inch-V8 formula is going to be the mass seller in Australia in five years' time."

Ford quietly slipped the ZB Fairlane onto the market a year later, in February 1968. Little was changed from a styling point of view except the new tail-light units had the indicator/reversing lens positioned horizontally across the bezel and not floating in it as on the ZA (the units were from the 1967 US Fairlane), the grille texture was new, the wheel trims were far more ostentatious and the body badges were new.

Under the bonnet were more far-reaching changes. The 'Super Pursuit' six was expanded in capacity from 200 to 221cu in, from 3.3 to 3.6 litres, the increase in capacity coming from a lengthened crankshaft stroke – from 79.2mm to 87.6mm (3.12in to 3.45in). With a slightly higher 9.3:1 compression and single-throat carburettor, the power output rose to 100kW (135bhp) at 4400rpm and torque to 282Nm (208lb-ft) at 2400rpm. And the 289cid V8 was replaced by the 302cid (5.0 litres) Windsor V8. Power was now quoted at 179kW (240bhp) at 5000rpm and torque at 413Nm (305lb-ft) at 2600rpm on a compression of 9.5:1 and with a single twin-throat carburettor.

Power-assisted front disc brakes were still an option, albeit an option taken up by more than 90 per cent of buyers. For the ZB, Ford's engineers quickened the steering ratio for those equipped with power steering making it slightly more direct. As for the interior, it was unchanged.

Wheels published a full road test of the six-cylinder Fairlane Custom in its September 1968 issue, one of the few tests on a Custom as Ford's press fleet consisted mostly of the better equipped Fairlane 500 V8s. Commenting on the engine, they wrote, "The new 100kW (135bhp) six helps the power-to-weight ratio. While not providing the lusty torque of the V8, it does give the Fairlane more tow than many mature owners will ever need." They achieved a maximum speed of 152km/h (95mph) with the standing quarter time of 19.3 seconds and a 0–96km/h (0–60mph) sprint in 12.8 seconds.

Of its handling, they said, "The Fairlane six is an excellent tourer.

Combined with this is a great stability factor inherited from the Falcon but emphasised by the extra length in the wheelbase." They did comment negatively, however, on the soft damper settings that promoted a 'floaty' feeling on some surfaces.

In conclusion, they wrote, "The ZB Fairlane has its sore spots like any car does. In terms of ride, comfort, sheer space and prestige the Fairlane is excellent value."

The recommended retail price of the Fairlane Custom was $3141 making it something of a bargain in the market.

In August 1969 Ford released the third edition of the Fairlane, the ZC. The winning formula remained basically untouched but was again improved in the details. Styling, this time round, came in for some attention with the result being a far more distinctive-looking luxury automobile.

Clearly inspired by the 1967 American Galaxie, the ZC adopted vertically stacked headlights with a new grille consisting of two broad, narrow rectangular sections stacked one above the other, each comprising four horizontal bars. The restyled front meant that the Falcon and Fairlane no longer shared fenders, those for the ZC now being unique.

The C-pillar area was restyled to permit a recessed rear window, another theme taken from the Galaxie. To prevent reflections from the sun the window surround was painted black. At the rear the tail-lights now wrapped around into the quarter panels although they retained their three-lens style.

The ZC was still very recognisably a Fairlane but now had a much stronger presence, a more purposeful appearance than previously.

Along with the far more distinctive exterior, the Fairlane interior adopted a more unique style from the Falcon. The dashboard consisted of a huge padded plastic moulding that was divided 60:40 across the width of the interior. Under the broad, rectangular hooded binnacle that occupied 60 per cent of the dash in front of the driver were the instruments and various controls. No longer were the instruments Galaxie-inspired, they were now fewer in number and less clear to read. The speedometer was a narrow-but-wide strip type with a fuel gauge at the left end and a temperature gauge to the right. A small glove compartment occupied the area left of the dash in front of the passenger.

Stacked in the centre of the vast dash were the radio and heater/demister (and air conditioning, if ordered) controls. All the various control knobs, and there were many of them, were now made from soft plastic and much larger in diameter than previously, in line with safety ideas at the time.

New also was Ford's 'Select Air' fresh air ventilation system that looked exactly what it was – an afterthought. Chromed, rectangular adjustable air vents were positioned either side of the interior, below the dash and not incorporated into it, and not reachable by a driver or passenger wearing a seatbelt.

As part of the upgrade Ford redesigned the seats, particularly those in front. They were referred to appropriately as "twin comfort lounge seats" such was their comfort.

Like the ZB, the ZC came in two versions: Custom and Fairlane 500. New on the options list for the 500 was factory-fitted air conditioning and a 351-cubic inch V8 engine, the 302 V8 remaining as the standard engine for the 500 series. With the 351 engine Ford was able to offer buyers prestige *and* performance.

The 351cu in V8 (101.6 x 88.9mm/4.00 v 3.50in bore and stroke) ran a high 10.7:1 compression and used an Autolite four-barrel down draft carburettor to produce 216kW (290bhp) at 4800rpm and a massive 522Nm (385lb-ft) of torque at 3200rpm. It was the same engine as in the Falcon GT. Amazingly, it was technically available with the four-speed all synchromesh manual gearbox but it is doubtful if any were actually built.

Powering the Custom was the 3.6-litre (221cu in) six-cylinder engine now rated at 104kW (140bhp) and 284Nm (210lb-ft) of torque. Standard engine for the Fairlane 500 was the 164kW (220bhp) 5.0-litre (302cid) V8.

Along with the under-bonnet changes came a number of other improvements. Standard brakes on the Custom were still 254mm (10in) cast-iron drums. For the 500 series the front brakes were now Kelsey-Hayes 286mm (11.25in) diameter ventilated and turbo-cooled discs with a power boost and dual circuits. 5JJ by 14 safety rims were fitted with either 6.95 x 14 low profile or 7.35 x 14 extra low profile tyres. V8-engined cars were available with 6JJ safety rims with either 185 x 14 radials or special ER70 x 14 wide oval radial ply tyres.

The 351 V8 gave the ZC a level of performance unheard-of in this class of car. In fact, so quick was it that it could out-accelerate the XR and XT Falcon GTs up to 160km/h (100 miles) an hour! *Wheels* achieved a maximum speed of 187km/h (117mph) from their test car, with a standing quarter of 16.0 seconds and a 0–96km/h (0–60mph) time of 7.8 seconds. 0–160km/h (0–100mph) took just 23 seconds, this in 1969 from a luxury sedan that weighed 1578kg (3472lb)! A ZC Fairlane 500 equipped with the 216kW (290bhp) 351cid V8 was a real wolf in sheep's clothing, a real Q-car.

Ford remained competitive with its pricing of the Fairlane. By the time of the ZC the basic price of the Custom – 3.6-litre six, three-speed manual gearbox, drum brakes and bench front seat – had risen from $3088 to $3490 despite rampant inflation. The 302 V8 was a $183 option, disc front brakes were an extra $66 and the three-speed automatic was $264. The Fairlane 500's basic price had risen to $4370 with the options being the 351 V8 at $407, air conditioning also $407, radio $123 and a sunroof at $163.

As predicted by David Morgan from the beginning, the biggest seller was the Fairlane 500 equipped with a radio that sold for $4493. The 351 V8 option that arrived with ZC came at a modest premium that also included mandatory limited slip differential and radial tyres. $4777 for the ultimate Aussie Q-car, what a bargain! The fourth generation Fairlane arrived late in 1970 and will be discussed in *Australian Cars of the 70s*.

CLUB PERMIT
CH·9116
VICTORIA

Chapter 3

CHRYSLER

Chrysler began the sixties in the same way it ended the fifties, somewhat in disarray. Its model range consisted of the modern and well-liked Simca Aronde sedan that was joined by the uniquely Australian station wagon in 1962, the under-appreciated Vedette Beaulieu V8 sedan that failed to grab the market's attention despite being a very well-engineered and well-styled car, and the ancient Chrysler Royal. Not a lot to get excited about but behind the scenes much was happening that would have a profound effect on the company's future.

SIMCA

Chrysler had established the Simca as a desirable small car in the lower segment of the market. In March 1960 it released the P60 Aronde sedan, which was immediately popular with buyers. In many ways the P60 was a large small car (or a small large car depending on your point of view) because it rode on a wheelbase of 2438mm (96in) and stretched 4191mm (165in) overall. It competed in the market segment (around the £1000 mark) dominated by the VW Beetle, but also against cars like the Hillman Minx, Austin Lancer/Morris Major, Ford Anglia, Fiat 1100 and Renault Dauphine. The Aronde's interior was roomier than any of those and it had a bigger boot, an important consideration in those days.

Powering the Aronde was the company's long-serving OHV four-cylinder engine of 1290cc (74 x 75mm) that developed 36kW (48.5bhp) at 4800rpm and 92Nm (68lb-ft) of torque at 2500rpm. It featured a cast-iron cylinder block topped by an aluminium alloy cylinder head with the intake and exhaust manifolds both on the right-hand side of the engine as on the Fiat; this was because the Simca engine was basically a copy of the Fiat design. Similarly, the crankshaft of this 'Flash' engine as it was known had three main bearings. It was coupled to a four-speed manual gearbox with synchromesh on the top three ratios, operated by a column shift, and an open drive shaft delivered the power to the live rear axle suspended on semi-elliptic leaf springs; the front suspension was by upper-and-lower wishbones with coil springs and concentric dampers. Braking was by enormous 254mm (10in) diameter drums all round (it had 14in rims with 5.60 x 14 tyres) while the steering was a worm-and-roller system. It was pretty much standard fare for almost all cars in that class at that time.

Styling of the P60 was quite a step forward from its predecessor by being more contemporary (the outgoing model was nearly ten years old) with a squarer rear end having vertical tail-light units each side, the roofline was flatter and the rear window curved around into the C-pillar. Up front was an oval-shaped concave grille with fine vertical bars. What was unusual was the windscreen wiper sweep: the driver's arm parked at the bottom of the screen while the passenger's arm parked vertically alongside the left A-pillar.

The Aronde dashboard was a plastic moulding with padding along the lower edge to protect passengers' knees. The French were leaders at the time in using plastics in their car interiors (Renault and Peugeot were the same) but the problem was the Australian sun, which played havoc with the interior. All instruments were in a simple rectangular panel in front of the driver (strip ribbon-type speedometer plus a fuel gauge and some lights) and in front of the passengers was an identically shaped panel for the glovebox.

Seating comprised a front bench with individual backrests and a rear bench so up to five passengers could be carried. In the Deluxe model, which was by far the most popular, a fresh air heater/demister with a fan was standard as were reclining backs to the front seats.

For 1962 Chrysler released an upgraded Aronde that featured the 'Rush' version of the 1290cc engine, the main difference being the use of a five-bearing crankshaft and a centrifugal oil filter on the front of the crankshaft. Externally the sedan had a brushed aluminium strip down each side, the gearshift mechanism was simplified and the shift quality improved enormously, windscreen washers were standard and the speedometer now had a needle pointer. It was the old story of if it ain't broke don't fix it! The Deluxe sold for £1045, while for price conscious buyers there was the Etoile version with the old engine available at £949.

Modern Motor carried a full test of the Aronde in its February 1962 issue. Tester Hanrahan was ecstatic about the handling saying, "The Simca's handling will bring joy to any man's heart – flat, light, utterly predictable. Exhilaratingly fast through corners." He described the engine as 'wonderful', the revised gearshift was "as good as any of its type", the front seats as "in the executive class" and that a lot of carmakers could copy the Simca's unusual wiper pattern. What were the negatives? The indicator lever (on the steering wheel hub) worked on a timer principle, the foot pedals (which sprouted up through the floor) were too close together, the automatic choke on the carburettor and the inaccuracy of the speedometer. For a design that originated in 1951 and had only changed in minor details apart from the body change for 1960, some of the criticisms were obvious. As for its performance, *MM* published figures of 130km/h (81.4mph) for a maximum and 14.6 seconds for the 0–80km/h (0–50mph) dash with 8.8–7.4 litres per 100km (32–38mpg) economy.

Sales of small station wagons had been growing as witnessed by the numbers of Hillman Minx, Austin A60, VW Type 3 1500, Skoda Octavia and others showed. Chrysler decided it wanted a part of this action and approached the French for assistance; after all, they had designed the P60 Aronde sedan, but they merely shrugged their shoulders in Gallic disinterest and walked away. The Australians made the decision to go it alone. In early 1960 an Aronde sedan was taken to the experimental workshops where a hand-built prototype wagon was constructed for management to inspect. Built on the Aronde floorpan, it had an extended roof with a Ford pattern tailgate that had a wind-down rear window, and the seats were redesigned and made to allow a number of load options. With the seats folded down there was space for two adults to sleep (it was 2.87 metres (9ft 5in) long), which was more than any other small wagon on the market.

A sturdy roof rack was standard equipment and it could take up to 90kg (200lb) of luggage in addition to the 364kg (800lb) that could be carried inside. To allow for this the engineers specified heavy-duty rear dampers and springs and larger tyres – 5.90 x 14 instead of 5.60 x 14.

The production Aronde station wagon appeared in showrooms in March 1962 and was immediately popular with family car buyers who appreciated the versatility of the interior, its roominess and spirited performance from the five-bearing 'Rush' motor.

Modern Motor extracted a top speed of 123km/h (77mph) from the wagon and a time of 15.1 seconds for the 0–80km/h (0–50mph) dash, the small difference in performance being due to the extra 51kg (112lb) of the wagon over the sedan. The only major difference in terms of handling came about when driving over rough roads with no weight in the wagon when the rear end could become skittish. At £1159 the testers believed the Aronde wagon to be excellent value for money.

There was another Simca in Chrysler showrooms during the early sixties – the Vedette. Small numbers were assembled beginning in 1959 with the last being sold some time in 1962. The Vedette was a 'kissin' cousin' to the popular Mark II Ford Zephyr but that association never helped the Simca and Chrysler seemed at a loss to know what to do to sell it. At £1395 it was more expensive than the Holden but it was only

VACUUM
AGENT
SMB 555

SIMCA 1

SIMCA 1

10 20 30 40 50 60 70 80 90 100
FUEL
TEMP

£30 more expensive than the Zephyr and £7 more than the Vauxhall Velox. Its styling was very contemporary, passenger accommodation was excellent and the boot was huge. Maybe it had something to do with the old Ford side-valve V8 engine under the bonnet? It was an engine with an enviable reputation for reliability and longevity and it provided the Vedette with 145km/h (90mph) performance (comparable to the Zephyr and Velox) but buyers stayed away. Every magazine that published a road test came away highly impressed with its performance, long distance cruising abilities and accommodation but despite good reviews sales were hard to come by.

In the August 1961 issue of *Wheels* a Vedette featured on the front cover and there was a full road test within headed 'Simca's Virile Vedette'. It was a most pleasing report to read because the testers found few faults – the use of side valves on the Ford V8 engine, relative lack of low speed torque, no interior bonnet lock, time delay on the indicator switch (same as on the Aronde) and that was about all. None were bad enough to prevent a sale, especially when the Vedette was better kitted out than most of its rivals. With 64kW (84bhp) at 4800rpm and 152Nm (112lb-ft) at 2750rpm, the Vedette ran out to 148.8km/h (93mph), took 17.7 seconds for the 0–96km/h (0–60mph) dash and returned 14.8 litres per 100km (19mpg) on test, 11.3 litres per 100km (25mpg) during normal driving which was more than competitive with the Zephyr and Velox.

Finding a Simca Vedette today is quite a challenge.

ROYAL

In June 1960 Chrysler released the AP3 version of the Chrysler Royal sedan. For a company with such limited resources and for a model that was selling in such small numbers the extent of the AP3 upgrade was remarkable. From the exterior it was notable for its four vertically-stacked headlights set in an extravagantly-styled grille while at the rear were reshaped quarter panels that formed fashionable fins (even though the styling fad had passed) that housed three light lenses set vertically each side. The styling idea for the rear came from the 1958 De Soto Firesweep although the actual individual lenses were manufactured locally by Hella.

Running full length along the side of the body was a chrome flash that began behind the headlights and progressed in a slightly downward path to then rise to the tip of the rear fin – it looked like a giant tick of approval.

Inside was a restyled dashboard made over the original structure. The speedometer was a broad horizontal unit set on top of the dash in front of the driver (it was a copy of the 1960 Plymouth unit) with the small square-shaped minor dials (fuel and temperature) set in a brushed aluminium strip below. If the Torqueflite three-speed automatic gearbox (it replaced the two-speed Powerflite) was ordered the five push buttons to operate it were on the right-hand end of the strip.

The ancient 250cid side-valve six and OHV 313cid 'Fury' V8 were carried over from the AP2 as were all the other mechanical components.

Motor Manual tested an AP3 V8 and expressed positive opinions about the car – huge luggage space, vast interior with comfortable bench seats, its quiet progress and ease of driving – but they were a little concerned about the braking system's capacity to cope with the enormous performance potential. They recorded a top speed of 168km/h (105mph) and a 0–96km/h (0–60mph) time of 10.4 seconds.

Production stumbled along until the summer of 1963 when the last of the old dowagers came off the assembly line and into motoring history.

VALIANT

In January 1962 the R Series Chrysler Valiant was released to great acclaim and with only 1008 units available it sold out in days. Chrysler Australia, led by ex-pat American David Brown, knew the Valiant was the make-or-break car for the company and it was he who forced the hand of the Americans back in Detroit. The Australian Valiant retained the extrovert Virgil Exner styling but differed from the American version in several important ways. Firstly, the engine mounts were different to allow the engine and gearbox to be moved fractionally to the left to allow room for the steering column shaft to squeeze between the cylinder head and engine bay side panel to the steering box that was bolted onto the lower body rail. It came as standard with the larger of the two engine options in America (the big 108kW (145bhp) 225cid 'Slant Six') and 14in road wheels shod with 6.95 x 14 cross ply tyres. Power went to the rear wheels through either a three-speed manual gearbox with a floor shift or three-speed Torqueflite automatic with push-button controls. The suspension comprised Chrysler's famous 'Torsionaire' front suspension using wishbones and longitudinal torsion bars allied to a live axle on semi-elliptic leaf springs at the rear. There were 228mm (9in) drum brakes all round with 153sq in of lining area.

Unusually, the Valiant was built on a relatively short 2705mm

RV1-4-1

(106.5in) wheelbase and had an overall length of 4666mm (183.7in) with quite a long rear overhang. Width and height were 1788mm and 1397mm (70.4 and 55in) respectively and it weighed 1200kg (2604lb). These dimensions made it just a tad bigger than the Falcon (that had a longer wheelbase) and the EJ Holden. Roominess inside was very good, with up to six people being accommodated on the bench seats even though the gearshift was on the floor. The Valiant lost out on boot space because of the slightly exaggerated slope of the boot lid and the intrusion of the fuel filler pipe.

CKD kits were dispatched to the old Mile End factory where locally sourced interior trim, glass, floor mats, paint and many accessories were added to the imported (for the moment) panels. What set the Valiant apart from all of its rivals (apart from its storming performance) was its distinctive Virgil Exner inspired styling that featured a prominent almost-square grille that echoed that from the fabled Chrysler 300 letter series sports sedans, quad headlights, six-window side glass, boot lid with a fake spare wheel stamped into it and cat's eye tail-lights. Inside was a deep instrument binnacle in front of the driver with two large round dials in a fake machine-turned finish panel, padding on the dash in front of the passenger, and bench seats – important in the Australia of 1962. If you bought an automatic the five buttons that operated it were positioned on the right-hand edge of the instrument binnacle. If a heater/demister was fitted its control buttons were on the left side of the binnacle.

When the media drove it they were stunned with the performance – it was electrifying compared with the fairly pedestrian performance of the Holden and Falcon. The Valiant was slightly more expensive than its two rivals, a deliberate move by the company and justified when compared with the others. For example, the Valiant would run to 158km/h (98.9mph) and dash to 96km/h (60mph) in 11.5 seconds where an EJ Holden could manage only 134km/h (84mph) and 21.0 seconds, the Falcon 139km/h (87mph) and 18.0 seconds. As for fittings, none of them had a heater/demister as a standard fitting and the floors were covered by rubber mats, door armrests were fitted to the Valiant but not the others and so it went. It was the 1960s …

Only two months later, at the end of March 1962, Chrysler replaced the R Series with the S Series that was more of the same but toned down a little, more's the pity. Gone was the fake spare tyre, the boot lid now being a plain sheet stamping with a circular chromed decoration on it, the tail-lights were now small round units recessed into the lower panel under where the cat's eyes had been, a small blanking panel being bolted on to plug the hole, the grille had a finer pattern and was no longer recessed while the previous floor gear shift was replaced by a conventional column lever. Little else was touched; after all, when you have a winner why mess with it?

What was not realised in 1962 was the impact that the R and S Valiants would have on the local market – they were literally the harbingers of change and changed *forever* the way Australian motorists would see their family sedan.

On the American market Chrysler offered buyers the option of a station wagon and a slinky two-door hardtop coupe but the ultra-conservative management in Australia decided not to bring them in because they did not have the factory space or capacity to add them to their model line. Full importation was apparently never considered even though at the time local content percentages were not an issue. A huge marketing opportunity sadly missed.

Finance had been approved by Detroit for the construction of a completely new assembly plant that would include the biggest and best stamping plant and tool room in the Southern Hemisphere; it would be erected on land the company had purchased some years previously at Tonsley Park.

Under pressure from the conservative and hawkish media in the US to conform to perceived market 'norms' Chrysler introduced their T Series which was coded as the AP5 here. The code, by the way, stood for Australian Production (not Plymouth) number 5. That saw a *very* conventional three-box design for the next generation Valiants. Chrysler's Australian stylist, Brian Smyth, made some necessary changes at the rear to raise the boot line and improve luggage space and gave it a much plainer face, plain to the point of being nondescript with single 7in round headlights each side of a straight grille with six horizontal bars topped by a chromed strip with the word Chrysler embossed in it. Released in May 1963, early production AP5s retained the parallel windscreen wiper sweep for America because initially the components were still US-sourced.

Body tooling for the rear of the AP5 was made in-house at Tonsley Park with local content pushing up past 70 per cent; amazing given the relatively short time frame. New with the AP5 was the arrival of the first Valiant Safari station wagon, a local design adapted from the American version. It retained the sedan's rear door window line, the side window of the wagon area curving down slightly at the top to meet it. The tailgate featured a wind-down window that had to be wound all the way down before it could be dropped. When closed and the rear seat back was up, the load space was 128 by 110mm (50.5in long by 43.5in) between the wheel arches; with the seat down the load space stretched to 2133mm (84in) in length.

Basic dimensions remained the same as before as did the mechanical components. Roominess was improved fractionally by the model change, mostly rear seat head room because the Valiant had adopted the flatter Thunderbird roofline. The dashboard was all new; it was now a plain straight across design with a padded upper edge, glove box in front of the passenger, provision for a radio and heater/demister in the centre. In front of the driver was a brushed aluminium panel containing the round instruments comprising the speedometer (large) and three smaller dials for fuel, temperature and amps, oil pressure being monitored by a warning light.

As part of the company's desire to match Holden and Ford, Chrysler introduced the Regal sedan and wagon that was distinguishable from its lesser siblings by exterior badges, a raised emblem on the bonnet, chromed fluted body mouldings and window trims, whitewall tyres and chromed dress trims on the wheels. To give a more upmarket ambience inside, Chrysler used a soft-to-touch vinyl upholstery, folding centre armrests were fitted front and back, the floors were carpeted with a better quality carpet, the steering wheel had two colours and a heater/demister came as standard. The sedan cost £1498 and the wagon was £100 more. Chrysler reduced the showroom prices of the regular Valiants too, by £35 for the manual and £40 for the automatic.

A *Wheels* four-car comparison (November 1963) showed the Valiant and the newly re-engined Holden were the two performance leaders with top speeds of 147km/h (91.9) for the EH Holden and 145.7km/h (91.1) for the Valiant, the positions remaining the same for the 0–80km/h (0–50mph) acceleration times at 10.1 and 10.4 seconds respectively. The Falcon was left way behind as was the Austin Freeway.

The AP5 gave way to the AP6 in March 1965 and, as with the R and S Series it was the most minor of upgrades that seemed to be done more for marketing purposes than any other reason. What changed? Well, there was a new grille that was far more distinctive comprising three parts using the horizontal theme again but the centre one-third section stood slightly proud of the sections either side and was painted body colour. A prominent bar carrying the parking/indicator light was in the centre of each of the side sections. The chromed strip on the side of the body was repositioned, beginning with a sharp hook on the front fender to then go all the way around the body on the waist line ridge and across the lower edge of the boot lid. On the wagons, the tail-lights were now round in place of the horizontal ones used previously. All other body panels were carried over from the AP5. In keeping with the apparent need to conform to rivals GM-H and Ford, Chrysler went to a normal steering column lever for the automatic forsaking the much-liked push-button system on the Torqueflite A904 gearbox.

New, too, with AP6 was the availability of the small block 273cid (4474cc) V8, another first for Chrysler in the local market. With cylinder dimensions of 92.2 x 84.0mm it developed 134kW (180bhp) at 4200rpm and 352Nm (260 lb-ft) of torque at 1600rpm on an 8.8:1 compression and using a Carter dual-throat carburettor. It was available only with an automatic gearbox with a console-mounted selector lever.

Intriguingly, the engine was only available at that stage in the Valiant V8 as it was badged (and *not* Valiant *Regal* V8); although to confuse the issue it was trimmed inside at Regal levels and could only be distinguished outside by the V-Eight badge on each front fender and boot lid. And despite weighing 1352kg (2957lb) and having a 172.8km/h (108mph) top speed and 10.9 seconds ability to sprint to 96km/h (60mph) the

CH·0859

AP 6225

RMS-435

VALIANT

Valiant V8 was still fitted with drum brakes, albeit now with a vacuum booster. All for £1775, around £250 more than the Regal.

In April, a month after the rest of the range, Chrysler announced the availability of the Wayfarer utility that was a totally Australian effort that resurrected an old name last used on the Royal utility in the fifties. This time it met a keenly receptive market response!

A year later came the VC Valiant that brought with it a comprehensive re-style that was the work of the Australian designers led by Brian Smyth. The passenger section was carried over but there were six new outer panels – three each end comprising fenders (x4) plus new boot lid and bonnet pressings; and new bumpers. Each end was squared up with the lights recessed behind the leading edge of the fenders. The grille retained the suggestion of a central section that was slightly vee-ed and again the theme was horizontal. The tail-lights were vertically positioned and vaguely triangular in shape; reversing/indicator lights at the rear had orange lenses and were positioned in the bumper while the parking/indicator lights at the front were also in the bumpers, the bumpers looking to the eye to be interchangeable front-to-rear.

Inside there was a revised dashboard that carried over the theme from the AP5 and AP6 although it was different insofar as the instruments were now contained in two large circular dials with round knobs lined up across the centre of the dash if the heater/demister was fitted.

If the V8 engine was specified the car came with a vinyl roof that included the A- and B-pillars and on the rear quarter panels were three discreet horizontal chrome strips, while the automatic selector was floor mounted, not on the column. Some months prior to the arrival of the VE, front disc brakes were made available as an option.

A complete model change came in October 1967 when Chrysler announced the VE Valiants, the code VD being skipped for obvious reasons! While it might have looked to be a carry-over body, it was in fact new according to stylist Smyth. The proportions of the body were exactly the same as before, the style was nicely refreshed and on a slightly longer wheelbase – 2743mm (108in), an increase of only 38mm (1.5in). The grille continued the horizontal theme with four bars that were stepped in shape to meet with a chamfer on the leading edge of the bonnet (a feature taken from the US Dodge Dart) that carried the Valiant model name. Tail-lights were now U-shaped but lying on their side with two mild depressions going across the back of the boot lid joining them. On the lower-spec versions these grooves were painted body colour but on the upmarket Regal brushed aluminium panels were used. Interestingly, the rear window had a slight 'turn-up' in the last 38mm (1.5in) at the top and was apparently free of distortion. And for the first time on Valiant, the side window glass was curved.

Mechanically it was carry-over VC, although a higher performance 119kW (160bhp) version of the slant six was now available (it had a twin-throat carburettor) and the 273cid V8's output was raised to 145kW (195bhp).

Inside was a new dashboard that featured a more thickly padded roll top with the facia part vee-ed in profile. In front of the driver was a new instrument cluster featuring a square speedometer with graduations up to 190km/h (120mph). In a bezel to the right were the three minor dials – fuel, temperature and amps – and to the left was another bezel with the oil and brake warning lights. All three bezels were edged in chromed plastic. In the centre of the dash was provision for a radio and the slides for the heater/demister system when fitted; a large glovebox was off to the far left.

Modern Motor tested a VE sedan with the 119kW (160bhp) engine and three-speed Torqueflite automatic that retailed for $2835. It was in so many ways a repeat of what Chrysler had served up for five years – conservative styling bordering on bland, nondescript even, allied to excellent mechanical components that had proved themselves to be virtually unbreakable, certainly long-lasting and reliable. The Valiant ran to a top speed of 158km/h (98.8mph) and dashed off the 80 and 96km/h (50 and 60mph) increments in 7.6 and 12.6 seconds each and consumed fuel at the rate of 15 litres per 100km (18.7mpg) on test, say 13 litres per 100km (22mpg) for normal driving. If the 119kW (160hp) engine was specified then power-boosted disc front brakes were generally recommended, although they were not mandatory, which was a surprise.

The 1968 range from Chrysler comprised three models, each available in sedan and wagon bodies. There was the base model with the 108kW

(145bhp) engine and three-speed manual gearbox starting at $2490, the Safari wagon was $200 dearer. Then there was the Regal sedan that started at $3095 – Safari plus $200 – and then the top of the range VIP which cost $3650 with V8 engine, automatic gearbox, power steering, power front-disc brakes and lap-sash seatbelts.

Chrysler raised the bar a little with the VE by making several key improvements including the fitting of an internal bonnet release, co-axial power steering with only 3.75 turns from lock to lock (only available on cars with the automatic gearbox; could not be fitted to cars with a manual gearbox because of the proximity of the clutch mechanism), more powerful windscreen-wiper motor now mounted on the bulkhead, windscreen washer switch incorporated in the wiper switch, and a dual braking system in case of a line failure making total loss almost impossible. However, with any Valiant model capable of more than 144km/h (90mph) the company persisted with 228mm (9in) cast-iron drum brakes as standard, power-boosted front discs were a $210 extra cost and the base Valiants rode on the cheapest cross-ply tyres.

Nevertheless, the people at *Wheels* were impressed enough with the VE range to vote it their Car of the Year, an award that came as a complete surprise to Chrysler's executives.

In March 1969 the VF took over and as with AP5-to-AP6 it was primarily a cosmetic touch-up, although the front fenders were reshaped at their leading edge and the parking/indicator lens was placed on top, above the headlight, on the angled face. It might have looked good in the styling studio but they would prove to be difficult to see in daylight. The bonnet now had a straight-across leading edge and the grille was convex in shape with six thin and four thick horizontal bars above slightly different bumpers and a three-quarter length chrome side spear starting from behind the front wheel cut-out extended to the tail-lights.

Reshaped rear fenders saw the fitting for the first time on an Australian car of side marker lights from the now vertical tail-lights. The side markers were not required by law on the local market but the stylists knew they were mandatory in the US and so adopted them here and marketing used the feature in the promotion of the car.

An additional model was added to the Valiant range with the VF – the Pacer sedan. Ford with their Falcon GT and Holden with their Monaro GTS were grabbing all the media headlines because of their racing successes while poor old Chrysler could only stand by and watch. Conceived and built on a shoestring budget, the Pacer proved to be one their better ideas. It featured a mildly reworked 225cid engine (higher compression ratio, twin-barrel Carter carburettor and dual outlet exhaust system) together with a slightly firmer suspension system that was set around an inch lower in ride height, 5.5in rims with 6.95 x 14 red line sports tyres and three wild (for Chrysler) body colours – Wild Blue, Wild Yellow and Wild Red – adorned with black stripes and a discreet Pacer badge on the boot lid. Inside were tombstone bucket seats, a floor gearshift and a tiny horizontal VDO tachometer placed on top of the dash to the driver's left.

Wheels published a four-car comparison (August 1969) between the Pacer, Capri 1600GT, Monaro 186GTS and the Mazda R100, which was enlightening for the fact that the Pacer dominated virtually all aspects of the test even though the testers expressed the view that in some ways it was a fairly crude car. It was quick – 171km/h (107mph) top speed, 0–80km/h (0–50mph) in 7.9 seconds, standing quarter mile in 17.8 seconds – and at $2798 was regarded as something of a performance car bargain. Certainly the market thought so because the Pacer quickly accounted for 20 per cent of all Valiant production. And with it Chrysler took its first tentative steps towards racing.

VIP

With Ford in particular doing well with their Fairlane that was derived from the Falcon, it came as no surprise that Chrysler would join the fray by announcing the VIP by Chrysler as part of the VE range. Unlike Ford who made major alterations to the Falcon structure when creating the Fairlane, Chrysler took the simpler (and cheaper, typically) approach and loaded the VIP with luxury fittings and left the wheelbase, for example, the same as for the Valiant sedan. Holden had taken a similar short cut with their Brougham and it, too, was a sales failure. The idea with the VIP was not only to challenge the Ford Fairlane but to also fill the marketing gap between the Regal and the Dodge Phoenix.

To differentiate the VIP by Chrysler from its lesser siblings the company de-specified the Regal slightly to create room for the VIP. From the outside the most noticeable difference was the thickly padded grained vinyl roof, VIP badges on the C-pillar, three horizontal chrome strips on the rear quarter panels and new dress trims on the wheels. Inside was thicker vinyl upholstery that looked a little like leather but definitely did not smell like leather, the individual front seats were fully reclining with headrests, the rear bench seat had a folding centre armrest, the floors were fully carpeted, the doors were upholstered up to the sill line and had a wood veneer panel around each door handle. The reality for Chrysler's marketing people was that there was too little difference between the Regal and VIP and so it was nowhere near the sales success that Ford's Fairlane was.

Unlike the Regal, the VIP was only available with the 273cid V8 engine together with the Torqueflite automatic gearbox.

Despite the lack of sales success, Chrysler retained the VIP in its VF series line-up. However, this time more far-reaching and significant changes were made, changes that should have been made to the VE. The wheelbase was extended from 2743mm (108in) to 2845mm (112in) by inserting a piece in the floorpan under the rear passenger's feet, a 'plug' was inserted into the rear window aperture to create a more formal look, the roof was covered with a padded vinyl, four headlights now graced the grille and the tail-lights were slightly different as were the wheel dress trims. Inside there were items such as a standard heater/demister, full carpeting (including the boot), wood-grained finish on the dashboard, vanity mirror in the glovebox and courtesy lights on all four doors, in the boot and engine compartment.

VIP buyers now had the choice of the 119kW (160hp) six-cylinder engine or the new 'Fireball' 318cid V8 that developed 171kW (230bhp) at 4400rpm and 460Nm (340lb-ft) at 2400rpm. If the six-cylinder engine option was selected, the price was $3595, $3998 if the V8 was ordered and a further $400 for the Airtemp air-conditioning system.

Chrysler came back for a third try with the VG VIP which will be covered in *Australian Cars of the 70s.*

DODGE PHOENIX

Despite the modest success that Chrysler enjoyed with the return of the famous Plymouth, Dodge and De Soto nameplates discussions were held with their colleagues in Canada and it was agreed to bring in one model only and to call it the Dodge Phoenix (the name came from the Dodge Dart Phoenix, top model in Dodge's low-range line which competed for sales in the US with Chev and Ford) beginning with the 1960 (May) model year. It would be the latest from North America, possess the latest specifications and be positioned well above the Chrysler Royal to avoid conflict on the dealer's showroom floor.

The 1960 models were the first senior Chrysler automobiles to feature the company's 'Unibody' unitary body construction. Chrysler was the first major US automaker (Nash was first but it was a minor player in the market) to move its entire model range away from the traditional body-on-chassis construction that had been a common feature of American cars since the turn of the 20th century. Needless to say, the American media expressed their cynicism towards this 'daring' move and predicted that the corporation would soon revert back. Despite the scepticism from the so-called 'experts' Chrysler was unmoved and continued with the practice from then on, although for the 1960–61 model years only the company did use a bolt-on separate front sub-frame.

Allied with the unitary body construction, the Dodge Phoenix also featured the company's famous 'Torsionaire' torsion bar front suspension that gave a far more stable ride and more responsive handling than the soft-and-floaty coil spring systems from its GM and Ford rivals. Its geometry incorporated anti-dive measures and was fully ball-jointed. The long torsion bars were anchored to the underbody beneath the front seat mounts and acted upon the lower wishbone; upper location of the front wheel was by a robust wishbone. Steering was a power-assisted recirculating ball system that used an external hydraulic ram for the locally assembled cars and braking was by cast-iron drums of 279mm (11in) diameter. If the Dodge had an Achilles heel, it was the braking system but in those long-forgotten times such deficiencies were glossed over.

The Phoenix sat on a wheelbase of 2997mm (118in) with an overall length of 5298mm (208.6in), width of 1981mm (78in), height of 1633mm (54.3in) with wheel tracks of 1562mm (61.5in) and 1529mm (60.2in) front and rear respectively. Kerb weight was a hefty 1577kg (3470lb) and the fuel tank held 75 litres or 16.6imp gal.

Under the bonnet was Chrysler's 318cu in (5.2 litres) OHV V8 engine, a slightly enlarged version of the 'poly' engine that had been introduced in 1956 and would power the Phoenix until 1966. With a bore and stroke of 99.3 x 84.0mm (3.91 x 3.31in) it developed 171kW (230bhp) at 4400rpm and 460Nm (340lb-ft) of torque at 2800rpm, figures that were regarded as excellent for 1960. Its specification included a dual-throat downdraft Carter carburettor and a dual exhaust system. This power went to the rear wheels through a Torqueflite A904 three-speed automatic transmission, regarded at the time as the best automatic gearbox in the world.

What set the Phoenix apart from other US-sourced family cars, other than its body construction, was its relatively restrained styling. Up front were quad headlights set into the leading edge of the fenders above a very broad vee-shaped grille with closely spaced vertical bars, the front bumper filling in the space either side of the vee with rubber over-riders at either end. At the rear were small(ish) fins on the upper plane of the rear fenders that culminated in large circular tail-lights; indicator lights were in similarly large pods at either end of the hefty chromed bumper. The glass area was large, from the semi-wraparound windscreen, deep side windows with a quarter-vent only in the front windows to a huge wraparound rear window. The boot was large in surface area – long and wide – but quite shallow with the spare wheel on the floor robbing it of much useable space.

Interior equipment was not what might have been expected given our standards today. Size was a luxury on its own in 1960; you had to order the Luxury Liner edition to have power steering, power brakes and a heater as a standard fitting, cigar lighter, air foam front cushions, tinted windscreen swept by variable speed electric wipers and a lockable glovebox were included but it was really a rather sparse place to be. Seating was by wide benches with carpeting on the floor and the dashboard was a massive piece of metal sculpture dominated by a broad horizontal speedometer pod that sat on the upper surface directly in front of the driver with the three minor gauges set in a brushed aluminium strip below that and the push buttons for the automatic transmission on the right-hand end of the panel. Unusually, the rear-view mirror was pivoted from a base on the top of the dashboard, just to the driver's left, where it must have hindered visibility. Prices for the Phoenix began at £2550 for the De Luxe.

The first Phoenixes, coded PD4, were really a Canadian Dodge with a Plymouth dashboard, an interior incidentally not dissimilar to that which had appeared in the AP3 Chrysler Royal.

Wheels carried out a full road test (November 1960) and was mightily impressed. The opening lines read, "This is possibly the fastest accelerating four-door car you can buy in Australia. The Dodge will frighten most sports cars off the road." With respect to its touring ability, the tester commented, "The beauty of the car is that the huge motor belts it along with a soft sort of performance without the slightest fuss or strain and with very little noise." He tempered his remark with the

26·691
Dodge

caution, "What a pity, then, that the Dodge's steering and brakes do not match its tremendous urge to go forward."

The firmness of the torsion bar front suspension was appreciated for its contribution to the relatively crisp handling for such a large saloon, and the roominess of the interior was commented upon favourably. On the test strip the Phoenix ran to a maximum speed of 166.4km/h (104mph), roared through the standing quarter mile in 17.5 seconds and the 0–96km/h (0–60mph) dash in 8.9 seconds, 0–112km/h (0–70mph) in 13.2 seconds and returned 19.5 litres per 100km (14.6mpg)!

In line with the marketing trends in America, the Phoenix for 1961 (the RD4) featured a body shell that utilised the cabin section from the PD4 with completely new front and rear sheet metal. The grille was a full-width concave piece with the dual headlights set low on each side with the parking/indicator lights in small pods on the ends of the bumper. At the rear it had an unusual reversed fin where the high point was facing the front and it sloped back and down to the tail of the fender. The tail-lights were slim horizontal units that wrapped around the corner just above the rear bumper, while the indicator lights were separate round units alongside. It all looked a little like they were an afterthought. The cabin interior was a carry-over from 1960.

For the 1962 SD2 there would be a completely new body with a 2in shorter wheelbase (2946mm instead of 2997mm (116in instead of 118in)) and corresponding reduction in length, and it was slightly narrower. From this model year the fully unitised body would no longer have the front sub-frame. This was also the first year that Dodge did not feature a fin of any description. However, to replace them, Chrysler's stylists came up with character ridges above the wheel arches. Up front was a most unusual grille design: it was almost elliptical but with flattened top and bottom sections, projected forwards from the bonnet, had vertical bars that were close together and two of the four headlights were embedded in it; the other headlights (low beam) were near the outer corner where the front panels joined the fender.

Swinging back horizontally from the top edge of the grille was a prominent horizontal ridge that petered out near the front door handle while another began low on the rear door at sill level and ran along the back door before rising up and over the rear wheel arch and ending with one of the round tail-lights pods that was joined to its opposite number by a horizontal chromed strip. A second round pod was positioned slightly below it and there was an eight-piece chromed decoration adornment in front of it.

Inside was a much plainer looking dashboard (very much like the Valiant's) with a visor over it to prevent reflections in the windscreen at night. Instruments included a large speedometer at the left with three small dials in a line off to the right, switches for lights, wipers and ignition under them. On either side of the panel were a vertical row of buttons – automatic transmission on the left, heater on the right. Chrysler was the only US manufacturer to use push-buttons to operate the automatic transmission, which was now the new A727 unit with an aluminium housing to reduce weight, and it now included a park brake 'sprag'.

For 1963 and the TD2 the lines were smoothed out a little although the grille continued to feature four headlights that were apart from each other. This time the second (high beam) light was below the main headlight and again inset into the grille, this one being rectangular in shape and full width with vertical bars. The front bumper was a carry-over but with rubber over-riders added; mounted on its upper surface at each end were the direction indicator lights. At the rear there were now horizontal tail-lights in the valance panel with the separate indicator lights being on the boot lid, put there as an after-thought by Chrysler Australia because amber indicator lenses were required by law here in our country. The C-pillar area was wider this year and the rear window was almost flat to give what some described as the 'Thunderbird' roof line, a styling feature added to the Chrysler range courtesy of ex-Ford Design Director Elwood Engel.

Wheels conducted a full road test and it mirrored each of their previous three road tests insofar as the towering acceleration and over-160km/h (100mph) maximum speed were still there as were the twin negatives of dreadful steering and brakes that were in no way up to the car's performance potential.

With the phasing out of the Chrysler Royal during 1963 the Dodge Phoenix assumed the mantle as the company's ultimate sedan, Chrysler Australia's 'halo' car to use today's terminology. The R and S Series Valiant sedans had hit the sweet spot where buyers were concerned and satisfying that demand was stretching the company's facilities to the limit.

Dodge's Golden Anniversary year was 1964, John and Horace Dodge having built and sold their first car in 1914. Styling was basically carried over although there was a lower cowl and new windscreen but it was allied to a more conventional front design that featured a full-width parallel-section grille with fine vertical bars, the outer headlights being in wide bezels and the inner high beam lights alongside. The massive bumper carried twin rubber over-riders either side of the licence plate, dips either end under the headlight bezel and small shield-shaped indicator lights below that. At the rear were four small square lights – red outers, orange inners – covering tail/stop and indicator/reversing functions. Along the body sides was a prominent ridge with a chromed strip to emphasise it.

Inside was practically unchanged from the previous year except that the minor dials (fuel, temperature and amps) now had squared-off bezels and the seats were large bench-style with fold-down armrests front and rear, and fittings continued unchanged as well. As a bonus in those times, the price still began at £2595.

Mechanically the Phoenix continued with the well-proven and admired 318cid V8 still with 171kW (230bhp) and 460Nm (340lb-ft) of torque driving through the excellent three-speed Torqueflite automatic transmission to a slightly higher 3.23 rear axle. The wheelbase was now 3022mm (119in) and overall length was up by almost 102mm (4in) to 5385mm (212in), width was an inch wider and the kerb weight was much the same at 1578kg (3472lb), 14in wheels and tyres were still specified and the much-criticised 279mm (11in) drum brakes and low ratio steering (5½ turns lock-to-lock) continued unchanged.

For 1965 a new design was introduced – the Corporate 'C' body, This time the Dodge Phoenix was a rebadged Canadian Plymouth Fury III body, a strategy that would apply through to the end in 1972. For 1965 the emphasis would be on making the Phoenix appear as large as it actually was by giving it vertically-stacked four headlights and body side decoration that went full length. The grille was of fine mesh with a horizontal peak running across it while at the back there were single lighting units each side of a valance panel that was slightly convex in shape. The glass area was still as large as ever as was the luggage compartment while the mechanical components continued unchanged. Inside was a new dash that featured huge twin nacelles over the two round instruments (the Phoenix retained the full set, unusually) that were a part of the vast moulded top in black plastic to eliminate glare in the enormous windscreen.

The 1966 was a minor variation on 1965 – new grille, new rear quarter panels, tail-lights and boot lid with crease lines that imitated the grille – including the vast dash. But new were twin front seats that had built-in adjustable head restraints and the passenger's seat could recline (the driver's did not because on left-hand drive cars the adjustable seat was for the driver!) instead of the divided bench. In their road test of the 1966 Phoenix *Wheels* lamented the fact that front disc brakes, tilt-and-telescope steering column and six-way power seats were overlooked by the marketing people at Chrysler and yet were all available ex-Windsor for what was the company's most luxurious offering that now carried a retail price of $5795. At the end of the test in which they praised its cruising capability, roominess, quietness and quality of assembly but criticised its steering, brakes and body rattles on rough roads, they concluded by saying, "We suspect that the Phoenix is not as tough and durable as its reputation would have it, but despite that it sells well to country people – probably better than any other big American. It is certainly the most luxurious and best handling of the locally-assembled big brothers, and thus the best for interstate work."

For the 1967 model year Chrysler offered buyers the choice of two body types for the first time – the regular four-door sedan and a four-door hardtop. The sedans used the 1965–66 roof pressing and glass areas while the hardtops had new roof and glass areas. Apart from the lack of a centre pillar and door window frames there was very little to tell the difference between the two models. Under the bonnet, however, were new engines. If the pillared sedan was ordered the engine was a new V8 of 318cid capacity but labelled the LA (some authorities say it stood for 'Light A', others suggest 'Late A' or even 'Lowered A'), its bore and stroke being the same as its predecessor as was its power and torque output. Essentially the LA engine was the original 318 cast-iron block with new, narrower, cylinder heads that were lighter in weight. Buyers of the hardtop sedan experienced the power of the 383cid (6.3 litres) V8 – 107.95 x 85.85mm (4.25 x 3.38in) bore and stroke – that was a member of the famous B series 'wedge' family of engines that powered the 1958 Dodge and De Sotos in 350cid capacity, and from 1959 in 361cid capacity and would be expanded first to 383cid, then 413cid and ultimately to 440cid. Power from the 383 was 216kW (290bhp) at 4400rpm and torque was a massive 528Nm (390lb-ft) at 2400rpm.

External dimensions continued unchanged and the vertically-stacked four headlight treatment continued for a third year, the lights being shielded from the side by prominent leading edges of the fenders, with the grille containing large horizontal bars and a thicker centre bar. On the rear doors there was a slightly raised crease line that was like a reminder of the coke bottle effects found on GM and Ford cars of recent history. At the back were slim, horizontal tail-lights set in a recessed panel.

During the latter part of 1967 Chrysler moved the assembly of the Phoenix from its new Tonsley Park factory over to the old Rootes Group factory in Salmon Street, Port Melbourne where an annexe had been set up exclusively for it; they would be assembled there until the last models ran down the 'line' in late 1971. In the opinion of many stalwarts those Melbourne-built Dodges were the least desirable as their quality was apparently appalling.

Wheels and *Modern Motor* magazines road-tested a four-door hardtop and published very complimentary articles but lamented the lack of decent brakes for such a big, heavy (1782kg/3920lb) and fast (171km/h (107mph), 0–96km/h (0–60mph) in 9.4 seconds) motor car that cost a rather hefty $6345, somewhat more than the sedan at $5895. These prices, however, compared reasonably well with the Chevrolet Impala sedan that retailed for $6230 and the Ford Galaxie that cost $5590 when fitted with the 289cid V8 and $5820 when fitted with the 390cid V8. Only Pontiac paralleled the Phoenix by offering the two body types and charged $5760 for its Parisienne V8 automatic sedan and $6555 for the hardtop variation.

In 1968 there was more of the same with most of the styling upgrade taking place at the rear where there was new sheet metal that raised the rear lines a little helping to create more luggage space while the tail-lights were now broad-but-narrow horizontal units that appeared to be full-width but were not. The option of body types continued, each with their own V8 engine variant.

New styling arrived for 1969 that was big and bulky but at the same time smooth with almost no extraneous body adornment. The full-width mesh grille housed four headlights, there being a slight dip under each light, and the tail-lights were broad, horizontal units each side; bumpers were quite restrained and lacked rubber over-riders. Wheelbase was now up another inch to 3048mm (120in) and overall length had grown to 5448mm (214.5in), while the front and rear tracks were out to 1575mm and 1542mm (62 and 60.7in) respectively. Kerb weight had held steady and the fuel tank was increased to 90 litres (20impl gal), tyres were 8.15 x 15 nylons on 5.5 x 15 steel safety rims, an increase of 1in. What was new mechanically were Kelsey-Hayse 299mm (11.8in) ventilated front disc brakes in unison with carry-over 279mm (11in) rear drums and vacuum assistance.

A rubber-insulated cross member to which the rear telescopic

dampers were mounted helped reduce interior noise levels in association with a redesigned and strengthened front structure which meant that the Phoenix's ride and handling were of a very high order.

Chrysler's interior designers had developed a new dashboard that curved slightly around the driver with a large square speedometer right in front of the driver and minor dials next to it plus the radio and heater/demister controls under the one broad hooded binnacle. It brought all the main controls into the one area and all were reachable by a driver wearing their seatbelt. Despite repeated criticism of the feature for the past decade by the media, Chrysler (along with GM and Ford) persisted with the foot dip switch rather than incorporating the feature into the column stalk like every other manufacturer had done. It was really the only criticism of the driving experience according to the *Wheels* road test that praised the bias towards handling over ride, the proverbial seven-league boots as well as the new braking equipment, but was critical of the lifeless steering.

Performance levels had been maintained despite the encroachment of engine exhaust emission controls, but with 383cu in at its disposal the Phoenix was always going to be quick but thirsty. Pricing had risen, too, the hardtop now retailing for $6850.

Modern Motor tested the Phoenix hardtop (number 161 out of 400) and said, "Despite its bulk, Chrysler's Dodge Phoenix 400 presents a fairly athletic image with good brakes, stable ride and plenty of go." They managed a maximum speed of 168km/h (105mph), a 0–96km/h (0–60mph) time of 9.8 seconds, 0–128km/h (0–80mph) in 18.3 seconds and ran the standing quarter mile in 17.2 seconds. It was thirsty, though.

The last Dodge Phoenix was the 1971 model that was a continuation of the basic 1969 model, each model year being characterised by the fact that Chrysler marketed them as the 400 Limited Edition series, each car – sedan and hardtop – carrying a discreet badge on the dashboard with a number on it. With the release of the long wheelbase Chrysler by Chrysler as an integral part of the vast Australian-designed VH/CH range of cars during 1971 the Dodge Phoenix had become redundant – the two cars were essentially competing for the same buyer even though the Phoenix was somewhat larger physically. In some respects Chrysler was merely following its two main rivals – GM and Ford – who had both discontinued their low-volume assembly of Chevrolets, Pontiacs and Galaxies respectively several years previously. The Dodge Phoenix was, literally, the last of the Mohicans.

ARROW

HILLMAN HUNTER

While the negotiations for the takeover of the Rootes Group by Chrysler were taking place, in the background, much activity was going on with an important new model development by the Rootes Group engineers. The Minx and Super Minx were both long in the tooth and used old ideas of body construction which meant that they were worthy performers with a body that was strong but heavy for their size. A completely new model that would use only the 1725cc engine and the all-synchromesh manual gearbox from the last of the Super Minxs was on the way.

Officially Chrysler took possession of Rootes Australia on 1 December 1965. Talk at the time suggested that Chrysler would submit the forthcoming Hillman Hunter for the 95 per cent local content plan. There was also talk of stamping the Hillman panels at Tonsley Park, but none of this ever eventuated.

It was introduced onto the Australian market in May 1967 and was available in two versions: the Arrow which was the price leader and the Hunter which was better equipped and by far the bigger seller. They were attractively styled medium-sized four–five seater family sedans that brought two firsts for Rootes – curved side window glass and the MacPherson strut front suspension. That might give you some idea of how far off the pace Rootes were …

The new Hillmans were comparable in size with the Ford Cortina, Mazda 1500 and Austin 1800 and were built on a new floorpan with a 2502mm (98.5in) wheelbase, an overall length of 4292mm (169in), width of 1613mm (63.5in) and height of 1422mm (56in) and weighed in at exactly 1000kg (2240lb) or one ton in the old measures. Inherited from the Minx/Super Minx was the 1725cc engine that developed 54kW (73bhp) at 4900rpm and 134Nm (99.5lb-ft) of torque at 2700rpm on an 8.4:1 compression and using a single Zenith 150 CDS carburettor. Compared with the engines under the bonnets of the Mazda 1500 and Datsun 1600 the Rootes engine was not particularly advanced in its technology, it could probably be best described as worthy because it got the job done.

They were reasonably comfortable four-seater saloons, five at a pinch, with a good boot of 18cu ft capacity; although the spare was positioned up against the back seat, just about impossible to get at – why, when this was a totally new body? The dashboard was a hard plastic moulding with padding on the upper surface; the instruments comprised a fan-shaped speedometer plus fuel and temperature gauges and some warning lights in a rectangular binnacle in front of the driver. Front seat passengers sat on bucket seats with a plain bench for rear-seat passengers. The Arrow was a bare-bones saloon with no heater, non-reclining front seats, no carpets, no reversing lights and was priced at $2038. The Hunter was a far better buy at $2188, just $150 more for a good heater/demister, carpeted floor, cigarette lighter, door armrests, reclining front passenger seat, reversing lights, boot light, wheel dress trims and whitewall tyres.

Modern Motor carried out a test of the Hunter (July 1967) and came away impressed with its styling, the ergonomics of the dashboard and driving position; although the various switches were recessed in chromed surrounds that reflected in the windows, the electric wipers had only one slow speed and the washers used an archaic plunger setup – all the Japanese cars used two-speed wipers with an electric pump for the washers – and the ventilation system was excellent. The quality of finish was definitely not up to the usual Rootes standards in their opinion – it was far inferior to that of its Japanese rivals – for which they blamed Chrysler cost-cutting.

While the maximum speed was a worthy 136.9km/h (85.6mph), the acceleration from 0–80 and 96km/h (0–50 and 60mph) was considered off the pace at 11.9 and 19.8 seconds respectively. The Mazda 1500, a bigger and heavier car with a 1.5-litre engine was quicker, for example. They concluded their test by saying, "What the Hunter really lacks is the sparkle and dash to go with its smart new lines."

A year later Chrysler added the Hillman Hunter Safari station wagon to the line-up. During late 1968 Chrysler added the Hunter GT to the range after basking in the glory of an unexpected win in the London to Sydney Marathon by Andrew Cowan and crew in a well-prepared Hunter sedan.

By early 1969 the HC range was released, its most obvious identifier being the rectangular headlights that replaced the round originals. The Arrow name was dropped and the Hunter name used on the price leader ($2098). What was the Hunter became the Hunter Royal that sold for $2385 with the GT available at $2565. *Modern Motor* tested the Royal in its April 1969 issue and was impressed by the improved paint and finish in general; as for its performance the top speed remained at 136.6km/h (85.4mph) but a couple of seconds were shaved off the previous acceleration times.

The GT was one of those cars that Chrysler did not know how to sell – it had everything like good styling, a well-appointed interior that boasted a dashboard that only the Brits could design consisting of a full set of Smith round gauges set in a polished walnut surround. It looked classy and was competitively quick, *Modern Motor* recording a maximum speed of 156.8km/h (98mph) with times for the 0–80, 96 and 112km/h (0–50, 60 and 70mph) sprints taking 8.3, 12.4 and 16.7 seconds respectively. This urge came from a revised 1725cc four-cylinder OHV engine that had the Sunbeam eight-port alloy cylinder head with a 9.2:1 compression, bigger valves, twin 1½in Zenith-Stromberg carburettors and twin Y-type exhaust headers. Maximum power was 70kW (94bhp) at 5200rpm with 145Nm (107lb-ft) of torque at a high 4000rpm. As they opined, “The Hunter GT is a very safe handler, it’s nicely decked out inside and should enjoy good sales.”

The HE range came along in 1970 with a new grille and tail-lights plus some components from the Valiant parts bin, most notably the collapsible steering column and wheel, plus there was the Hustler to replace the GT. It was powered by the 70kW (94bhp) GT engine but had the plain Jane Hunter interior making it a Valiant Pacer clone. However, where the Pacer was super successful for Chrysler the Hustler was a dismal failure. By 1973 the Port Melbourne plant had closed and the Rootes heritage needlessly destroyed.

HILLMAN
SAFARI

NTROL
HUSTLER

The Motor
COPYRIGHT

Chapter 4

BRITISH MOTOR CORPORATION

BMC Australia began the sixties full of confidence having only recently released two new cars both of which featured styling by the famous Italian *carrozzeria* Farina, who was the Big Thing in international automobile styling at the time. Not only BMC but Peugeot and Fiat also adopted his themes. The first to be released in late 1959 was the A40, a two-box sedan over the A35 mechanical components, and the second was the A60 Cambridge that was a roomy and plain-but-competent sedan that replaced the A55. Both met with good responses from the media and public alike. Continued on from 1957 were the Austin/Morris twins, the Lancer and Major respectively. All four models were front-engined and rear-wheel drive, very conventional and very conservative.

Rounding out the wide and somewhat disparate range was the locally-assembled Morris Minor and Oxford, and Wolseley 15/60, all but the Minor having Farina-designed bodies. There were also the MGA and Austin-Healey Sprite sports roadsters that were being assembled locally by Pressed Metal Corporation.

The differences between each marque and model were minor and consisted mainly of grilles and badges, although the Wolseley 15/60 required different front sheet metal around the traditional upright, ever-so-British grille. The Wolseley also featured more traditional wood, leather and carpet club-type interior which set it apart from the humdrum Austin/Morris models for not a lot of extra money.

BMCA had invested a huge amount of money – believed to be around £13 million – during the mid-'50s and by 1958 could boast that local content of some of its models was up to 98 per cent. As a part of the expansion of the Zetland site the company now had its own press shop as well as machine shop to manufacture the B series four-cylinder engine locally. It had a capacity of 1489cc and developed 37kW (50bhp) in the Major and Lancer, 1622cc capacity and 45kW (60bhp) in the Cambridge, Oxford and 15/60 sedans and 65kW (86bhp) in the MGA Mark II. It is interesting to note that the Australian engineers went against the 'advice' from their peers in Longbridge in creating the 1622cc version of the engine because the Poms said it could not be done! The Australians were desperately in need of more torque (they actually wanted a six-cylinder engine) to better cater for our lazy style of driving but Longbridge would have none of it. Intriguingly, once the Aussies had shown *how* it could be done the Poms adopted it immediately as their own!

For family-car-oriented buyers BMCA opened their account for the sixties with two bang-up-to-date models. The smallest of these was the Austin A40, a cute-looking two-box design that pointed the way towards the hatchback cars that are so common today. It was a two-door sedan with a fixed rear window and a drop-down lid that gave access to a remarkably large boot.

Built on a wheelbase of only 2108mm (83in) it stood 1422mm (56in) tall, was 1752mm (69in) wide and only 3657mm (144in) in length; kerb weight was 802kg (1764lb). Mechanically it carried over components from the A30/35 so it featured upper and lower front wishbones with coil springs and lever action dampers incorporated into the upper wishbone mounting, semi-elliptic leaf springs and live axle at the rear, cam-and-peg steering and 203mm (8in) diameter cast-iron drum brakes all round. For the time it was considered par for the course and was well-proven.

Inside was a pressed-steel dashboard with a semblance of padding along the top edge, a rhombus-shaped combination dial in front of the driver (it was used in other BMC cars) that had a speedometer as the main dial with a tiny fuel gauge below it in the centre and some warning lights. To the left was a slot for a radio and a lockable glove box in front of the passenger. The ignition key/start was on the far right with three switches in the top centre; below was a full-width parcel shelf with a lip to stop items flying out under acceleration. The high-low beam dipper was a floor button and there was a neat floor shifter for the four-speed gearbox that had synchromesh on the top three ratios only. Small bucket seats seated those in front, a simple bench in the rear; upholstery was cheap vinyl, rubber mats were on the floor and a heater/demister was an option.

Road tests of the time revealed it to have a top speed of 105–110km/h (66–69mph) with 37/56/100km/h (23/35/63mph) available in the lower gears, acceleration from 0–64km/h and 80km/h (0–40 and 50mph) taking 12.2 and 19.5 seconds, fuel economy was 8.6 litres per 100km (33mpg) around town, 7.8–7 litres per 100km (37–40mpg) when cruising. Remember, we're talking about the 948cc A series engine putting out 26kW (34bhp) and 68Nm (50lb-ft) and running a low 4.55:1 rear axle ratio designed to make around town driving more pleasant but long-distance cruising noisier than need be. As a package retailing for £915 it was felt to be good value.

Introduced in Australia at the end of 1959 by BMCA which assembled it from CKD components plus much locally-sourced material, the A40 took a little while to be accepted by the market mainly because of its styling. Interestingly, the A40 was never badged as anything other than an Austin, much like the Morris Minor was never badged engineered. The A40's nemesis on the local market was, in fact, the Minor even though at the time it was more than a decade old as a design.

By 1962, its last year on the Australian market, BMC released the A40 Countryman that featured what many said it should have had from the beginning – a lift-up rear hatch and fold-down rear seat.

The A40's big brother was the A60 Cambridge, a six-seater sedan (just!) that had a local content of more than 95 per cent. Like the A40, it carried over most of the chassis and running gear from the A55 except that the B series engine had been increased in capacity from 1489cc to 1622cc. The need for more torque was what drove the Australian engineers to disobey their Longbridge overlords and go it alone! Its bore and stroke were now 76.2 x 88.9mm, power was 42kW (55bhp) at 4250rpm and torque was 117 Nm (86.5lb-ft) at 2100rpm. It was a

MARK II.
WOLSELEY
24/80

relatively large four-cylinder family car having a wheelbase of 2514mm (99in), length was 4521mm (178in) by 1600mm (63in) wide and 1498mm (59in) high while its kerb weight was quite heavy at 1120kg (2464lb), much of which came from the very strong monocoque body.

Inside was seating room for up to six people on bench seats front and rear, both being upholstered in washable vinyl as was the custom in those days, and there were plain rubber mats on the floor. The dash was a body-coloured steel pressing with two round Smiths dials in front of the driver, the speedometer on the left and combination dial – water temperature, fuel contents and engine oil pressure – on the left with (curiously) the ignition switch between them where it was most awkward to use. A heater/demister was not a standard fitting but provision was made to install it at the dealers plus a radio if ordered and a large glovebox was on the left for the passenger. At the rear was a large luggage compartment, the spare wheel being on a tray that wound down outside and the fuel tank was located behind the back seat. Unlike the UK cars, our A60 Cambridge rode on 15in wheels for better ground clearance.

Despite the fact that it was a four-cylinder car competing in a six-cylinder market it gave a good account of itself under test, *Wheels* achieving 125km/h (78mph), a time of 0–80km/h (0–50mph) in 13.7 seconds and fuel consumption of 10.5 litres per 100km (27mpg) on test, more than 8 litres per 100km (35mpg) on a cruise. An FC Holden was only marginally quicker! No development work took place with A60 between its 1959 release and 1962 replacement.

In April 1962 BMCA released their last locally-developed four-cylinder rear-wheel drive sedan, the Morris Major Elite. It was the final flowering of the model that came onto the market in 1958 and had almost 100 per cent local content. The Series II had the stretched body and the Elite was a tidy-up of that car with a new full-width grille, different chromed strips each side for easier two-tone colouring, the 1622cc engine in 37kW (50bhp) form and four-speed manual gearbox, an automatic not being on offer. At £940 including a heater/demister it was one the decade's better value-for-money buys and was a popular car during its time on the market. Various road tests were published that credited the Major Elite with a top speed of between 120 and 128km/h (75 and 80mph) with acceleration to 80 and 96km/h (50 and 60mph) taking 14.5 and 22.7 seconds respectively, fuel economy being around 8.8–7.8 litres per 100km (32–36mpg). Today we would think a car with a 1.6-litre engine should perform far better than the Elite did but in those post-credit squeeze days it was viewed as a very well performing small family car.

BMC discontinued the Major Elite in late 1964 in preparation for the release of the Morris 1100 having two years previously discontinued the Minor to make room on their production lines for the Mini.

Staying with the conventional models for a moment, BMCA's management had been badgering Longbridge to manufacture an all-Australian car designed specifically to cope with local driving styles and road conditions. Longbridge studiously ignored the requests and advised the Australians to make damn sure they built what England sent them. Apart from some minor strengthening of the body and suspension components and far better dust sealing, an Australian Austin A60 was the same as the English version except for the 15in wheels and tyres on the local version and local paint colours. The A60 did get a good rap from the media – it was modishly stylish and had a remarkable amount of interior room plus a big boot (always important in Australia for some reason). However, no matter how good the report it always said the A60 (or Oxford or 15/60) was still a *four*-cylinder car in a *six*-cylinder market and therefore always at a disadvantage.

That situation was resolved when BMCA released a thoroughly revised new model that featured the one single item that had been missing for all those years – an in-house designed six-cylinder engine! The model was called the Austin Freeway and its release on 21 May 1962 ended some five years of rumour and conjecture. It was built on a tight budget using as much carry-over A60 componentry as possible, which was most of it. What was new apart from the engine? The rear quarter panels now had reverse-slope fins taken from the UK MG Magnette, new front grille that was full-body-width with larger indicator/park lights each side, revised seating and other minor improvements inside. It now ran on 4.5J x 14 rims with 5.90 x 14 cross-ply tyres and had a locally-sourced Borg Warner three-speed manual gearbox with a column shift as standard, a Borg Warner Type 35 three-speed automatic was an option. The engine, labelled on the rocker cover and in the brochures as the 'Blue Streak', was an extension of the company's famous B Series engine with a new cast-iron block and head (both cast at Birmid in Geelong), cast-iron camshaft and forged four-bearing crank. It shared the 76.2 x 88.9mm bore and stroke and so had a capacity of 2433cc from which it developed 60kW (80bhp) at 4250rpm and 175Nm (129lb/ft) of torque at 1750rpm.

Modern Motor published a full road report in its July 1962 issue and came away highly impressed. At £1130 they felt it represented excellent value for money because it came equipped with a heater/demister, windscreen washers, padded dash, twin horns and a cigarette lighter, none of which was standard in the Holden Special or Ford Falcon Deluxe. Too, the dash featured large round Smiths dials, the one on the left containing the speedometer while the right one had proper gauges for fuel, engine temperature and oil pressure. The car's dynamics met with approval as did the comfort of the interior that was felt to be better made than its rivals. As for performance, the car posted a top speed of 131km/h (82mph), 0–80 and 96km/h (0–50 and 60mph) times of 12.0 and 18.3 seconds respectively and returned 11.2 litres per 100km (25mpg) overall for the test. It was more than a match for Holden and Ford, and the company's dealers were extremely enthusiastic at their prospects in the sales race. The problem for BMCA was that Chrysler had released the 145bhp Valiant four months earlier.

While developing the Freeway the BMCA engineers busied themselves with one of their brighter ideas and upgraded the 15/60 to the 24/80 and created one of the nicest and most endearing sedans ever made in Australia. It was a neat combination of the Farina body with the new 2.4-litre six-cylinder engine and the typical wood, leather and carpet interior that could only have been British. Priced at £1395 for the automatic version compared with £1280 for the sibling Freeway, the 24/80 was excellent value. In many areas of Australia, the Wolseley was actually the better seller of the two. *Wheels* tested both cars in Mark II guise in its December 1964 issue, the changes being new rear quarter panels for the 24/80 that lowered and softened the formerly pointed fins, reprofiled bumpers, minor retuning of the engine to lift power and torque slightly, vacuum servo for the brakes, re-rated springs and dampers plus redesigned seats. Not earth shattering but typical of the low-key way BMC went about its business.

If the Freeway and 24/80 could be criticised, and they were, it was because the resources were not available to retool the floorpan and widen it by (say) 4in to significantly increase the body width, and therefore interior room, to better match the Holden, Ford and Chrysler opposition. A single example of such a car was built by the Australian engineers and when their Pommy overlords saw it they were not best pleased and immediately ordered it to be destroyed. If only …

The *Wheels* people said of the Mark II 24/80 and Freeway, "Although their acceleration is not particularly quick – 0–50mph in 15.1 sec and 0–60mph in 22.8 secs maximum speed of 82mph – they are surprisingly fast on a long trip, cruising at 70–75mph presents no problems." They went on to say, "The revisions have made the Wolseley into one of the nicest and plushest sixes available."

MORRIS 850

In the meantime, the Issigonis-inspired front-wheel drive revolution had arrived at BMCA, at first in the form of the Morris 850 as it was badged in Australia. The local marketing people were apparently not comfortable with the name Mini Minor. English prototypes were imported (believed to have been only three) and tested in western New South Wales (around Lake Cargelligo) and were found to be deficient in several areas that were important in Australia – body strength, dust and water sealing, subframe and suspension mountings and, of course, those tiny 10in wheels and tyres.

Despite initial misgivings, the Waterloo plant was re-equipped to manufacture the 850 and sales began following the announcement on 23 March 1961. It was an immediate sales success and quickly sold out. At the same time, it brought a whole new client demographic to BMCA as buyers were primarily much younger than before. Initially it was assembled from CKD packs with local content being restricted to tyres, batteries, paint and interior trim.

The Australian engineers were unable to alter the 850's design and construction to any great extent – instructions from Longbridge, old chap – despite wanting to as there were some glaring deficiencies. The gearshift was not liked although as one or two former engineers said, "You did get used to it!" Also, the engineers had misgivings about the unusual Moulton rubber cone suspension that was totally untried under the harsh local road conditions although to be fair it was never a major issue in the field. In very quick time the 850 became a cult car and BMCA's fortunes rose dramatically. As a package the 850 was undoubtedly a stroke of genius being able to accommodate four people in a car built on a wheelbase of just 2032mm (80in) with an overall length of 3048mm (120in) and a kerb weight of around 582kg (1280lb). Under the bonnet was the smallest version of BMC's ubiquitous A Series engine having a bore and stroke of 62.9 x 68.26mm for 848cc, power output being a modest 25kW (34bhp) at 5500rpm. That was enough to pull the little 'brick' to a top speed of just over 112km/h (70mph) with around 19 seconds needed to accelerate from rest to 80km/h (50mph). In 1962 that was considered quite acceptable.

In November 1962 BMCA introduced the first of the Mini-Coopers that had been developed in conjunction with the Cooper Car Company, then of Formula One racing fame. It had a 997cc version (62.43 x 81.28mm) of the A Series engine which with twin HS2 SU carburettors and 9.0:1 compression developed 42kW (55bhp) at 6000rpm and was able to propel the brick-shaped box-on-wheels at speeds of up to 145km/h (90mph) and dash from 0–96km/h (0–60mph) in 15.0 seconds. Other upgrades included the fitting of tiny 178mm (7in) diameter Dunlop disc front brakes, drilled 4.5 x 10 wheels, Dunlop radial tyres, a seven-horizontal-chromed bar grille, over-riders with corner nudge bars, a redesigned remote floor gearshift and a new oval-shaped instrument binnacle in the centre of the dash containing a (very) large Smiths speedometer recalibrated to 160km/h (100mph) (with the fuel gauge in the lower segment) flanked by temperature and oil pressure gauges; intriguingly, no tachometer was fitted! New also was a key start rather than the floor push-button.

Around 2000 were built using UK-sourced panels but then production converted to locally pressed panels for the 850 in early 1964. In March or April 1964, the Mini-Cooper quietly switched to a 998cc version of the engine that had the cylinder dimensions of 64.58 x 76.2mm; with an 8.3:1 compression and dual SU carburettors it produced the same 42kW (55bhp) but at 5800rpm and a fraction more torque at lower revolutions. Initial stocks used imported engines but from September 1964 the engines were assembled at Waterloo. From April (1964) the local content of the Mini was increased with the body panels being pressed at Zetland.

August 1965 saw the arrival in BMC showrooms of the definitive Mini-Cooper S, sufficient of which had been built in time for approval for the Hardie-Ferodo 500 at Bathurst that year. Where the UK also offered 970 and 1071 Mini-Coopers, in Australia BMC went from the 998cc units to the 1275cc models, although a small number of 1071cc Coopers were imported for racing.

BMC 850

Although the Australian-built Cooper S used the same mechanical package as the UK, the bodies were locally pressed and assembled, and the interior trim was the same as the Australian Mini De Luxe. The Cooper S continued with the three-dial dashboard, twin fuel tanks were standard (they were an option in the UK), an engine oil cooler was standard, the rubber cone suspension gave way to the Hydrolastic system that had been seen first on the Morris 1100 and there were corner nudge bars on the bumpers. To facilitate production at Waterloo, BMC Australia imported the Cooper S mechanicals (engine, transmission, drive shafts and disc brakes) as a built-up unit ready to be installed into the cars.

The engine now had a bore and stroke of 70.63 x 81.33mm for its 1275cc capacity, power rising to 56kW (75bhp) at 5800rpm on a 9.5:1 compression and breathing through two HS2 SU carburettors. Braking was by 190mm (7½in) diameter solid discs up front and 178 x 31.75mm (7 x 1¼in) drums at the rear with a vacuum booster and it continued to use the 10in wheels, now shod with 145–10 Dunlop SP41 radial tyres. John Bolster writing in *Autosport* said of the Cooper S, "It is one of the most delightful cars to drive that one could imagine. Capable of 160km/h (100mph), it is also a practical four-seater family saloon with not a sign of temperament." He recorded speeds of 51, 88 and 123km/h (32, 55 and 77mph) through the gears and ran the 0–80 and 96km/h (0–50 and 60mph) sprints in 6.6 and 9.0 sec respectively while returning 11.2 litres per 100km (25mpg). The Mini-Cooper S really was a giant-killer in its day. And to prove the point, the Cooper S was victorious in the 1966 Gallaher 500 mile race at Bathurst driven by Bob Holden and Rauno Aaltonnen, Cooper Ss coming in second (Bill Stanley and Fred Gibson) and third (Bruce McPhee and Barry Mulholland) for a clean sweep. It was one of the more remarkable and largely unexpected wins in the race's history.

A Mark II Cooper S was released in April 1969 and it was with this model that a full-synchromesh transmission became available for the first time. BMC made a big deal out of it but what has to be remembered was that every other manufacturer in the world had long ago adopted full-synchromesh manual transmissions. Included in the Mark II package were wheel arch flares, a second muffler (both these additions were as a result of police actions in NSW believe it or not) plus new badges and better quality interior trim. However, the model was now over four years old and in some respects rivals had caught up with the Cooper S but at $2420 it still had plenty to offer. The Cooper S was not a comfortable car in which to travel because of the angle of the bucket front seat's backrest and depth of upholstery, it was noisy despite the added muffler although tyre/road noise was as big a culprit, luggage space was minimal (but everybody knew that) and its ride was very firm.

Modern Motor tested an S and said, "Responsive is a key word with the Cooper. There is a tremendous physical bond between car and driver, no doubt brought about by the car's tiny size, engine vibrations, noise and generally the car's willingness to do as it's told." The firm ride was attributed to the viscous fluid in the Hydrolastic suspension which was different in its composition from the Mini K, for example, and this gave it a distinctly firm ride. And the gearshift to the new all-synchromesh gearbox was, in their opinion, the best that they had tried on any British Leyland fwd car.

The Mark II tested ran to 56km/h (35mph), 94km/h (59mph) and 133km/h (83mph) in the indirect gears and to 155.2km/h (97mph) in fourth, dashed from 0–80, 96 and 112km/h (0–50, 60 and 70mph) in 8.1, 11.4 and 15.8 seconds respectively which was still pretty quick, and returned 8.9 litres per 100km (32mpg) for the test, suggesting around 7.2–7.0 litres per 100km (38–40mpg) was possible on a long cruise and with 50 litres (11gal) on board you could travel around 640km (400 miles) before needing to refill.

In March 1965 BMC released the Mini Deluxe – the brochure said De Luxe, the car's badge said Deluxe – which featured wind-up windows with swivelling quarter vents, an Australian design initiative by BMC engineers Chris Rogers and Frank Lee using Morris 1100 components. These windows appeared on the Mini panel van in May 1965 and the base Mini from February 1966. All Australian-built Mini-Cooper S also had the wind-up windows. The Hydrolastic suspension system, key-start ignition and the remote gearshift also found their way into the Mini from this time along with a diaphragm clutch, mechanical fuel pump, redesigned bigger brakes, door operated courtesy light and improved quality interior trim. The base Mini and the van retained the rubber cone suspension system and did not get all the new features.

Powering the Deluxe was the 998cc version of the A series engine that developed 28kW (38bhp) at 5250rpm. Compared with the standard 850 the Deluxe felt more robust and had much stronger performance according to the *Modern Motor* testers (May 1965). It conquered hills easily and a 112km/h (70mph) cruise was well within its capabilities – maximum speed was timed at 124.8km/h (78mph), 0–80km/h (0–50mph) took 14.0 seconds – and braking was more powerful because of the new two-leading-shoe system that needed less pedal pressure. What was noticeable from other Minis was the ride and handling improvement given by the Hydrolastic suspension – a huge bonus. At £833 it was outstanding value for money.

Released in September 1967 was the Mini Deluxe with the optional AP four-speed automatic gearbox with a floor selector. Power from the 998cc engine was raised to 31kW (42bhp) to cope with the power losses and there was an 'Automatic' badge on the boot lid. Included in the price of $1919 was a heater/demister and three-point seatbelts. The selector was in a large quadrant on the floor and had the positions of reverse, neutral, then 1-2-3-4 and D for Drive; there was no Park position because once the engine was turned off the transmission locked in whatever gear it was in. Cold starts were a problem in the test cars that *Wheels* drove (March 1968) because it was difficult to select a gear. Shifts were also jerky and often too sudden as well. The auto Mini possessed all the usual roadholding and handling characteristics expected but added the ease of driving an automatic that could be driven as a 'manual'. They coaxed 113.6km/h (71mph) out of it and times of 15.6 and 24.1 seconds for the 0–80 and 96km/h (0–50 and 60mph) sprints with better than 8.8 litres per 100km (32mpg) economy.

April 1969 saw the release of the Morris Mini 1100 K (for Kangaroo allegedly) that was officially listed as the De Luxe Mark II and featured an Australian-assembled 1098cc engine with the Hydrolastic suspension, remote gearchange, dished steering wheel with padded hub, blinker/horn stalk on the steering column, three-dial dash à la the Cooper S, round bonnet badge without the wings, a three-part Morris Mini 1100 badge on the boot lid and a Mini K decal on the left fender. The base Mini and the van also received the 1098cc engine but retained the rubber cone suspension and 'magic wand' gearshift lever while the 998cc Mini Automatic was also continued.

The 1098cc engine developed 37kW (50bhp) at 5100rpm (a 20 per cent increase) and torque went to 80Nm (60lb-ft) at 2500rpm, up from 70Nm (52lb-ft), and a Lucas alternator now supplied the electricity. *Modern Motor* tested a Mini K in the June 1969 issue and liked it. Its around town flexibility was better than before as was climbing hills and they found it would cruise comfortably for long stretches at 112km/h (70mph). They recorded a top speed of 125km/h (78mph), 0–80 and 96km/h (0–50 and 60mph) times of 12.0 and 18.6 seconds which was par for the course in 1969, and the fuel consumption was 8 litres per 100km (35mpg) for all tests, indicating a figure of less than 7 litres per 100km (40+mpg) on a long trip which with a tiny 25-litre (5.5gal) tank gave barely enough range for our huge country. The Hydrolastic displacers gave the passengers a comparatively level ride, only getting choppy on really rough surfaces.

Any complaints? A few with the front seats being high on the list because of their upright backrest which made long drives uncomfortable, the seats were too narrow, there was no heater/demister, the foot pedals were too small and too close together, the fuel tank was too small and the engine bay was very crowded. But at $1780 it still represented great value for money in their opinion.

MINI MOKE

BMCA sprung a surprise on the Australian motoring public when it released the Moke on 31 March 1966. It *looked* military but was not even close, in fact the British Army had rejected it on a number of grounds. BMC went ahead with production in the UK but sales were abysmal so all the production equipment was shipped out to Waterloo where from late 1968 the Zetland factory became the supplier of Mokes to the world.

BMCA imported a handful of UK Mokes in 1965 for evaluation. Out of the test program several adjustments had to be made for it to be in any way suited to local conditions. For example, the ride height was raised by an inch, a hefty steel sump guard was specified with a ground clearance of 5in (130mm), a second engine stay bar was fitted to stop the engine-gearbox assembly 'rocking' on its mounts, a lower 4.121:1 differential ratio replaced the 3.765:1 used in the Mini, the hood design was greatly improved and its profile changed. The hood changes looked better compared with the Pommie version and gave better weather protection. 'Our' Moke also had the pretence of a proper dash insofar as there were open parcel shelves either side of the centrally-mounted single instrument and our seats had tubular steel frames with seat cushions slung over the frame and tied with cord and the seatback cushions were designed to slide over the frame; the English seats were pressed steel with padded cushions. Seatbelts were standard as were dual windscreen wipers and a washer; passenger grab handles and a heater were options.

The Moke was a buckboard-type of car based around a simple punt chassis built from virtually flat sheet metal with the Mini engine (still with a generator, not an alternator) and four-speed manual transmission unit up front and the rubber cone suspension and 178mm (7in) drum brakes with 74sq in of lining area, all coming from the donor Mini. It even retained the Mini's 10in wheels and 5.20 x 10 tyres which meant a low ground clearance, which in turn limited where it could be driven, particularly off-road. If inclement weather was encountered there was a crude folding canvas top for some (but not all!) protection.

Powering the original Moke was BMC's ubiquitous A Series engine in 998cc form (64.6 x 76.2mm) that developed 28kW (38bhp) at 5250rpm and 70Nm (52lb-ft) of torque at 2700rpm on an 8.3:1 compression and using a single SU carburettor. The front wheels were driven through the Mini gearbox with a non-synchromesh first gear.

Physically the Moke was close to the Mini, having a wheelbase of 2095mm (82.5in), length of 3225mm (127in), width of 1447mm (57in), height of 1600mm (63in), it weighed 620kg (1367lb) and could carry up to 254kg (560lb) of load. At the time of its release its retail price was just $1295.

To counter criticism about the lack of clearance BMC offered 13in wheels and tyres from April 1968. Dealers had suggested fitting the Morris Minor's 14in rims but there were clearance problems with the rear wheel arches. As a running change BMC fitted slightly longer trailing arms to the suspension and changed the shape of the rear wheel arches for the 13in rims. This change widened the wheel tracks slightly, which necessitated welding on wheel-arch extensions. The steering rack had to be modified and the turning circle increased marginally. The only other change was to a slightly lower 4.267:1 differential ratio.

A year later came the Moke Mark 2 and this had the 1098cc engine (64.6 x 83.7mm) that developed a healthy 38kW (50bhp) at 5100rpm and 80Nm (60lb-ft) of torque at 2500rpm, and full-synchromesh gearbox from the Mini K, a revised bonnet pressing and new single-unit tail-lights. The engineers had planned some additional improvements such as extra fuel capacity, better waterproofing and self-parking wipers. A single prototype was built with a second fuel tank mounted in the right-hand side pannier which meant that the battery had to be relocated to the engine bay, and for this to fit a smaller capacity windscreen washer bottle was necessary … and so it went on.

Evolution of the Moke continued into the next decade and this will be discussed in *Cars of the 70s.*

MORRIS 1100

With the 850 generating much-needed sales volume (and a modest profit), BMCA began a similar process of development with its bigger brother, the Morris 1100. Again, myriad minor changes had to be made to make it better suited to the local conditions and again they did not go nearly as far as the BMCA engineers wanted. Nine cars were imported from the UK and converted to Australian specifications before embarking on a program that totalled 297,000km (186,000 miles) of testing under every conceivable condition. There were a number of changes made including repositioning the handbrake to the right of the driver, reshaped gear lever to fit around the bench front seat, stone guards fitted to protect the fuel tank, pump and wiring, body reinforcements added to eliminate minor cracking at high mileages on rough roads, dirt and dust sealing of the remote gearshift significantly improved and a host of other minor items that made the local Morris 1100 a better car.

It was released and embraced by an expectant public on 17 February 1964, replacing the Elite on the dealer's showroom floors. Although physically smaller than the Elite, its transverse engine and transmission meant that it was vastly superior in space utilisation. The interior was in fact roomier and considerably more comfortable with the bench seats using Pirelli webbing rather than steel springs to support the passengers' bodies. Only the boot space was smaller, something that would become as issue with BMCA's dealers and their relationships with the clientele. Nothing was ever done about it which contrasts with earlier days when the Series I Morris Major was transformed to the much longer Series II for 1960, the redesign being *specifically* to create a larger boot!

It was the Morris 1100 that introduced Australian motorists to the wonders of the Hydrolastic suspension, a remarkable system developed by Alex Moulton (a friend of Issigonis) and adopted by BMC as a part of their 'new technology' process. In theory it gave motorists most of the advantages of the magnificent Citroën hydro-pneumatic system but at a fraction of the complexity and cost. That might have been true (the Morris 1100's ride and handling was brilliant, no doubt about that) but the downside was the poor reliability of the system that was prone to the displacers leaking causing the suspension to collapse. Regular

maintenance was imperative and repair was not inexpensive. The displacers were sourced locally, most likely from Dunlop Australia where they would have been made under licence from the UK.

The Hydrolastic suspension system was disarmingly simple, comprising four displacer units (one for each wheel), those at the front positioned vertically above the top wishbone while those at the rear were horizontal and operated by a pushrod that was part of the rear trailing arm. Steel pipes running under the car interconnected the front and rear displacers on each side. Within each displacer was an alcohol-based fluid that was moved by the action of the piston at the bottom which was attached to the suspension arm. The movement of this fluid would pass through a damper valve and out along the pipe towards the rear unit. This movement back and forth kept the car on an even keel with the suspension absorbing most of the bumps before they reached the passengers, body roll was limited so the 1100 cornered with a flat stance and back-and-forth pitching was eliminated. It really was a remarkable system.

The 1100 was built on a completely new platform using a wheelbase of 2375mm (93.5in), the overall length being 3727mm (146.75in), width 1534mm (60.38in) and height 1340mm (52.75in); kerb weight was 842kg (1852lb) and the car rode on 4J x 12 steel rims shod with 5.50 x 12 tyres. Like the 850 the engine and transmission unit was mounted transversely, the transmission located under the engine sharing the same oil. The engine was a development of the A Series BMC engine, having a bore and stroke of 64.56 x 83.72mm for a capacity of 1098cc and a power output of 38kW (50bhp) at 5100rpm, torque was 80Nm (60 lb/ft) at 2500rpm. As with all BMC transmissions to that point, the 1100's was a four-speed manual system with a non-synchromesh first gear.

Like the English Morris 1100, the Australian-manufactured version had the same dashboard that had a binnacle in front of the driver containing the instruments (fan-shaped speedometer graduated to 145km/h (90mph), fuel and temperature gauges plus warning lights) with open 'glove boxes' to the right and stretching across to the left with the ashtray dead centre. The fresh air heater/demister controls were mounted low down under the centre. The driving position was less bus-like than the Mini (but not much!) and because of the bench front seat the gearshift lever had an S-shaped bend near the top to follow the seat's contour but later this was changed to a 45-degree bend halfway up the stick to clear the leading edge of the seat. Going with a bench seat meant that the handbrake could not be positioned in the centre and was relocated to the right between the seat and the sill; a cross-shaft connected it to the existing cables.

Australian Morris 1100s had vinyl floor coverings, painted interiors on the door pillars and tops of the doors, adjustable door armrests, no

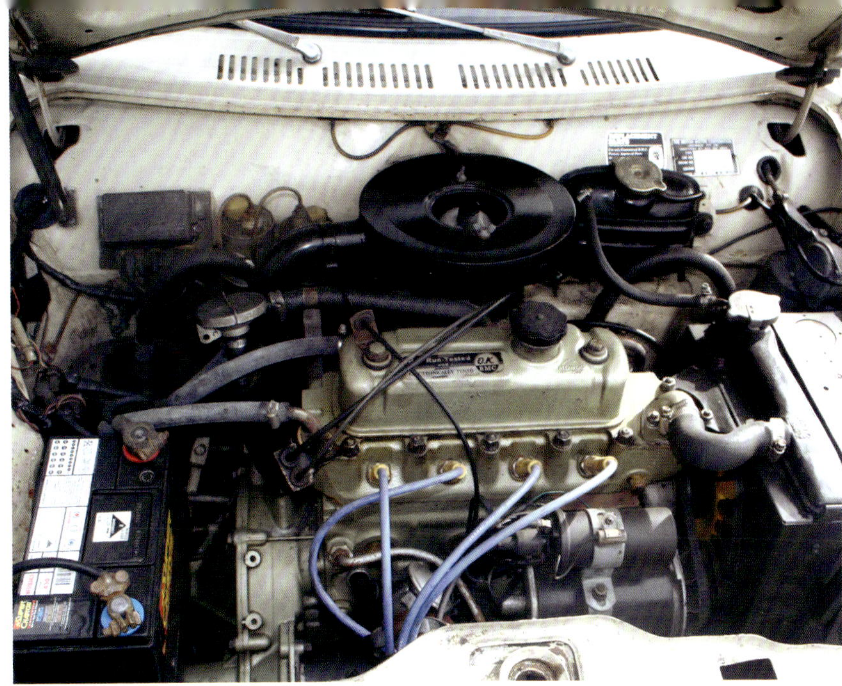

door pockets and stencilled names for the switches in the instrument nacelle (the Pommie version was unlabelled) and the road wheels were painted Silver Birch rather than white or body colour.

The media raved about the 1100 to the point where *Wheels* magazine voted it their Car of the Year for 1964. The public, too, liked what they saw and soon BMCA had a six-week waiting list. All 1100 production was of the Deluxe version until late 1967 when BMC introduced a Standard version but few were made – was it a government order?

Interestingly, apart from the suspension displacers leaking and the CV joints wearing and 'clicking' when on lock owners had little to worry themselves with where the 1100 was concerned. It was generally a trouble-free car.

In its April 1964 issue *Modern Motor* carried a full road test and came away to write a most pleasing (from BMC's point of view) article. The Hydrolastic suspension in particular was highly praised as were most aspects of the car's design. In conclusion they said, "At £960 the 1100 is undoubtedly good value even though it is right in the middle of a highly competitive section of the market." They extracted a maximum speed of 120km/h (75mph) out of it with a 0–96km/h (0–60mph) time of 21.7 seconds and between 8.9 and 7.3 litres per 100km (32–38mpg). It was not the fastest small family car available but it was one of the nicest and certainly one of the most innovative.

Through 1965 and 1966 the 1100 held top spot in the small/medium-sized car segment heading off the VW Beetle, Ford Cortina and its sibling, the 850, and achieving a 13 per cent market share. 1967 proved to be a busy year for BMC, which released the 1100S in August that had the 1275cc engine from the UK range plus the option of the AP four-speed automatic arrived at the end of the year. The introduction of the more powerful 1275cc engine did not require any mechanical changes over the 1098cc version, which spoke volumes for the rightness of the original package. *Australian Motor Sports* magazine tested an 1100S (November 1967) and found that the extra power (now 47kW (63bhp) and 95Nm (70lb-ft)) made quite a difference on the road where it would now run to 139km/h (87mph) and dash to 96km/h (60mph) in 15.8 seconds and return well over 9.4 litres per 100km (30mpg) in normal driving. It was a win-win for buyers, many of whom loved their 1100 but wanted more power. At $2074 *AMS* thought it a bargain.

All through its long production life the 1100 remained as it was when first introduced. Australian buyers might have longed for a bigger boot and maybe even 13in wheels for more ground clearance, especially under the vulnerable cast alloy sump, but neither seemed to be a barrier to sales on the showroom floor. The 1100 was superseded by the Morris 1500 in June 1969.

BMC 1800

ABF·455

AUSTIN

AUSTIN 1800

The third of the BMC front-wheel drive triumvirate arrived in October 1965 in the form of the Austin 1800. It was the largest of the Issigonis cars to be made locally and interestingly was a better seller in Australia on a per capita basis than in England! Of all the cars the 1800 truly showed how clever the Issigonis packaging was but it must be said that the car's styling and rather drab interior let the side down badly. Within what were quite compact dimensions – it was only 4166mm (164in) long on a 2692mm (106in) wheelbase (a Mark II Cortina was 4318mm/170in long on a 2489mm/98in wheelbase and was regarded as roomy for a conventionally engineered family sedan) – it easily seated five people in comfort (the Hydrolastic suspension again) and had ample luggage room.

What escaped most industry critics at the time (still does) was just how clever and advanced the 1800 was vis-à-vis its contemporaries from GM, Ford and Chrysler. Apart from the front-wheel drive and Hydrolastic fully independent suspension system, the 1800 had rack and pinion steering, power-assisted front disc brakes (241mm/9.5in diameter) with a pressure reducing valve in the circuit between the front and rear brakes, radial ply tyres, an effective heater/demister and flow-through ventilation system was standard equipment as were floor carpets, adjustable front bucket seat (down to full recline if needed), two-speed electric windscreen wipers with washers and a body that proved to be one of the strongest to have ever been built for a mass-produced saloon in the world. The dash was a thin strip across the front of the passenger compartment with a padded top and the instruments (speedometer, fuel and temperature gauges plus warning lights) were in a strip in front of the driver. Stretching full-width below that was a parcel tray storage area with large adjustable air vents either end. It looked cheap and probably was compared with its rivals' interiors.

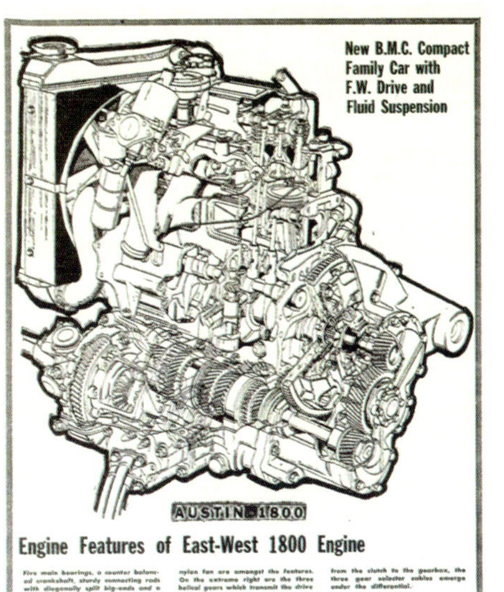

Initially the local 1800s were virtually identical to their British cousins but BMCA quickly began introducing changes that better suited the car to local conditions. Examples of this include the slight raising of the car's ride height, a heavy-duty sump guard to protect the vulnerable cast alloy sump, progressive rate throttle cam with a non-jamming plastic-lined cable, revised ratio steering rack, stronger wheels and better dust seals. However, despite the changes the 1800 Mark I was typical of many 1960s British cars insofar as it was fitted with Girling brakes and a Lucas positive earth electrical system that still used a DC generator. The Poms were way behind most of the rest of the world and in particular the Japanese, their nemesis.

Unlike its smaller siblings, the 1800's manual gearbox was a very robust unit with the familiar arrangement of the drop gears outboard of the clutch, the disadvantage being that a clutch replacement required the whole power pack to be removed from the engine bay; the 850's and 1100's clutches could be replaced without removing the engine. The optional Borg Warner Type 35 automatic had a separate oil sump from the engine (unlike the 1100 AP unit) and there was a chain drive from the torque converter to the input shaft. And because there was only a front oil pump the 1800 automatic could not be tow started.

As the car's name implies, it was powered by an 1800 engine, in this case the largest capacity then possible from the B Series production engine, its bore and stroke were 80.26 x 88.9mm for 1798cc, power being 63kW (84bhp) at 5300rpm and torque 134Nm (99 lb/ft) at 2100rpm using a single HS6 SU carburettor and an 8.2:1 compression ratio. This engine was a cousin to that in the MG B sports car and came with the five-bearing crankshaft from the start.

Sadly for BMCA the media critics judged the car primarily on its

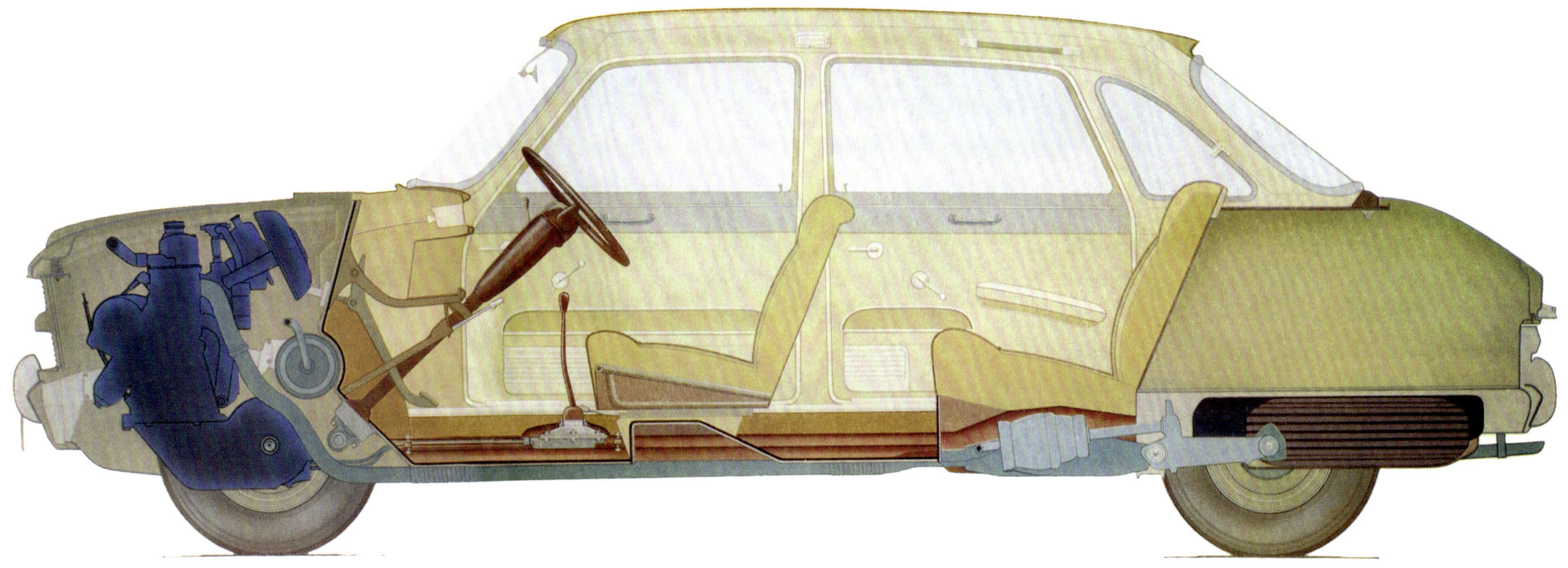

performance, which was not competitive with an HR Holden Special, XP Ford Falcon or AP5 Chrysler Valiant all of which had much larger capacity six-cylinder engines with vastly more power and torque, considerably more weight and were much less economical to run. The 1800, which weighed 1145kg (2520lb), would run to a maximum speed of 135km/h (84mph) and take 17.6 seconds for the 0–96km/h (0–60mph) sprint through the gears if that was necessary. However, what the 1800 was, and this was its ace in the hole, was a most delightfully relaxing and comfortable long-distance cruiser.

In almost every road test the media praised the 1800's ride and handling – "class-setting" were words used often to describe the Hydrolastic system – as well as the accurate rack and pinion steering although some thought it too low-geared (no power assistance offered) and the brakes were terrific. The only negatives were the styling, the wide turning circle and the upright driving position. As *Australian Motor Manual* summed up, "Despite some controversial features – shape, power, etc. – the Austin 1800 is a valuable contribution to our over-crowded new car market. It introduces a new dimension in road holding and road safety and in addition is quite luxuriously equipped considering its price."

For the most part the 1800 was a reliable and trusted family sedan but it was not long before suspension displacer issues arose as well as CV joints in the drive shafts. Opposition marketing people seized on these to show the buying public that it was all very well to be technically clever but 'our' cars did not suffer the same expensive breakdowns. The fact that 'their' cars were same old, same old was irrelevant then and the strategy sadly worked.

As with most BMC cars, the best came for those who were prepared to wait, and so it proved with the Mark II Austin 1800 that was released in October 1968. The styling received some attention given that the proportions of the original made any major changes both awkward and expensive and so it was an economy upgrade. The rear quarter panels were lengthened slightly and raised to accommodate vertical tail-light units with a side bonus of raising the boot line a fraction thereby giving slightly more room in the boot. Up front the grille was a new plastic moulding that was flush with the surface, not recessed as on the Mark I, and there was now a full-length chromed strip just below the door

handles and the front parking/indicator light units were larger. Inside, the switches for the various functions were now of the rocker type to meet forthcoming safety requirements.

Mechanically it was pretty much carry-over, although there were some significant (for BMCA) upgrades. A raised compression ratio and slightly larger valves in combination with a new log-type intake manifold yielded slightly more power, second gear had a higher ratio, the brakes were now sourced from PBR and had dual circuits, the electrics had a negative earth and an Email alternator and there was now a spin-on oil filter. While it looked like a minor styling upgrade to freshen interest in what many perceived to be a dull motor car, the 1800 Mark II was a much better made car.

From March 1969 the handbrake was relocated to the floor between the seats, a tandem braking system was installed and the door window winders were now made from a soft plastic.

As far as road performance was concerned the Mark II was identical to the Mark I – adequate without being startling – and it was a superb touring car.

When it was announced by the *Daily Mirror* in London that in November 1968 there would be a London to Sydney marathon with a first prize of £10,000 many car companies and individuals rushed to enter cars and teams. One of those companies was the newly formed British Leyland, which entered a three-car team while a total of 12 1800s were entered; some were Austins, some were Morrises. Lead driver for the factory team was Irishman Paddy Hopkirk with team-mates Tony Fall and Rauno Aaltonen. Of the 12 1800s entered nine completed the marathon, Hopkirk being an unlucky second (he should have won and in fact was declared the moral winner) with Aaltonen coming home in fifth and Fall in 24th position. While second place was a disappointment for the company it proved beyond a doubt the ruggedness of the car; although to be truthful it is doubtful if it caused more 1800s to be sold either in England or Australia.

BMCA continued selling the 1800 Mark II in modest numbers until the arrival of the X6 twins in 1970 and they will be discussed in *Australian Cars of the 70s*.

MORRIS 1500, NOMAD

Back in England the Leyland takeover had taken place in May 1968 and the only new product found to be undergoing development was the Austin Maxi, a hatchback derivative of the 1800. Under its bonnet was a completely new E Series in-line four-cylinder engine, the first entirely new production engine from BMC since the C Series six-cylinder unit of 1954! Can you believe that? The E Series showed the lack of engine expertise at Longbridge – it comprised a heavy cast-iron cylinder block (the rest of the world had gone to light-weight cast-iron technologies or even aluminium alloys) and cylinder head sporting a single chain-driven overhead camshaft; the expectation was the head would be a cross-flow design but, no, both intake and exhaust manifolds were on the same side! In the sump was a new manual gearbox with a cable gearchange mechanism. The new E Series engine's dimensions were 76.2 x 81.28mm for a capacity of 1485cc. On a compression of 8.6:1 and using a single SU carburettor it developed 55kW (73bhp) at 5500rpm and 110Nm (81lb-ft) of torque at 4000rpm.

BMCA engineers were involved in prototype development in England and flatly refused to accept the Maxi for assembly or manufacture in Australia. What they did take was the E Series engine and the new manual gearbox, initially as a four-speed and later as a five-speed. The Australians did point out to the Brits that the gearshift, as they had designed it, would not work but were politely asked to return to Australia and leave well enough alone. You guessed it, the cable gearshift was an unmitigated disaster and an enormous source of annoyance and frustration for owners of the Maxi and a huge warranty expense for the new British Leyland Motor Corporation. Because they were not allowed to make modifications off their own initiative, those same issues blighted Morris 1500 owners in Australia and BMCA and its dealers.

What BMCA had done locally was to adapt the existing 1100 bodyshell to take the less pointy rear fenders from the UK models, changed the bonnet pressing to one with a bulge to clear the taller engine, design a new grille, fit flush door handles and burst-proof door locks, use slotted steel wheels, install the original Austin 1100 dashboard from England and voila, there was the Morris 1500.

Announced simultaneously with the 1500 sedan in June 1969 was the Morris 1300 automatic and 1500 Nomad, a uniquely Australian vehicle that was trying to take some of the Renault 16 market by offering a versatile and adaptable interior within quite compact dimensions.

BMC advertised the 1500 as 'The Civilised Sports Car' which was a bit ambitious of them because there really was nothing about the car that could be in any way described as 'sporting'! The 1500 carried over most of the annoying foibles of the 1100 including the dreadful windscreen wipers that had only the one speed, which gave a clue as to what little development was taking place at BMCA. They were too slow in a decent shower but the most frustrating part was that they were set for left-hand drive for all those years!

In various road tests the test drivers were less than enthusiastic about the performance of the engine – it was noisy and not very responsive – and the cable gearshift was vague in the extreme; however, much of the rest of the car gained praise. Most tests returned with a maximum speed of 136–140km/h (85–88mph) with a 0–96km/h (0–60mph) acceleration time of 15.9 seconds and a fuel economy figure of 27–30mpg, not brilliant for a new 1.5-litre engined car but acceptable in 1969. And for 1969 they felt that the lack of a flow-through ventilation system was a big minus, there were no reversing lights, the wipers had only the single (slow) speed, they were set for left-hand drive, the washers were of the old-fashioned plunger type, there was no fan in the heater/demister system, the interior rear view mirror was too small and it vibrated, and the foot pedals were better suited to children rather than adults.

It was true that Holden, Ford and Chrysler also lacked most of these items, but the important reality was that the several Japanese manufacturers' products had them as a standard fitting and that really was the big issue for BMCA.

Owners soon found that the Morris 1500 was something of a lemon – head gaskets blew unless extreme care was taken during servicing, the cable gearshift could select more than one gear at a time, or none(!), and the suspension displacers would leak; with the Nomad, owners had to tolerate the rattles from the rear seat area or dispose of the car, which most did. Many ex-BMCA people believe earnestly that the Morris 1500 was the straw that broke the camel's back.

The 1500 soldiered on until the arrival of the Morris Marina in 1972 and that will be covered in *Australian Cars of the 70s*.

SPORTS CARS

Almost forgotten in the rush to become the nation's leading provider of technologically advanced family cars were the sports car lines, the Austin-Healey Sprite, its badge-engineered cousin the MG Midget, the big Austin-Healey and MG A. BMCA assembled the Sprite and MG A at Pressed Metal Corporation's factory at Enfield under contract.

BMCA imported the Healey Sprite beginning in November 1958. It was a cute thing that used as many existing mechanical parts as possible wrapped in a cheeky-looking two-seater body that was intended to have pop-up headlights but ended up with the headlights perched on the bonnet that led inevitably to it being called the 'frog-eyed Sprite'! It featured a monocoque body in which the front section (wings and bonnet) lifted as a single unit for access to the engine for servicing, a short rear with no boot lid and just enough space in between for two medium-sized passengers. The interior was minimalist in keeping with the so-called sports car tradition that was important to the English; the occupants sat on tiny bucket seats with the driver having two round Smiths dials in front and a combination dial for fuel and temperature, a stubby floor gearshift and little else by way of creature comforts.

The engine was the A series OHV four of 948cc capacity developing 31kW (42bhp) at 5000rpm using twin SU carburettors, the gearbox was from the Morris Minor/Austin A30 and had four speeds with first gear non-synchronised, a stubby remote floor shifter, the rear suspension used quarter-elliptic leaf springs, at the front was a double wishbone setup with coil springs and the brakes were 203mm (8in) drums all round.

Road tests saw the little fella reach 128km/h (80mph) with 0–80km/h (0–50mph) in 15 seconds which seems lethargic today but in 1958 that was pretty exciting stuff. Australian CKD assembly began in March 1960 at Pressed Metal Corporation's factory and brought with it a significant reduction in the retail price (down to £998 from £1174) much to the chagrin of early buyers.

In August 1962 BMCA introduced the Sprite Mark II that was based on the Mark I 'frog eye' but styled to look more conventional. It retained the centre structure but now had the headlights at the top of the fenders, a simple rear-hinged normal bonnet and at the rear the lines were squared up with vertical tail-light units off the A40 Farina, and a boot lid! It was a typically 'corporate' design where the original 'frog-eyed' Sprite had been the vision largely of one man, Donald Healey.

We're talking here about a small sports car sitting on an 2032mm (80in) wheelbase, 3454mm (136in) in overall length by 1346mm (53in) wide and 1270mm (50in) high at the top of the windscreen and weighing just 585kg (1288lb) at the kerb, all for only £950!

Mechanically the Mark II carried over the same components although the 948cc engine now produced 34kW (46bhp) at 5500rpm. Some months later, in March 1963, BMC substituted the 1098cc version of the A Series engine that produced 43kW (56bhp) at 5500rpm and changed the front brakes from tiny drums to small discs and baulk ring synchronisers were used in the gearbox. Top speed now was 136–140km/h (85–88mph) and the 0–96km/h (0–60mph) time was around 18.5 seconds. This sounds rather tame today when any ordinary 1.3-litre hatch will blow it away but in 1962 the Sprite was a cheekily quick car that was fun to drive, a commodity that is sadly missing in today's sanitised cars.

The Mark III arrived in October 1964 and was virtually indistinguishable from the Mk II except for the slightly deeper windscreen. Under the skin, however, changes had been made – a more powerful 46kW (61bhp) engine and the rear suspension now utilised conventional semi-elliptic leaf springs to suspend and locate the live axle in place of the previous quarter-elliptic leaves. Inside there was a new dash with an electric tachometer, wind-up door windows, self-cancelling indicators and a three-spoke steering wheel.

In August 1965 the last version of the Sprite, the Mark IV (called the Mark IIIA in Australia), was announced. It was the culmination of nearly a decade of (painfully slow) development and was regarded as the best of the breed. Under the bonnet was the engine that many believed should have been there much earlier – but we are talking about BMC here, remember – and it was the 1275cc A Series engine, a more powerful version of which had powered Mini-Coopers for some time. Power rose only 4bhp to 48kW (65bhp) but it had more torque and mid-range oomph. Possibly the most significant new feature was the foldaway soft top – no longer did you have stand out in the rain building the top up like a Meccano set!

With the formation of the British Leyland Motor Corporation in May 1968 it quickly became obvious that certain models in the vast range being produced in England were on borrowed time because managing director Lord Stokes loathed paying royalties to people like the Healeys and Coopers and by late 1968 the Sprite was withdrawn from local production and replaced by the MG Midget. It was in many ways a sad day for sports car enthusiasts and kind of highlights the inept thinking of British Leyland management.

There were two Midgets assembled and sold in Australia, the Mark I (as it has retrospectively been labelled) was current from November 1967 and ended in March 1970. It was identifiable by the vertical chromed bar grille; Mark Is all had their electrics wired with a positive earth, had thin cast cylinder blocks that required nitride crankshafts for rigidity. Late in the production of the Mark I BMCA introduced cylinder blocks with thicker walls, a negative earth wiring system with an alternator (at last!), plastic window winders and internal door handles, cross-flow radiator running at a slightly higher pressure, and just before the changeover to the Mark II the differential ratio was raised to 3.9:1. All locally assembled Midgets were fitted with radial tyres, an engine-oil cooler, front sway bar, twin horns and wire wheels as standard – they were options in the UK market.

A 'Spridget' as the car was colloquially known in Australia was tested by *Modern Motor* and they enjoyed their time with it but commented, "we loved every moment in the endearing little roadster but we were quite happy to step out". They felt the concept was a little outdated and despite spirited performance – 0–96km/h (0–60mph) in 12.0 seconds, top speed of 163km/h (102mph) – they found getting sprayed by diesel exhaust at traffic lights, poor levels of equipment inside, noisy non-synchromesh first gear and firm ride all a bit much. Were they missing the point of what the Sprite/Midget was all about?

Included in the Midget's specifications as part of the slow evolution of the model was a diaphragm spring clutch along with a revised close-ration four-speed gearbox still with no synchromesh on first gear, and separate master cylinders for the brake and clutch. *Racing Car News* achieved a top speed of 155.2km/h (97mph) and a 0–96km/h (0–60mph) acceleration time of 12.8 seconds. They were, however, scathing in their comments about the windscreen wipers, "they were completely out of place in a near-100mph car and were quite useless above 30mph in a moderate city downfall", and the headlights that were "nowhere near up to scratch and pretty feeble at any speed above 50mph".

Big brother, the MG A continued into the new decade in 1600 form having been upgraded in late 1959. A further revision, the 1600 Mark II, arrived in December 1961 that looked similar to its predecessor except for new horizontally placed tail-lights (that in truth looked like after-thoughts) and a recessed grille but had the 1622cc engine that had another 6kW (7bhp) on offer under the bonnet. More important was higher gearing for more relaxed touring. Top speed just breasted the 160km/h (100mph) mark.

Even though the MG A had been in production for seven years and was greatly admired internationally, it was in need of replacing with a new model and in March 1963 the company announced the MG B. CKD kits had been dispatched from Abingdon in November 1962 with the first assembled B coming off the PMC line on 4 April 1963.

The MG B was a total redesign insofar as it was the first monocoque MG sports car – yes, really! – and it was quite a bit roomier in the cockpit than the A, despite having a shorter wheelbase of 2311mm (91in, 76mm/3in less) and an overall length of 3894mm (153.3in), also

76mm (3in) less; it was wider at 1516mm (59.7in) and heavier at 919kg (2030lb) versus 904kg (1988lb).

The engine was the B Series 1798cc unit, initially with the three-bearing crank, developing 70kW (95bhp) at 5400rpm. Apart from the availability of a Laycock overdrive unit much of the rest of the B was carry-over A with minor refinements. It was not until March 1965 that the five-bearing crank 1.8-litre engine arrived but this was only a running change; an electric tachometer arrived at the same time. Bill Tuckey, the doyen of Australian motoring journalists, wrote a full test of the MG B for *Sports Car World* in September 1965 and said of the new engine, "It is much more flexible than its predecessor, with more torque and lugging ability low down and surprising smoothness under 3000rpm; but it is also much noisier and will not spin anywhere near as freely." The tachometer was redlined at 6000rpm but as Tuckey noted, "We rarely saw that figure." He liked the road dynamics and handling as well as the braking and found plenty of feedback in the steering but found the foot pedals were poorly positioned. The top was difficult to erect but once up was draught-free. Against the clock the B achieved a top speed of 161.6km/h (101mph) with acceleration through the gears to 80, 96 and 112km/h (50, 60 and 70mph) taking 8.9, 12.8 and 16.8 seconds each. In his opinion BMC and MG had softened the MG B too much – it was more a fast cruiser than a proper sports car – but it quickly became the top-selling sports car in Australia.

In October 1968 the MG B Mark II was announced (it arrived simultaneously in the UK with the MG C which never came to Australia, thank goodness) which featured the new all-synchromesh manual gearbox, the Borg Warner Type 35 three-speed automatic as an option, twin reversing lights were added on the rear valance panel, there were now anti-burst door locks, an alternator (at last!) with a negatively-earthed wiring loom and a boot lid badge that read 'Overdrive'. In this form it soldiered on into the seventies.

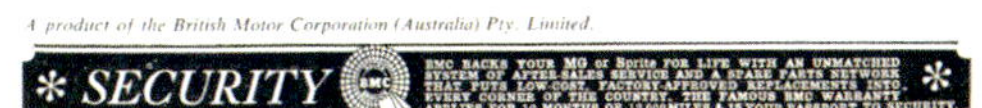

Despite the passage of time there were no significant improvements to the B. As *Modern Motor* said, "When you take a hard look at the car you realise that it is something of a relic. Its ancestral ties with MG TDs, TFs and MG As are painfully obvious – through its dated rigid rear axle, its rack and pinion steering with so much castor action that self-centring is virtually non-existent, its jarring ride on poor surfaces, its giant steering wheel, its stuffy, badly ventilated cabin and its awkward collapsing hood." Nevertheless, despite the short-comings and the availability of quicker, quieter and more comfortable sports sedans, around 1200 people each year paid around $3500 to buy an MG B.

The new five-bearing engine was fitted with twin SU HS4 carburettors and on an 8.8:1 compression developed the same 70kW (95bhp) at 5400rpm and 149Nm (110lb-ft) of torque at 3000rpm. Through the gears maxima were 51, 80 and 120km/h (32, 50, 75mph) with overdrive third running to 144km/h (90mph), direct top gear to 160km/h (100mph) and overdrive 171.2km/h (107mph). Acceleration took 8.0, 11.1 and 15.0 seconds from rest to 80, 96 and 112km/h (50, 60 and 70mph) which were not startlingly quick. But that did not diminish the desire by many to own an MG B, foibles and all.

BMC did the unthinkable with the Mark II by introducing the MG B Automatic! There were howls of protest from the traditionalists but the B Automatic soon became a modest sale success, mostly to women owners. It was only fractionally slower taking 11.7 seconds to 96km/h (60mph) and running to a top speed 162km/h (101mph).

The final years of the MG Midget and B will be discussed in *Australian Cars of the 70s*.

HILLMAN
56-056

Chapter 5

ROOTES GROUP

Like its British rivals, BMCA, Rootes Australia approached the sixties with some confidence. Their share of the local market had remained consistent at around 4.5 per cent and the company appeared to be quite happy with its achievements and position as the fifth largest provider of cars for the Australian market behind GM-Holden, Ford, BMCA and Volkswagen Australia and ahead of Chrysler and AMI. At the beginning of the sixties the very idea that there would be an invasion from the many Japanese manufacturers was unthinkable. Life for Rootes, however, was about to change … dramatically.

As with their fifties range of motor vehicles, those for the sixties would be assembled in their factory at Fishermans Bend from components shipped from England, in other words it was strictly a CKD operation. There had been talk from Rootes at various times about manufacturing a six-cylinder commercial vehicle engine in Australia and rumours abounded in the early sixties of the company utilising the land it owned at Dandenong for the manufacture of the company's four-cylinder passenger car engines. However, these ideas remained just that, ideas.

MINX

Carried over from the fifties was the Series III Hillman Minx that had been steadily developed since its 1957 release. For the Series IIIA released in November 1959 Rootes gave the Minx a tail lift(!) in the form of roll-over 'fins' and new vertically mounted oval-shaped tail-light units. The 1494cc engine continued, now with 40kW (53bhp) at 4600 (up from 34kW/49bhp) and in place of the former Manumatic semiautomatic gearbox (how many of those were sold locally?) came the new Easidrive full automatic developed by Smiths Industries in collaboration with Rootes. Unlike conventional automatic transmissions that featured a large and relatively inefficient torque converter filled with oil to drive gears that were clamped by hydraulic bands when selected, Easidrive used couplings that contained a metallic powder that became magnetised when a gear was selected. It was a genuine attempt to break the mould of Borg Warner-type automatic transmissions that were heavy and inefficient, but ultimately it failed in the market place not through any design flaw but because of Rootes' inability to mount a sufficiently strong marketing campaign to counteract entrenched dogma. There was considerable hoopla at the time in the media about this new 'breakthrough' form of automatic gearbox and the car was fitted with marginally bigger brakes. In November 1960 the IIIB arrived and was virtually indistinguishable from the outside but now was equipped with a hypoid rear axle.

The Minx was a typically British small–medium-sized car having bench seats front and rear, rubber mats on the floor, the instruments were in a central binnacle with open cubbies either side, the gearshift was on the steering column and a heater/demister was an option. We would consider it very basic today but in the sixties that was what you expected. If the car wore a Deluxe badge it merely meant more chrome.

Australian Motor Manual published a full road test of an automatic Minx and was impressed. They noted that from the driver's point of view it had a quadrant on the steering column with positions D, 2, N and R just like the Humbers that had a Borg Warner automatic gearbox. The engine had to be started with the selector in Neutral and when D was engaged they noted that there was no jerk and absolutely no evidence of creeping at idle; gear changes were notable by their smoothness. As for its on-road performance, the Minx auto would run to 128km/h (80mph) with 0–80 and 96km/h (0–50 and 60mph) times of 17.9 and 26.7 seconds each, ever-so-slightly slower than for the manual car. The Easidrive gearbox added around £150 to the car's price, the Minx Deluxe costing £1249.

The Series IIIC arrived in March 1962 and was discernible externally because it wore 1600 badges on both front doors (the engine's capacity had been raised to 1592cc by widening the cylinder bores to 81.5mm) and the Minx name on the boot lid; it remained unchanged until 1963 when the Series V appeared. What happened to Series IV you ask? That appellation was assigned to what became the Super Minx! The Series V was released in November 1963 and was a major restyle of the existing model with a new bonnet, a flatter roof pressing to go with four new fenders and new rear doors that were necessary because the rear window was now larger in area and no longer curved around into the C-pillar; the oval-shaped tail-lights were retained and the grille was a narrow

The Magnetic Particle Coupling

Smiths magnetic particle coupling consists basically of three main components. The stationary field member, housing a copper exciting coil, is secured to the engine crankcase. Attached to the engine crankcase is the driving or input member, while an output member is fixed to the gearbox input shaft.

All three members are assembled concentrically and are separated by small gaps. The inner gap between driving and output members contains a quantity of fine magnetic powder. When a direct current is passed through the coil, a magnetic flux is created and passes around the stationary field member, through the driving and output members, crossing the air gaps as shown in Figs 1 and 2.

When the magnetic flux passes through the magnetic powder the particles are attracted between the pole faces in such a way that a turning force is transmitted from the driving to the output member via the powder. The amount of 'drive' or torque is almost directly proportional to the current supplied to the coil. This allows a gradual and smooth engagement or disengagement of drive merely by varying the amount of current through a special control mechanism.

horizontal opening with four bars and prominent indicator/parking light units at each end.

Inside there was a new dashboard with the round Smiths instruments in front of the driver – hooray! Also included in the upgrade were front disc brakes, a larger (45 litres/10gal) fuel tank, 13in slotted steel wheels to go with a 3.89:1 rear axle ratio along with the elimination of the many suspension grease points. For motorists who wanted an automatic gearbox, Rootes were now using the industry standard Borg Warner Type 35 three-speed unit; and from early '65 the manual gearbox was a new all-synchromesh unit and the model was then given the Series Va name.

At the end of March 1966 the last version of this long-running and successful model rolled off the Port Melbourne assembly line, the Series VI with the 1725cc engine. Dimensions were now 81.5 x 82.5mm, with a five-bearing crankshaft and slightly more power; externally it was recognisable by the '1725' badges on the guards and if you looked closely there was a single small Pentastar badge to signify Chrysler ownership of the company. Accompanying it was the slightly more luxuriously equipped and more powerful Hillman Gazelle. The Minx's retail price was $1998 (manual), $2218 (automatic) while the Gazelle sold for $2187 (manual) and $2398 for the automatic.

Chrysler was attempting to cover a wider spectrum of the small–medium car market with the Minx and Gazelle. Externally the Gazelle had a completely different grille – it was the British Singer grille, upright centre section with side grilles encompassing the same indicator/parking light units as the Minx – and chrome wheel trims plus of course the new badges. Under the bonnet was where the major differences lay, the Minx having the single-barrel Zenith carburettor and an 8.4:1 compression ratio to produce 55kW (70bhp) at 4800rpm and 132Nm (98lb-ft) of torque at 2100rpm; by comparison the Gazelle used a high compression eight-port alloy cylinder head (9.2:1) in conjunction with a dual-barrel Solex carburettor to produce 66kW (85bhp) at 5500rpm and 144Nm (106lb-ft) of torque at 3500rpm. Acceleration and top speed were improved – 137km/h (86mph) for the Minx, 148km/h (93mph) for the Gazelle – and the media opined that they were now much more competitive cars in their market segment although they both were recognised as a decade-old design.

Inside they shared the same (new) dashboard and instruments but the Gazelle had reclining front bucket seats with better shaping and upholstery material, the heater/demister was a standard fitting and there were carpets on the floor front and rear.

HUSKY

In late 1958/early 1959 Rootes replaced the Mark I Hillman Husky with the Series I that was based on the new Minx design. As before, the front part of the body (up to the windscreen) shared panels and structure with the Minx but from there back it was unique to the Husky. The wheelbase was shorter by 203mm (8in) at 2184mm (86in) and its length was 3797mm (149.5in), 50mm (2in) longer than the previous model.

Apart from the more modern styling, the Series I Husky was now fitted with the 1390cc OHV four-cylinder engine but in a de-rated form producing 36kW (51bhp) at 4400rpm and 98Nm (72lb-ft) of torque at 2200rpm. It continued with a four-speed manual gearbox with a non-synchromesh first gear and a floor shift, its suspension, steering and brakes were from the Minx parts bin; it also continued with 15in wheels shod with 5.90 x 15 cross-ply tyres. Its kerb weight was a solid 990kg (2180lb).

Two body types were available with the plain windowless van for people who required a small delivery van to use in congested city conditions or tradies who needed something small, strong and economical to run. It was popular as a small four-seater station wagon as well, especially for those couples with two young kiddies; there was a reasonable space behind the rear seat for stowing all the paraphernalia that goes with young kids (accessible through the rear door) or the seats could be folded for carrying other loads. Either way it was an economical and versatile little wagon that retailed at £1042.

The interior was pretty basic, as perhaps might have been expected. The dashboard was a simple body-coloured steel pressing that housed a simple instrument binnacle in the centre – it was a British car, remember – that contained only a speedometer with a fuel gauge in the lower section plus some warning lights. Stretching full-width across the body, below the dash, was a parcel tray to stow odds and ends. A hangover from the past was in the form of the old Lucas combined ignition switch and rotary light switch.

Wheels carried out a full test of a Husky wagon and was impressed with its performance (116.8km/h (73mph) top speed, 0–80km/h (0–50mph) in 15.8 seconds and 10–7.8 litres per 100km (28–36mpg) economy) and the careful build quality and paint; although the painted (not chromed) grille was felt to be needless cost saving and the bare interior was not particularly inviting.

A Series II Husky followed in late 1960, the biggest change being the completely new all-synchromesh four-speed manual gearbox. Other changes (very hard to spot) were a slightly lower roof line (why bother?), a deeper windscreen and better front seats. By 1964 sales had slowed to a trickle and Rootes quietly discontinued assembling it from the CKD kits. There was no wake.

SUPER MINX

With the Minx successfully launched the attention of the designers and engineers in Coventry turned to a successor that was supposed to be the Minx Series IV for release in 1963. However, as often happens, the new model grew in size to the point where it was obviously going to be more expensive to produce and not suit the original buyer profile. Rootes, therefore, made the decision to continue manufacturing the Minx and in fact planned the Series V upgrade, and to build the new model for a different buyer profile. Marketing decided to name it the Super Minx. There is a certain amount of logic there but it did mean the two model ranges were very closely aligned which must have created marketing

issues that Rootes kept very much to themselves.

Dimensionally the Super Minx sat on a 2565mm (101in) wheelbase, was 4166mm (164in) in overall length, 1581mm (62.25in) wide, 1479mm (58.25in) high and weighed in at 1070kg (2355lb). Both four-door sedan and station wagon body styles were offered. The faithful 1592cc engine provided the power (49kW (66bhp) at 4800rpm) and the same four-speed manual gearbox from the Minx was offered. The wheels were slotted steel 13in in diameter with 5.90 x 13 cross-ply tyres and initially the front brakes were 228mm (9in) drums.

From a styling perspective the Super Minx was quite different from the Minx. At the front was a plain, horizontal eight-bar grille with the Hillman badge in the centre flanked by a single headlight each side with the semicircular shaped indicator/parking light above. At the rear were unusual strakes along the top of each rear quarter panel that dipped at an angle over the same oblong tail-light units as on the Minx and were joined across the boot lid by a chromed strip. The Hillman name was spelled out in individual letters above the chrome strip. The front windscreen was semi-wrap-around (a little like that on the Humbers that were styled by the same people) and the rear window curved around into the C-pillar just like on the 56-through-63 Minx. Jack Green and Jack White were mainly responsible for the car's exterior styling and Bernard Winter for the car's conservative engineering.

The spacious interior featured bench seats front and rear, floor carpets, a floor gearshift (which was an option, column shift was standard) and the ribbed metal dashboard contained three round Smiths dials in front of the driver (speedometer on the left, small fuel dial (showing gallons and litres) in the middle and a combination dial containing only a temperature gauge and provision for amps and oil pressure (plus warning lights) on the right) and an efficient heater/demister was a standard fitting. In the centre of the dash was also provision for the fitting of a clock.

The Mark I lasted exactly a year on the market before being replaced by the Mark II version that brought disc front brakes, individual front seats, relocated fuel tank (from under the boot floor to behind the back seat) and the option of the Borg Warner Type 35 automatic gearbox.

Wheels magazine road-tested a Mark II sedan (September 1964) and came away highly impressed. They particularly liked the interior, commenting, "the cockpit of the car is one of the better examples of British design". The dashboard, a full-width steel pressing with discreet ribbing on its lower half, was neat and attractive with nice large Smith dials and a parcel shelf below. The seats were regarded as excellent giving good support for

the shoulders and under the thighs and there was carpet on the floor front and rear. The finish inside was to a high standard. The same opinion was expressed regarding the build quality and exterior paintwork.

The only real disappointment was the Super Minx's tardy acceleration which was timed at 9.6 seconds for the 0–64km/h (0–40mph) run, 16.2 seconds to 80km/h (50mph) and 23.8 seconds to 96km/h (60mph). These times were almost identical to those achieved with a Series V Minx that utilised the same mechanicals. But the Super Minx was 55kg (120lb) heavier so perhaps it was not as slow as perhaps it felt. Like other models in the Rootes Group range, the basic handling characteristic was understeer which made for a safe car but hardly an exciting one.

Late in 1964 the Mark III was released with considerably revised styling. From the waist up it was all-new. The windscreen had less wraparound, the roof was slightly longer and flatter, the rear window was now almost flat and a third side window was incorporated in the C-pillar. It completely transformed the appearance of the Super Minx. Mechanically it continued with the 1592cc engine, four-speed gearbox now with synchromesh on all four gears or the Borg Warner Type 35 as an option.

Rootes allowed the Super Minx to waft along with little by way of promotion until mid-1966 when it was quietly withdrawn from the range. It was replaced by the Hillman Hunter which is covered in the Chrysler chapter of this book.

IMP

In February 1964 Rootes Australia released one of the most anticipated small cars onto the local market – the Hillman Imp. It had been the subject of considerable hype (for a Rootes car) – although not to the same extent as the Mini 850 – and the dealers could not wait to get their hands on it.

It was a rather remarkable little car, quite possibly the most attractive small car ever to be put into mass production. The styling proportions were near enough to being perfect. However, as many hapless owners discovered, that neat styling hid a multitude of issues that really ought to have been exorcised out of the car *before* it went into production.

The Imp was a clean-sheet design and bore no resemblance to any other Rootes Group car, before or since. It was also the most ambitious project that Rootes ever undertook. It was small in size, its wheelbase was just 2082mm (82in), it was 3505mm (138in) in overall length by 1524mm (60in) wide and 1346mm (53in) high; its kerb weight was 714kg (1570lb) and the fuel tank held only 27 litres (6gal), which might have been fine in the UK but was marginal in Australia. The fully independent suspension – a Rootes first – was unusual insofar as the front used swing axles that were pivoted close to the car's centreline, with coil springs and had an obvious negative camber when the car was standing, at the rear were semi-trailing arms also with coil springs. Rack and pinion steering and four-wheel drum brakes completed the technical specifications.

Under the stubby rear bonnet was the Imp's pièce de résistance – the Coventry Climax-based 875cc SOHC four-cylinder in-line all-alloy engine. It was a glorious piece of engineering and visually delightful; having a bore and stroke of 68 x 60.3mm, on a 10:1 compression and with a single tiny semi-downdraft Solex carburettor it produced 29kW (39bhp) at 5000rpm, and 70Nm (52lb-ft) of torque at 2800rpm. A chain drove the overhead camshaft that operated on bucket tappets to the valves. Mated to the engine was an all-new four-speed all-synchromesh transaxle driving the rear wheels through flexible rubber couplings on the inner end of the driveshafts.

Offered at £799 – a Mini retailed at £763 – the initial sales were brisk although they were never at the level of the Mini, even though that was Rootes' declared target. That begs the question: Why was the Imp not as successful as the Mini? There is no simple answer unfortunately but one that takes in several issues like poor reliability, constant malfunction of the pneumatic accelerator pedal, the engine ingesting dust and scoring the cylinder bores which increased oil consumption dramatically and often required an engine rebuild, poor assembly quality, Spartan equipment levels (although the Mini was no better) and having the engine at the wrong end of the car. By 1964 most of the rest of the world's automobile industry was following BMC's lead in bringing out new small family cars with a transverse engine and *front*-wheel drive. Rootes definitely zigged when everybody else zagged! I am quite sure if the existing alloy engine was relocated transversely up front with an end-on gearbox driving the front wheels and using the same attractive body (which would then have a decent boot) the Imp could easily have been a huge success. Ah, hindsight … it's wonderful!

Wheels, *Modern Motor*, *Australian Motor Manual* and the many newspapers around the country devoted pages and pages to the Imp and found that it had excellent manners on the road, was ideal for women to drive because the controls were light and precise and the little engine would push it along at 118–120km/h (74–75mph) top speed and it would run from 0–80km/h (0–50mph) in 15.2 seconds while returning more than 7 litres per 100km (40mpg). By way of comparison, the Morris 1100 which was released at virtually the same time could manage only

123km/h (77mph) and at 16.2 seconds to 80km/h (50mph) was actually slower in acceleration!

In December 1964 the Imp Super was released with a retail price of £815. It was a vastly better car (in fact, many would say that Rootes erred by not specifying the original Imp this way), and there were a number of other technical improvements as well – a Bowden cable replaced the troublesome pneumatic accelerator system, the air pickup for the engine was relocated, a stronger clutch was fitted, while bumper over-riders, two sun visors and better quality trim featured inside.

The Imp II arrived in February 1966 with two identifiers: the Imp II badge on the doors and a discreet Pentastar badge low down on the left front fender. Many more improvements were wrought by this time including a bigger diaphragm clutch (6.25in replacing 5.5in), lighter brake pedal pressures, better designed air cleaner, sealed crankcase ventilation, a new carburettor, improved fuel filtration, more efficient water pump and sealed for life universal joints in the drive shafts. In addition, there were protective shields under the radiator and manifolding, a built-in ventilation system (a heater/demister was still an option), seatbelt anchorages, headlight flasher and windscreen washers.

In April 1967 Chrysler released the Hillman GT. Note, they never badged it as the Hillman *Imp* GT although that is what everybody called it. The GT was not simply a hotted up regular Imp, it was a thoroughly re-engineered car based on the UK Singer Chamois. Attention to details in the engine and the use of dual Stromberg CD125 carburettors, free-flow exhaust system, engine oil cooler and dual valve springs saw it now produce 42kW (55bhp) at 6100rpm, servo-assisted drum brakes did the stopping (admirably, I might add) and the safety rimmed 12in wheels were now shod with 145 x 12 radial tyres. As for performance, it would run to 140km/h (87mph) and take 9.9 seconds for the 0–80km/h (0–50mph) run and still return around 7 litres per 100km (40mpg). At $1799 it was something of a performance bargain.

In April 1968 Chrysler released the Imp III that was something of a hybrid initially using an English Mark I body (obsolete by 1965 in the UK!) before the Mark II body came on stream. A third body was used from early 1969 when the Imp III used the ex-GT body, which makes identification difficult today. The last Imp rolled off the Port Melbourne assembly line in November 1970 but it took almost a year before they were all sold.

HUMBER

The sixties began with strong prospects for the Humber marque. Market acceptance of the excellent Hawk and Super Snipe twins had been strong and with added refinements coming along regularly there seemed no reason to doubt the continuation of this success. However, the winds of change were blowing and Humber would unwittingly become a victim despite having the best cars ever to carry the proud name.

In March 1960 Rootes released the Series IA Hawk which had been subtly upgraded, its specification now including a heater/demister with booster fan and a cigar lighter as standard equipment. The only obvious change for car-spotters was the use of twin parallel chromed strips an inch or so apart along each side of the body and from June 1960 the only transmission on offer was the Borg Warner Type 35 automatic. A Series II was introduced in May 1961 and its specification included vacuum-assisted Girling disc brakes (279mm/11in diameter solid rotors) on the front wheels, wider rear brake drums, slightly softer spring settings to give a better ride, the intermediate gear hold for the automatic was operated by depressing the column lever in place of the push-pull knob on the dash, pump-type windscreen washers to go with the two-speed wipers and a reversing light was fitted to the plinth over the number plate on the boot lid.

Modern Motor tested a Series II in August 1961, the report being written by Bryan Hanrahan who loved Humbers. After several hundred miles of driving during which he posted a top speed of 142.4km/h (89mph), a 0–96km/h (0–60mph) time of 22.0 seconds and got 12.4 litres per 100km (23mpg) from the 1454kg (3200lb) luxury saloon powered by a 58kW (78bhp) 2.2-litre four-cylinder engine he said, "The Hawk is quiet, capable and beautifully finished. And I'm not sure that I prefer the Snipe, for all its extra power and six cylinders."

In March 1960 Rootes also released the Series II Super Snipe in Australia and this brought a raft of improvements. Under the bonnet was now a full 3-litre version of the superb cross-flow six, the cylinder bore being increased to 87.3mm (the stroke remained unchanged) for 2965cc, power rising to 90kW (121bhp) at 4800rpm using a new Zenith carburettor. The drum front brakes were replaced by Girling solid rotor

S590 AAM

SNIPE 3

SEV 744

SNIPE 3

S590 AAM

SNIPE 3

279mm (11in) diameter solid discs with a vacuum boost to reduce pedal pressures. The floating grille remained up front and a second chromed strip was added to the body sides (it was not parallel like on the Hawk but dropped away to the rear) and this could be used to add a second body colour. *Wheels* magazine road-tested a Series II and headed their report by saying, "Modest price, good finish and bags of performance make the biggest Humber about the greatest value money can buy in Australia." They eulogised over the car's ability to cover vast distances in supreme comfort for the occupants and in complete safety. The quality and ambience of the interior drew very high praise. Against the clock the revitalised Super Snipe ran to 148.8km/h (93mph), ran the 0–80 and 96km/h (0–50 and 0–60mph) dashes in 11.5 and 15.7 seconds respectively and would return 12.4 litres per 100km (23mpg) when cruising. Interestingly, when *Modern Motor* tested the Snipe they recorded a top speed of 163.2km/h (102mph) and a 0–96km/h (0–60mph) time of 17.6 seconds..

A year later the Series III was released. To the casual observer the most obvious changes were at the front where there was a new full-width grille consisting of nine chromed horizontal bars that swept around the corner to the leading edge of the front wheel arch; the park/indicator lenses were under the new four-headlamp front, a first for a British saloon. This necessitated a modified fender pressing each side compared with the Hawk which retained the original two-headlight front.

Inside, the walnut dash now featured new square air vents at either end for the flow-through ventilation system that was independent of the heater, which now had simpler controls. The manual choke control was now a slide – a dash light came on to advise the driver it was in use – and the intermediate hold for the Borg Warner gearbox was now in the column-mounted selector. Small detail changes admittedly but all worthwhile for the driver/owner. Performance was little different from the previous model, running to a top speed of 150.4km/h (94mph), a 0–96km/h (0–60mph) time of 15.8 seconds and 16.5 litres per 100km (17mpg) driven hard.

Little else was changed (when the product is right why change it?) until October 1964 when the Series V Super Snipe was announced. Visually this brought far more obvious changes to the styling, particularly where the cabin was concerned. New for '65 was a completely revamped roof and window line, the roof having a flatter profile with an almost flat rear window within slight buttresses and new sixth side windows were now where previously the wraparound rear screen had been. Also new were the tail-lights which now had three round lenses. The new style added renewed energy to the big car's appearance and from a sales perspective reinvigorated demand for the sedan.

From a technical point of view there was virtually no change, again the Rootes engineers working on the basis that if it ain't broke you don't need to fix it. Power was raised slightly to 102kW (137bhp) at 5000rpm and torque to 226Nm (167 lb-ft) at 2600rpm, and the only gearbox now available was a Borg Warner Type 35 automatic. Performance was still spirited with its top speed at 166km/h (103.8mph) and the dash to 96km/h (60mph) taking 14.9 seconds, good for a luxury saloon that weighed 1636kg (3600lb) and cosseted its occupants all of the way.

Despite being a decade-old design the Super Snipe continued to sell well to politicians, bankers, the medical profession, lawyers and rural people in consistent numbers years after year. However, with the takeover by Chrysler in 1966 of the entire Rootes Group one of the first casualties of their new marketing strategy was Humber. The Chrysler brains trust tried to sell long-time Humber buyers their Valiant Regal and wondered why they were rebuffed! An excellent example of commercial stupidity by people who should have known better and who ignored their market demographic.

During the early months of 1964 the Humber Hawk was quietly discontinued from assembly and sale in Australia as it was no longer fashionable to have an admittedly good car, if a very conservative good car, powered by a big and old-fashioned long-stroke four-cylinder engine and whose price was not significantly less than its larger and better-selling sibling. To bolster sales of premium brand small family saloons Rootes Australia began assembling the Humber Vogue locally from December 1962. This model was a badge engineered Hillman Super Minx that shared the same physical dimensions but was really the English Singer Vogue with Humber name badges applied here (the Singer name was long gone from the local marketplace where Humber was a highly respected name). This meant that it had new front quarter panels to accommodate the four-headlight system and a new bonnet pressing to accept the Humber grille. At the rear were three small round lights each side in place of the larger single unit.

The Vogue's interior was what buyers expected from a Humber, being very English Club in atmosphere with its polished walnut dashboard and door cappings, leather upholstery and Wilton carpet on the floor. Where the Super Minx had round Smith dials the Vogue had a rectangular instrument unit with a fan-shaped speedometer that had a fuel gauge at one end and a temperature gauge the other plus some warning lights. Heater/demister slides were in the centre of the dash with provision for a radio underneath and in front of the passenger was a deep glovebox with a mirror for the ladies to powder their nose while husband drove.

Mechanically the Vogue shared the 1592cc four-cylinder engine with the Super Minx and with a single Solex carburettor and 7.8:1 compression developed 46kW (62bhp) at 4400rpm and 116Nm (86lb-ft) of torque at 2400 rpm. Two gearboxes were available – either the Rootes four-speed with synchromesh on the top three ratios or the Borg Warner Type 35 three-speed automatic. A rear axle ratio of 3.89:1 was specified regardless of what gearbox was ordered.

Modern Motor tested a manual Vogue in its July 1963 edition and came away very impressed with every aspect of the car except its on-road performance. In a nutshell, it was far too highly geared and the engine was insufficiently powerful to pull the high ratio. That limited its maximum speed to 120km/h (75mph), its 0–80 and 96km/h (0–50 and 60mph) acceleration times to 18.0 and 27.3 seconds! It was much slower than the Super Minx! Rootes described the Vogue as a luxury car where the media believed it could so easily have been both a luxury and sporting compact saloon. The fixtures, fittings and assembly quality were first class in keeping with the Humber name and image and at £1192 they regarded it as something of a bargain.

With Ford adding substantially to its sales of the Cortina by adding the GT model to the line-up, Rootes followed suit with their Vogue Sports in November 1963, but it was not the bare-bones car that the Cortina was. No, this was a Humber and a certain level of gentility was expected so the Sports featured the full English Club interior and, surprisingly, the most unsporting ex-Singer dash with its fan-shaped speedometer and not a tachometer in sight. This is rather surprising because it was not as if a proper sporting dashboard was not available – it would have been a simple matter of adding it to the CKD kits being dispatched from Coventry.

To go with the Sports badge Rootes specified the aluminium alloy eight-port cylinder head that was fitted to the English Humber Sceptre and Sunbeam Rapier along with a twin-choke Solex carburettor and 9.1:1 compression ratio, this combination giving the Sports a power output of 62kW (84bhp) at 5000rpm and 123Nm (91 lb-ft) of torque at 3500rpm.

Despite its apparent lack of 'sportiness' in appearance matters, the Humber Vogue Sports was no slouch. *Wheels* magazine (October 1964) conducted a four-car comparison with the Vogue Sports being compared with the Ford Cortina GT, Volkswagen 1500S and the Fiat 1500. Three were neck-and-neck for top speed – the Fiat was the fastest on 149.9km/h (93.7mph), the Vogue next on 147.2km/h (92.0mph) and the Cortina GT on 147km/h (91.9mph) – while the VW 1500 S trailed on 128.1km/h (80.1mph). As for acceleration, it was again a three-horse race with the Cortina GT fastest from 0–80km/h (0–50mph) at 9.7 seconds followed by the Fiat at 10.0 and the Vogue at 10.7 seconds, the VW again lagging behind at 13.6 seconds. The Cortina GT and VW were the lightest in weight at 852kg (1876lb) and 862kg (1896lb) each, the Fiat was next at 963kg (2118lb) and the Vogue Sports was heaviest at 1069kg (2352lb) so its performance was all the more remarkable.

From a pricing point of view, the Cortina GT was the cheapest at £1203, the Fiat cost £1290, the Vogue Sports £1299 and the VW was

the most expensive at £1329. What those prices do not tell the reader was just how much of a bare bones stripper the Cortina was – no heater/demister, no vanity mirror, only half padding on the dash, no reversing lights, no internal bonnet lock and so on, all of which (and more) were in the Vogue Sports.

On the subject of ride, they expressed the view that "for general ride on good–average bitumen the Vogue seems to be best. As the road deteriorates the Humber's stiffer suspension makes it pitch rather smartly, the Cortina begins to leap about and the Fiat follows suit." On dirt the VW was unassailable. The only complaint they levelled at the Vogue Sports was the heavy steering (no power steering in 1964!) and preponderance for understeer all the time.

Rootes discontinued the Sports in July 1965 and upgraded the regular Vogue to the 62kW (84bhp) engine but the Sports badge was conspicuous by its absence. It coincided with the release of the Vogue Mark III that brought with it the same roof and window line that was on the Super Snipe – a flattish roof extended slightly with an almost flat rear window and a third side window. Little else was changed although reclining front seats were added and the manual gearbox was now a full-synchromesh unit. As *Wheels* commented in its January 1966 issue when they tested the Vogue, "In performance the car is right up into the Cortina GT class, although fractionally slower everywhere. It handles remarkably well, stops equally well, and fuel consumption is not excessive for a medium-high performance light four. This would be good enough. But the Vogue sets very high standards of comfort, trim and equipment to go along with this good road performance." The Vogue was timed at 139.2km/h (87mph) for top speed and ran the 0–80 and 96km/h (0–50 and 060mph) sprints in 11.0 and 15.8 seconds respectively while giving 10 litres per 100km (28+mpg) when cruising.

Rootes Australia was absorbed into Chrysler Australia from 1966, the ex-Rootes cars remaining pretty much as they were apart from the application of a single small Pentastar badge low down on the left front fender. Sadly for Humber enthusiasts the Super Snipe was quietly discontinued in late 1967 despite engineers in the UK fitting a Chrysler 273cid V8 under the bonnet of several examples and testing them extensively before doing what Chrysler did best in those days, canning the project allegedly on cost grounds. As for the Vogue, it too quietly faded from the local motoring scene in 1967 as the company prepared to place its marketing efforts behind the Hillman Arrow and Hunter cars, which represented the next generation and the future.

F JM 126

Chapter 6

AUSTRALIAN MOTOR INDUSTRIES

Although the directors of AMI may not have known it, the decade of the sixties was going to be momentous in every way, from bust to boom, and involve new partners – American Motors from the USA and Toyota from Japan – who would join the fray with stunning results.

MERCEDES-BENZ

The model changeover from the W121 and W180 Ponton saloons took place in Germany in September 1959 with the showing of the new W110 and W111 220S and 220SE sedans at the Frankfurt IAA. However, it was at least a year later before the new 'fintail' Mercedes-Benz 190 and 220 saloons came off the AMI assembly line. Local content consisted of tyres, trim, battery and paint.

Modern Motor published a full test of a 220S in the January 1960 issue, which was only a month prior to the release of the new models. Apart from being highly impressed with the big saloon's performance – 165km/h (103.2mph) top speed, 16.0 seconds for the 0–96km/h (0–60mph) run – from just 2.2 litres, the consummate way in which it devoured the vast distances of our country and the quality of the interior fittings writer Hanrahan felt that rubber mats on the floors and the lack of armrests front and back to stop passengers sliding about when the driver was pressing on was a bit poor in a saloon costing £2852.

The first batch of 'finnies' off the assembly line were W111 220S sedans and they arrived on showroom floors in March 1960. These sedans had stunning and very individualistic styling for their time, especially so for Daimler-Benz, which was one of the most conservative companies in the business. There was a touch of the then fashionable Farina style about the overall shape of the W111 but the Italians had no input at all to the Mercedes-Benz design – it was the work of Karl Wilfert and his protégé Paul Bracq.

From the front their style was dominated by the upright, regal Mercedes-Benz grille topped by the three-pointed star and flanked by tall, vertically arranged headlights under the one glass cover. At the top were the direction indicators with low beam lights below and high beam lights at the bottom. Nobody had ever done that before. The design had prominent front fenders over the wheels and swept back along the bonnet to a broad semi-wraparound windscreen and a cabin with very formal-looking windows with flat side glass. At the back the rear window swept around slightly into the C-pillar and as their nickname implies, there were vestigial fins atop the rear quarter panels and they were adorned with discreet chromed strips. There was a reasonable overhang at the back that gave the car a huge luggage compartment that had the spare wheel clamped in the left rear well. Across the rear was a full-width light assembly; there were substantial chromed steel bumpers front and rear. Incorporated into the body structure of the new family of Mercedes-Benz passenger cars were front and rear crumple zones designed to protect passengers in the event of a crash.

The W111 sat on a wheelbase of 2750mm (108in) and stretched 4875mm (192in) in overall length by 1795mm (71in) wide by 1450mm (57in) in height and weighed 1330kg (2940lb) in 220S form and 1360kg (2992lb) as a 220SE making them slightly larger and heavier than the W180.

Under the bonnet the W111 was very similar to the outgoing W180. The engine remained the SOHC in-line six with cast-iron block and alloy cylinder head, the intake system initially comprising dual twin-choke Solex carburettors that helped the engine develop 92kW (124bhp) at 5200rpm on an 8.7:1 compression. By substituting a Bosch mechanical fuel injection system for the carburettors the power was raised to 100kW (134bhp) at 5000rpm. Initially only a four-speed all-synchromesh manual gearbox was available with the obligatory steering column gearshift, an automatic (a four-speed unit designed and manufactured by Daimler-Benz!) not being available until the end of 1962.

The engine, gearbox and double wishbones with coil spring front assembly again sat on a sub-frame (the German word for it was *fahrschemel*) and while the rear suspension looked the same it was quite different in its details. It was still a swing axle arrangement with a low pivot point but now had a coil spring mounted horizontally above the differential unit. Brakes were still by four-wheel drums (with a vacuum booster) but for the W111 they were now finned to assist in their cooling. Disc brakes were still some way into the future at Mercedes-Benz!

Inside, passengers sat on sumptuously upholstered seats, adjustable bucket seats in front and a wide bench with a centre armrest in the back where the floor was carpeted, but in the front there were rubber floor mats! The Mercedes-Benz designers came up with something special for the instrumentation: the instrument binnacle was a tall, vertical unit directly in front of the driver; the speedometer was positioned vertically with graduations either side of a coloured strip indicator and every local road test complained about how hard it was to read. Among its party tricks was its changing of colour as the car's speed rose, from yellow to red above 40mph. Other dials included fuel contents, engine temperature and warning lights with dashboard switches for lights and wipers.

Bryan Hanrahan from *Modern Motor* tested a 220S in the May 1960 issue and waxed lyrical about the big sedan all the way through. He managed a top speed of 169.6km/h (106mph) which was very impressive from a big, heavy family sedan with only a 2.2-litre engine, acceleration times from 0–80 and 96km/h (0–50 and 60mph) took 10.3 and 14.9 seconds respectively and he returned a fuel mileage of 11.4 litres per 100km (25mpg) for the 280-mile test. At £2870 including tax he believed the 220S to be one of the best cars on the market.

Modern Motor followed the test of the 220S with one on the 220SE in its October 1960 issue, this time tested by racing driver and journalist David McKay. The price was £230 more but the payoff was faster acceleration and greater flexibility. The Bosch mechanical fuel-injection system (*Einspritzung*) helped produce another 7kW (10bhp) from the engine (100kW (134bhp) at 5000rpm) and the 0–80 and 96km/h (0–50 and 60mph) acceleration times dropped to 9.0 and 12.2 seconds and it covered the standing quarter mile in 19 seconds exactly. As before, the report was full of superlatives for the big sedan.

An automatic 220SE became available towards the end of 1962 at a showroom price of £3327, an increase of £227. Again, the test team poured superlatives on the Mercedes-Benz for its all-round exhilarating dynamics, brilliant roadholding, powerful braking and its ability to travel vast distances at high speed in complete safety. Maximum speed was down to 153.6km/h (96mph) and the 0–80 and 96km/h (0–50 and 60mph) acceleration times were actually quicker than the manual at 9.05 and 12.0 seconds while fuel consumption was quoted at 15.5 litres per 100km (18.3mpg) for the test – thirsty!

Shortly afterwards examples of the W110 four-cylinder 190 'finnie' sedan appeared on showroom floors around the country. From the bulkhead back they were identical to the 220 so passenger accommodations were the same as was the boot space. However, the wheelbase was shorter at 2692mm (106in) and overall length, too, was reduced to 4737mm (186.5in). Weight, too, was down to 1247kg (2744lb). In reality it was not really *that* much smaller! The front fenders were a different pressing because they had a single round headlight each side rather than the unusual (and doubtless expensive) combination units on the six-cylinder cars. At the rear were different (cheaper) tail-light units that performed the same functions as those on the W111.

Under the bonnet was the same engine that powered the W180, a single overhead camshaft in-line four-cylinder engine of 1897cc capacity that with a single Solex carburettor and an 8.7:1 compression developed 67kW (90bhp) at 5000rpm. The four-speed all synchromesh manual gearbox was carried over and the suspension was the same as for the W111.

Considering the fact that it was quite heavy and only had a 1.9-litre engine the fact that it reached only 136km/h (85mph) (*Wheels*, May 1963) should surprise nobody; acceleration times were not fast at 12.2 seconds for the 0–80km/h (0–50mph) dash and 21 seconds for the quarter mile. While the test driver complained about the brake pedal pressures (no booster) he never doubted their ability to stop the car. In conclusion he wrote, "Although there are many cars with higher top speed and slicker acceleration and, perhaps, some to which is attached greater prestige, there are few if any that can give the driver a greater sense of driving pleasure, better roadholding and more comfort at what, comparatively, is quite a moderate price." The price was £2390.

Local assembly continued at AMI until early 1965 when Daimler-Benz ended the contract after customer complaints over poor quality of some fittings, poor rust-proofing and paint that was not up to Stuttgart standards. From early 1959 through to early 1965 a total of 6390 Mercedes-Benz cars were assembled and sold by AMI. From that time on all Mercedes-Benz passenger cars were full imports.

TRIUMPH

The final chapter for the Phase III Vanguard came in 1961 with the announcement of the Vignale d Six. Under the bonnet was a completely new in-line six-cylinder engine that had been derived from the Standard 8 engine, as surprising as that may seem, especially when the refinement of the six was experienced. The original Standard 8 engine was a very small in-line OHV four of just 803cc from its 58 x 76mm cylinder dimensions. By siamesing the cylinder bores into pairs the Standard engine designers were able to expand the bore to 74.7mm and retain sufficient rigidity in the block casting and give ample thickness to allow for bore wear over the life of the engine. Sadly for many Vanguard enthusiasts the arrival of the six meant that the time honoured 'wet sleeves' were now a thing of the past. With a bore of 74.7mm and the original 76mm stroke of the (now) four-bearing crankshaft the new six had a capacity of 1998cc. On a compression ratio of 8.0:1 and by using dual semi-down draft Solex carburettors it produced 60kW (80bhp) at 4500rpm and 145Nm (107lb-ft) of torque at 2500rpm.

As a bonus for the engineers, the new six was only 2in longer than the four that it replaced, and was a remarkable 27kg (60lb) lighter. A sway bar was now fitted to the front suspension while the low profile cross-flow radiator was continued along with the three-speed all-synchromesh

3784 KV

9082 VC

HDO 352

TRIUMPH

manual transmission and column shift, while buyers now had the option of a Borg Warner three-speed automatic, or from mid-1962 a four-speed manual transmission with a long and ungainly-looking floor shift lever.

Differentiation between the new six-cylinder Vanguard and its immediate predecessor (which was for the moment continued) was confined to a 'Vanguard 6' badge on the boot lid plus a host of minor changes inside. Of these, the most obvious and notable was the new elliptical instrument binnacle that housed a complete set of circular Smiths white-on-black dials in place of the previous semi-circular speedometer, a padded facia top and knee pad, crushable visors and map pockets in the doors.

Although the four-cylinder models continued in England, management at Australian Motor Industries made the decision that once the four-cylinder Vanguard stock had been sold only the Vanguard 6 would continue to carry on the name.

A full test was published in *Wheels* April 1961 and would have pleased AMI such was the tone of the article. On the car's dynamics the tester wrote, "Combined with the lighter engine and mild resetting of the spring levels has given the Vanguard a better ride and greatly improved stability." All through the article were references to the quietness and smoothness of both the new engine and the car's ride and comfort inside. In conclusion they said, "There is no question this is the finest Vanguard yet produced." Against the stopwatch it was only marginally quicker, running to a 134km/h (84mph) top speed with a 0–80km/h (0–50mph) time of 12.1 seconds, 0–96km/h (0–60mph) in 18.4 seconds and returned between 13 and 10 litres per 100km (23 and 28mpg). At £1352 it was only £54 more expensive.

At the lower end of the range, sales of the Triumph Herald sedan and coupe were running at factory capacity after a successful launch to the media and public in November 1959. Unfortunately for AMI and the Herald – its main volume-selling car – its early sales success was blunted somewhat by the federal government's credit squeeze introduced in 1961 causing the company to resort to severe price cutting (from £950 down to £750) to move stocks of cars, which it managed successfully. Something like 1500 units were sacrificed as the company struggled to survive.

Introduced at the end of 1960 was a revised range comprising four models – Saloon, Coupe, Convertible and the Herald 51 Saloon – the numbers of the latter referring to the engine's power output which was a response to the media and dealers for improved performance and better finish. AMI had worked hard to eliminate the sundry squeaks and rattles that plagued early production cars and the paint finish was vastly better. However, it was the engine that received at least as much attention. It was fitted with twin SU carburettors and used an 8.5:1 compression but remained at 948cc (it was the Coupe's engine) and developed 38kW (50.5bhp) at an excruciating 6000rpm. According to *Australian Motor Manual*, December 1960, the 51 recorded a top speed of 128km/h (80mph), a 0–80km/h (0–50mph) time of 16.8 seconds and returned 7.6 litres per 100km(37mpg) on test. Its retail price was £1060. Its quick rack and pinion steering with a 25-ft turning circle was found to be a joy to use, the ride was thought to be too hard even if the cornering capabilities were of a high order, although at high speed care was needed because of the camber change from the rear wheels, braking was excellent as was fuel economy. The tester was of the opinion that a higher rear axle ratio should be fitted because engine speed at a 104km/h (65mph) cruise was very high, "there was a tendency when cruising to keep looking for another gear", and the boot was roomy for a small car.

The Herald was upgraded to the 1200 in April 1962 and it was this much-improved car that AMI used to return to profitability. Externally there were few differences apart from more substantial chromed bumpers front and rear, the large handle on the bonnet was gone and replaced by a thin chrome strip, body colours were now single tone and on the boot was a '1200' badge. A bare-bones version, the 1200A, was released with

little fanfare in November 1962 and priced at £885 compared with £952 for the better-equipped version.

Inside the former 'cardboard' dash was upgraded to a black vinyl covered unit that looked much better, there were rubber mats on the floor and the back-seat squab no longer folded down to supplement the boot, the front bucket seats were slightly higher and there was better instrumentation. The main (large) dial was for speed (with total and trip odometers) while there was a small temperature dial to the right, fuel dial on the left and various unlabelled switches in the centre. A heater/demister remained an option.

Under the lift-up bonnet was a reconstituted engine, the cylinder bores were taken out by 6.3mm to 69.3mm, the crank stroke remaining at 76mm, for a new capacity of 1147cc, power was up from 29kW (39bhp) to 32kW (43bhp) at 4500rpm, torque rose from 65Nm (48lb/ft) to 82Nm (61lb/ft) at 2250rpm. In conjunction with a 4.1:1 rear axle ratio (it was 4.875!) and higher first and second gear ratios, the Herald 1200 was a far better car on Australian roads. Compared with the 948 Herald, the 1147 was much quicker against the clock, recording a top speed of almost 120km/h (75mph) (105km/h/66mph for the old model) and the 0–96km/h (0–60mph) time was reduced from a l-o-n-g 38.5 sec to a more respectable 22.35 sec. Fuel economy was virtually unchanged at better than 8 litres per 100km (35mpg).

In a *Wheels* test the driver said, "the 1200 is a vastly different proposition when cruising. The happy speed is now anything between 96 and 112km/h (60 and 70mph), and it cruises in this range smoothly and without strain." It was also noticeable that the Herald was far better screwed together and felt more solid than before.

Despite intensive competition at the lower end of the market AMI and the Herald carved out a worthwhile segment for themselves. In December 1963 the Triumph 12/50 (the Herald name was nowhere to be found) was released to further enhance the model's popularity. The 12/50 was unique to Australia insofar as it combined certain attributes of the English Vitesse (a six-cylinder version of the Herald not seen here) and elements of the Spitfire sports car.

The Vitesse provided the one-piece bonnet/fender assembly that for this model replaced the single headlights with dual units each side that were angled downwards slightly to give it an Oriental appearance; on the boot lid was a 12/50 badge. The interior was carry-over 1200 but with a heater/demister now as a standard fitting (with an electric fan) and windscreen washers via a plunger type pump under the right-hand end of the dash. What was unseen was a strengthened chassis, made better from lessons learned in the field, and Girling front-disc brakes. *Wheels* magazine tested a 12/50 and found it to be a most enjoyable and easy car to drive and thought it now far better suited to local conditions. They liked the style, the penetrating headlights on high beam, the neatness of the interior and the powerful fade-free brakes. The poorly labelled switches in the centre of the dash came in for criticism (still!) as did the lack of synchromesh on first gear. All-in-all, though, they were impressed.

The engine now had a Spitfire-derived cylinder head with a higher 8.5:1 compression, a sportier camshaft and a new intake manifold with a single Solex carburettor (the Spitfire sports car used twin carburettors and a higher compression in the same head). Power was rated at the same 38kW (51bhp) at 5200rpm and the differences against the clock were minimal. Top speed was up to 128km/h (80mph) but the 0–96km/h (0–60mph) time was still 22.3 seconds. Pricing was keen at £989 for the sedan and £999 for the coupe. These cars soldiered on until they were quietly withdrawn from production in May 1966 and not replaced. They had long ceased to be competitive with the ever-increasing number of Japanese cars that were coming onto the market.

During April 1963 AMI introduced the Triumph Spitfire sports car based on the Herald's chassis and running gear. Again, its styling was by Michelotti and he produced a design that was both sporty and cheeky as Triumph took on the might of BMC and MG. Strictly a two-seater, the Spitfire's engine developed 47kW (63bhp) at 5750rpm through the use of a higher 9.0:1 compression, twin SU HS2 carburettors, extractor exhaust system and a sportier camshaft. Weighing only 712kg (1568lb), the Spitfire would run to 147.2km/h (92mph) and dash from 0–96km/h (0–60mph) in 15.4 seconds according to *The Motor* magazine in England in 1962. *Modern Motor* achieved a top speed of 150km/h (93.8mph) and a 0–96km/h (0–60mph) time of 15.0 seconds in its test of October 1963. *Australian Motor Sports* achieved a top speed of 145.6km/h (91mph) with 43km/h, 73.6 and 115km/h (27mph, 46mph and 72mph) in the indirect gears and 0–80, 96 and 112km/h (0–50, 60 and 70mph) in 10.8, 14.9 and 21.2 seconds respectively.

Included in the price of £1070 were instruments comprising matching large diameter Smiths speedometer and tachometer (redlined at 5750rpm) with smaller fuel and temperature dials either side, heater/demister, wind-up windows and a passenger grab handle.

From February 1966 the Mark II Spitfire became available. It had undergone strenuous development to fix some of the well-known problems of the Mark I – stronger chassis, improved bonnet catches with rubber blocks to minimise flexing, reinforced mounting for the rear suspension radius rod, better quality channels for the wind-up windows, improved rear dampers and so on. The engine now developed four more horsepower (50kW (67bhp) at 6000rpm) thanks to a higher-lift camshaft, four-branch water heated inlet manifold, four-branch tubular exhaust manifold, sealed cooling system and a four-blade fan. Inside, the former rubber mats were replaced by carpeting, the dash was trimmed in non-reflective matt black vinyl, the steering wheel rim had a non-slip finish and windscreen washers were standard. For all this the price was £1099.

A Mark III appeared in March 1968 and featured the raised front bumper – it must have blocked a lot of cooling air from passing over the radiator – and the 1296cc version of the old Standard engine that had been developed for the Triumph 1300 saloon was fitted. The engine's stroke remained at 76mm but the cylinder bores were widened to 73.7mm to give the extra capacity. With twin SU carburettors it produced 56kW (75bhp) at 6000rpm. Other changes included the fitting of reversing lights and wood veneer around the instruments. A vastly improved folding top, too, came with the car. The Spitfire's maximum speed was now up to 153.6km/h (96mph) – much quicker than the MG Midget – and the 0–96km/h (0–60mph) acceleration time was 14.5 seconds. It was a sports car bargain at $2348.

Standard-Triumph as the company was now called (Leyland Motors had bought it in 1961) was determined to move forward from the base created by the Vanguard with an entirely new model that came as a result of a further collaboration with Giovanni Michelotti. By combining his bodywork with a completely new floorpan accommodating MacPherson struts and coil springs for the front suspension, and a BMW-like semi-trailing arm independent rear suspension and a revised 2-litre OHV six-cylinder engine, the company developed the Triumph 2000 saloon, one of the stand-out British medium-sized saloons of the time. Remarkably, Rover had released their equally adventurous P6 Rover 2000 in the UK a week earlier!

The British motoring media raved about the Triumph 2000. Accolades flowed into the head office at Canley and deservedly so.

Built on a long 2690mm (106in) wheelbase and measuring 4415mm (174in) in overall length, 1650mm (65in) in width and a low 1420mm (53in) in height, the 2000 was most things that the old Vanguard was not. The 2000 had a wide and more raked windscreen that flowed back into a roof that curved only slightly back to the rear window, the window being slightly recessed, and it featured the classic six-window side treatment. Up front were dual round 5in headlights either end of a slightly pointed and jutting prow, beneath which was a narrow six-horizontal-bar grille with the parking/indicator lights either end wrapping around the corners. As was the style with Michelotti at the time, the 2000 had a recessed panel at its truncated rear with a vertical tail-light unit each side of the boot lid that opened down to the bumper.

As befitted its place in the market, the interior was well appointed for the time having nicely padded reclining front bucket seats, a wide rear bench with pull-down armrest in the middle, carpets on the floor and in the boot, a powerful heater/demister, polished wood cappings on each door, a vanity mirror in the glove box lid, courtesy lights on all four doors and so on. The dash was modern and stylish with the instruments deeply recessed directly in front of the driver. The Smiths speedometer (with trip and total odometers) was on the right and the combination dial on the left comprising temperature, fuel and amps plus warning lights. Tumbler switches on either side of the instruments operated the lights and wiper/washers.

Under the forward-hinged bonnet was a thoroughly revised six-cylinder OHV engine of 1998cc that with dual Stromberg 150 CD carburettors and a mild 8.0:1 compression ratio developed 67kW (90bhp) at 5000rpm and 158Nm (117 lb-ft) of torque at 2900rpm. The four-speed all-synchromesh manual gearbox sported a short console mounted shifter and later a Borg Warner Type 35 three-speed automatic was made available.

Released by AMI in April 1964, *Modern Motor* magazine was very quick off the mark and published a full road test in the May 1964 issue and came away highly impressed. Bryan Hanrahan, their journalist, managed a top speed of 150km/h (93.8mph) with 48, 78.4 and 116.8km/h (30mph, 49mph and 73mph) in the gears, a time of 9.9 seconds for the 0–80km/h (0–50mph) sprint and 14.3 seconds to 96km/h (60mph), which for a 1136kg (2500lb) sedan was good going for the time. He was truly enamoured with the Triumph 2000's dynamic capabilities writing, "only one car does it better – the Citroën DS", in reference to the ride, and found the near 50:50 weight distribution gave superb fore-and-aft balance and the boosted disc/drum braking system could "stop an overloaded semi on Bulli Pass". The report was not dissimilar from many others on the 2000 at the time. The media loved the car and said so.

AMI soon had a problem because it found that buyers were more than willing to pay the £1537 price and soon dealers had waiting lists. To their credit AMI did not panic and refused to compromise on build quality to get cars out in the market – the company had gained a solid reputation for excellent assembly quality and this was evident in the 2000. All panels and mechanical components arrived at Bertie Street, Fishermans Bend from Canley to be assembled using local paint, tyres, glass, upholstery and many other sundry items.

AMI's managing director, Ken Hougham, conceived the idea of building a limited edition of the 2000 to appeal to those who desired something different, something more than just a vinyl roof, for example. Where other manufacturers gave their specials initials like GT or GTO or S, AMI chose to call their car the Triumph 2000 MD, for managing director. It was easy to spot on the road or in the shopping centre car park because it came standard with a neat set of chromed wire wheels shod with Dunlop SP41 radial tyres, chromed stone guards over the quad headlights and the air intake at the base of the windscreen was also chromed. Inside, a push-button radio was installed in the centre console and two VDO instruments in pods (tachometer and electric clock) were positioned above the existing instruments, a slightly smaller steering wheel with a genuine wood rim and three aluminium alloy spokes and the gear knob was in a matching wood. An extra lever on the steering column controlled the electric overdrive unit that operated on third and top gears, giving the driver access to six gears. A lower rear axle ratio (4.3 in place of 4.1:1) helped to boost acceleration slightly.

Under the bonnet the only work done was to match the cylinder head ports to the manifolds for better gas flow (the same 90bhp was quoted) and to chrome both the rocker cover and radiator cap!

Wheels road-tested a 2000 MD (November 1965) and was mightily impressed with its build quality, interior fittings, roadholding, steering response and the way the engine could be revved easily to 6000rpm without apparent harm. They came away with a true top speed of 160.6km/h (100.4mph), 0–80 and 96km/h (0–50 and 0–60mph) times of 8.6 and 12.0 seconds respectively and it returned 10 litres per 100km (28mpg) on test. They loved it even if at £2075 it was a touch under £500 more expensive. An uprated MD was released in July 1968 and it featured an engine with triple Stromberg carburettors. AMI suggested the power was now 74.5kW (100bhp) at 5000rpm and *Motor Manual* recorded figures of 8.6, 12.6 and 17.2 seconds for the 0–80, 96 and 112km/h (0–50, 60 and 70mph) sprints with in-gear speeds of 48, 84.8, 126.4, 147 in overdrive, 153.6 and 161.6km/h in overdrive fourth (30mph, 53mph, 79mph (92mph in overdrive), 96mph and with overdrive engaged (101mph). Good going for a 1170kg (2576lb) luxury sporting saloon. Price was a high $3940.

I wonder how many have survived?

The Series II 2000 slipped onto the market in February 1967 and was changed only in details like two round air vents in the centre of the dash panel above the repositioned heater controls, air outlets above the rear window and rubber-faced bumper over-riders.

In June 1969 AMI quietly introduced the Triumph 2.5 PI, the letters standing for Petrol Injection, and this model replaced the MD in the range. The engine's capacity had been increased to 2498cc by lengthening the stroke of the crankshaft from 76mm to 95mm and a Lucas Automotive Mark II mechanical injection system was adapted to replace the carburettors, this for a car that was already five years old. Power output rose to 98kW (132bhp) at 5450rpm, torque to 206Nm (152lb-ft) at 2000rpm and was delivered to the rear wheels through the same four-speed all-synchromesh manual gearbox as the 2000 but the final drive was raised to 3.45:1. Few other changes were made other than the use of an alternator in place of a generator (Triumph, like the rest of the British car industry was way behind the rest of the world on this) and quartz halogen high-beam lights were fitted in place of ordinary sealed beams.

Triumph's designers were very discreet about the identity of the 2.5PI; the most obvious exterior point was the application of black vinyl on the D-pillar with a small circular badge containing the letters PI, fake magnesium alloy wheel trims and an INJECTION badge front and rear.

A full road test was published by *Wheels* magazine (September 1969) and they headed the article by saying, "Greater capacity and hotter tune puts a breath of fire under Triumph's conservative 2000. Local assembly keeps price down while there's comfort, brakes and handling to match the sizzling performance; real value for the $3850 tag." The only points of criticism were the wipers – set for left-hand drive and useless at speeds above 112km/h (70mph, they lifted off) and the fact that there was no tachometer was in their opinion a major blunder for such a "businessman's express" as they called it, and the lack of power steering. They recorded a top speed of 176km/h (110mph), 0–96 and 112km/h (0–60 and 70mph) acceleration times of 9.4 and 12.8 seconds respectively, a standing quarter mile time of 17.1 seconds. By way of comparison, *Modern Motor* recorded the same top speed and acceleration times of 10.0 and 13.3 seconds, quarter mile in 17.0 seconds.

Unfortunately for Triumph owners (and AMI) the fuel injection system was poorly engineered and quickly gained a reputation for unreliability in the hot Australian conditions. The rest of Triumph's history will be discussed in *Australian Cars of the 70s*.

NEVADA
336·FKL

RAMBLER

AMI began assembling American Motors Corporation's (AMC) products towards the end of 1960. They were always badged as Ramblers in this country although it was not always that way back in the USA. Company executives went to Kenosha, Wisconsin to secure distribution and assembly rights for Australia following several events that had caused financial difficulties for the company. It had lost the lucrative Ferguson tractor franchise when Massey-Harris won the rights from Harry Ferguson and the flirtation with Fiat tractors that followed cost a lot of money for little result. The Triumph Herald was not the money-spinner that AMI hoped it would be and then the federal government instigated a credit squeeze. To remain in business AMI sold its share of Mercedes-Benz Australia back to Daimler-Benz AG. Luckily for AMI, boom market conditions followed the bust of 1961–62.

Rambler cars were never technological trailblazers in America although they did adopt unitary body construction well before Chrysler. They were number four on the shopping list in America but it must be said they were sturdy cars, good meat-and-potatoes-type cars. By the standards of the time (1960) Rambler cars could be regarded as medium-sized compared with the products of GM, Ford and Chrysler. To begin with AMI assembled the six-cylinder Rambler Classic sedan and station wagon plus the V8 Rambler Ambassador sedan, all models being available only with an automatic gearbox. From a styling perspective the new Rambler could only have been American. Up front were four headlights below which was a wide-but-shallow three-bar grille, a large chromed bumper and the name Rambler spelled out in separate letters in a space between the headlights. At the rear were almost vertical tail-light units under shallow fins that began on the rear door and were joined by a horizontal line across the boot lid – it looked a little like the Hillman Super Minx and it is quite possible that the Rambler inspired the Hillman. The C-pillar had a reverse slope with the back window curving around into it; again the Hillman possibly followed the same theme.

For an American car the Rambler was nowhere near the size most people would have expected. It sat on a wheelbase of 2743mm (108in), was 4800mm (189in) in length, 1828mm (72in) wide and 1447mm (57in) high and weighed 1425kg (3136lb) at the kerb. Of unitary construction it rode on a very conventional suspension system comprising coil springs mounted on the upper wishbone at the front and a live axle on semi-elliptic leaf springs at the rear, braking was by cast-iron drums on all four wheels with a vacuum boost to lessen pedal pressures, and the steering was a recirculating ball system with 4.7 turns lock-to-lock for a 37-foot turning circle.

Power was provided by a cast-iron in-line six-cylinder OHV engine that was again of conventional design; it had a bore and stroke of 79.5 x 107.95mm for a capacity of 3206cc (195.6cid), not large by US standards, and developed 94.7kW (127bhp) at 4200rpm and 244Nm (180lb-ft) of torque at 1600rpm with the aid of a single Holley carburettor and an 8.7:1 compression. This was hooked up to a Borg Warner three-speed automatic gearbox driving the rear wheels.

Australian Motor Manual tested one in July 1960 and gave it a complimentary report which was normal back then. They liked the twin front seats that had reclining backrests even down to a bed if necessary, the excellent heater/demister and ample room for up to six passengers and their luggage. Performance was average for the day with a top speed of 134km/h (84mph) and 0–80 and 96km/h (0–50 and 60mph) acceleration times of 12.4 and 17.0 seconds which made it fractionally quicker than an FB Holden. The price, however, was somewhat more at £2535.

AMI provided locally sourced items like paint, tyres, some electrical items, glass and upholstery as well as labour and other minor items to qualify for tariff relief.

Within a year the Rambler Ambassador V8 was added to the local range and this was a larger (but still not that large) sedan with, surprisingly, a lower price tag at £2429. The lower price came about through savings made by added local content. In its styling the Ambassador was not dissimilar to the Classic insofar as it had the semi-wraparound front windscreen and reverse-slope C-pillar with the rear window curving around into it and very restrained fins at the back over similar-looking tail-light units. At the front was an 'eyebrow' over the four headlights with a rhombus-shaped plain grille featuring eight thin horizontal bars with the badge Ambassador at an angle on the left.

Inside were bench seats front and back, the fronts having fully reclining separate back rests, carpets on the floor, armrests on the doors and a powerful heater/demister with a multi-speed electric fan, a clock and cigar lighter. The dashboard was quite plain being flat and straight across the interior with a small oval-shaped binnacle containing the few instruments perched in front of the driver. All the driver had was a speedometer, fuel and temperature dials plus some warning lights and switches for wipers and lights below. What was a little unusual was the number of foot pedals – *five* of them! From the left they were the foot plunger for the windscreen washers, headlight dipswitch, foot brake, accelerator and then the parking brake. The Rambler must have been one of the first cars available on the local market with a foot-operated parking brake with a release lever on the dash.

The wipers had a 'clap hands' sweep pattern with a considerable overlap in the centre which made it easy for left-to-right hand drive conversions but they were vacuum operated … enough said!

There was ample room for up to six people to travel in comfort, the seats being upholstered in locally-sourced vinyl, they gave good support and there was plenty of head and leg room. And the boot was suitably commodious.

Physically the Ambassador was larger than the Classic, sitting on a wheelbase of 2972mm (117in) and stretching 5054mm (199in) overall by 1854mm (73in) wide and 1447mm (57in) high and kerb weight was 1636kg (3600lb). As big as it was, the Chevrolet Bel Air, Dodge Phoenix and Ford Galaxie were even larger and certainly not as conservative in their styling. Under the bonnet was a cast-iron OHV V8 engine of 5450cc (327cid) capacity (101.6 x 95.2mm) that on an 8.7:1 compression and using a twin-throat Holley carburettor produced a lazy 186kW (250bhp) at 4700rpm and 460Nm (340lb-ft) of torque at 2600rpm. This power went to the rear wheels through a three-speed Borg Warner automatic gearbox to a hypoid rear axle with a 2.87 ratio. Suspension up front comprised upper-and-lower wishbones with the coil springs and concentric dampers operating on the upper wishbone; at the rear was a typical for the day live axle with semi-elliptic leaf springs and telescopic dampers. Braking was by power-boosted four-wheel cast-iron 254mm (10in) drums with 167-sq in of lining area, and the steering was by a non-boosted recirculating ball system with 5.5 turns lock-to-lock. It was a specification typical of what you would expect to find on a US car of the day.

Ian Fraser, writing in *Wheels* magazine, September 1961, conducted a full test of an Ambassador and came away impressed with the care that AMI had used in its painting and assembly. As for its dynamics, Fraser was less impressed with the slow steering saying, "It was impossible to wind and unwind the wheel quickly enough." On the Ambassador's brakes he said, "I'm afraid that the brakes caused raised eyebrows. Power-assisted, they require only the lightest pressure. On test they were vicious." He further added, "There was unpredictable locking of individual wheels", which made him rate them as unsatisfactory. He loved the smooth power delivery through the automatic gearbox and the lively performance of the big sedan. Its maximum speed was 162km/h (101mph) with 0–80, 96 and 112km/h (0–50, 60 and 70mph) increments coming up in 8.0, 12.5 and 17.1 seconds while delivering just 21 litres per 100km (13.4mpg) on test, up to 14 litres per 100km (20mpg) on a long distance cruise meaning you would need all of the 76 litres (16.7gal) in the tank on a long interstate drive. The heavy V8 engine made the Ambassador very front-heavy, which made it a distinct understeerer, which was probably safer than the alternative given the power, unsophisticated suspension and dodgy brakes.

An updated Classic appeared in February 1961 with new front sheet metal, the rear staying pretty much as was. The new front was far more modern in appearance and more integrated with the four headlights now included in the grille that had an egg crate texture and the Rambler name was relocated at the bottom of the grille. Also new were the chromed side strips that started at a point just behind the headlights and went full-length of the body with a slight downward kink of the lower strip at the tail-light end. Robust looking straight chromed steel bumpers were fitted either end.

Accommodation and other amenities were basically carried over from the previous model.

What was different for Australian buyers of the Classic was under the bonnet. AMC in America had been experimenting with aluminium alloy cylinder blocks and heads as a means of reducing weight over the front wheels but being the ultra-conservative company that it was and knowing the hawks in the US media and the condemnation they would write the company opted to send their aluminium alloy engines to Australia. Small numbers were sold in the US and, you guessed it, the all-knowing media wrote disparagingly about it and after a little more than a year AMC closed the program. Much the same happened to Chrysler who produced aluminium alloy 225cid slant sixes for a brief period.

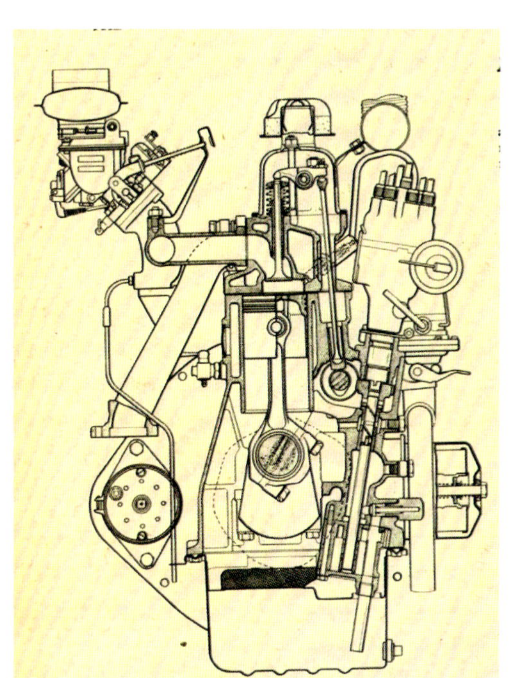

The 3.2-litre OHV six under the bonnet of the Classic looked like the engine Ramblers had used for years but a closer inspection showed it to be aluminium, not cast-iron. It was 36kg (80lb) lighter but retained the same cylinder dimensions and capacity as previously as well as the same power and torque. Despite the twirly steering, the reduced weight made handling of the Classic one of the best American cars in that respect. Understeer was much reduced and the ride was far better. As before, its top speed was 136km/h (85mph) with the 0–96km/h (0–60mph) dash taking 17.95 seconds with the fuel economy being around 15.8 litres per 100km (18mpg) on test. At £2125 it was regarded as good value.

April 1962 saw the release of a mildly restyled Classic, the majority of the new style being at the rear where there was new sheet metal for the fenders and boot lid as well as different tail-lights. New to the range was the Automatic Six Custom sedan that had a more powerful 103kW (138bhp) version of the engine using a four-barrel Holley that in turn pushed the top speed up to 139km/h (87mph).

In March 1963 came a completely new body style developed by AMC's chief stylist Ed Anderson and his team that brought with it curved side glass, a first for an American car. It was a veritable breath of fresh air from an American manufacturer and was characterised by completely smooth sides, a smooth bonnet and a C-pillar that sloped in the conventional fashion ending a decade of reverse-slope pillars. The roofline was flatter, overhangs front and rear were shorter, it was 63mm (2.5in) lower overall and 68kg (150lb) lighter. Only the grille showed any glimpse of adventure, being a concave vee-shaped affair with a wide chromed surround, four headlights and the name Rambler at the deepest point of the vee. Plain chromed steel bumpers adorned both ends. It was available as a four-door sedan or station wagon.

Inside Rambler offered a new dashboard, still straight across between the A-pillars, but there was a new stylish hooded binnacle with a fan-shaped speedometer with fuel and temperature dials in the lower section. Either side were flat panels where there once had been the automatic transmission buttons but now the control was a simple column lever on the left of the steering column. As a cost-cutting measure AMI took the heater/demister out and made it an option and the front seats no longer reclined.

Mechanically it was carry-over from before although the automatic gearbox was now the Borg Warner Type 35 which was locally sourced and was lighter and smoother in operation; it rode on 14in wheels with 6.50 x 14 tyres. The Classic sat on a 2844mm (112in) wheelbase, was 4775mm (188in) in overall length (the wagon was an inch longer) by 1386mm (54.6in) high with tracks of 1478mm and 1458mm (58.2 and 57.4in) respectively while the brakes were 228mm (9in) cast-iron drums with 153.8 sq in of lining area. Under the bonnet was the AMC

195.6cid in-line six that produced 95kW (127bhp) and 244Nm (180lb-ft) of torque. New with the Classic came parallel action wipers that were set for left-hand drive so there was always a blind spot in the top right of the screen on rainy days – why were they not converted? – and they were still vacuum operated. As for the suspension, up front it was the usual AMC coil spring acting on the upper wishbone while at the rear was now a torque tube drive with the axle suspended by coil springs.

As far as performance went, *Motor Manual* (May 1963) recorded a top speed of 134km/h (84mph) with 0–80 and 96km/h (0–50 and 60mph) acceleration times of 12.4 and 17.0 seconds which was good but not sensational for the time – it was on a par with a 170cid Falcon, way behind an AP5 Valiant; no doubt the people who bought the car were more impressed by other aspects, like its ability to cover long distances in comfort and quietness at 12.4 litres per 100km (23mpg). What did surprise the *MM* folks was the plain painted dashboard that was devoid of any padding.

Good news for buyers was the reduction in prices, the Classic automatic now retailing for £1799 (down £200), the station wagon now cost £2145 (down £151) and the Ambassador V8 was reduced by £115 to £2265.

The Classic name would run for two more years with the Classic 660 being released in February 1964 using the year-old body. A new grille accompanied this model, the grille now being flat with horizontal strips and faint vertical lines with the Rambler name in the top surround. A luxury version was added to the range featuring a 287cid (95.2 x 82.5mm, 4689cc) OHV V8 engine developing 147kW (198bhp) at 4700rpm and 380Nm (280lb-ft) of torque at 2600rpm. Interior fittings included reclining front seats while power-assisted drum brakes came with the package. For the next year (1965) AMC added five inches to the rear overhang, widened the body by three inches, and gave it a new grille texture and new rear lights. Included in its specification were front seatbelts, push-button radio, heater/demister with fan, a clock, windscreen washers, vanity mirror, floor carpets and courtesy lights in every nook and cranny. It was undoubtedly the best equipped US car sold here and retailed for $4496.

In a road test by *Wheels* (September 1966) they were generally complimentary but of the dashboard they said, "The facia layout comes as quite a surprise. It is a complete throwback to the Ramblers of five years ago – garish, old fashioned in concept and badly done." As for its dynamics, they said, "The Rambler is a very quiet car, with only engine noise over 4000rpm to remind you that you are travelling fast;" to "It runs dead straight at all speeds and the ride is very good; firmer than the GM and Ford cars, but pleasantly so." This could be attributed to the new coil spring live axle rear suspension. The 287cid (4.7 litres) V8 was powerful and so performance was lively running to 156.8km/h (98mph) with 0–80, 96 and 112km/h (0–50, 60 and 70mph) increments taking 8.6, 11.4 and 15.3 seconds respectively while fuel consumption was 17.8 litres per 100km (16mpg) for the test. Braking was by a dual-circuit disc front/drum rear system with vacuum boost and was a vast improvement on previous Rambler systems.

A new model arrived in May 1964 in the form of the Rambler American that was pitched against the Falcon, Corvair, Valiant and Lark in the USA but was competing in a higher (priced) segment when it arrived here. From a styling point of view the passenger compartment sheet metal looked remarkably like that on the Classic of 1963/64 but with shorter front and rear ends. That was not a criticism because the Classic was a very attractive sedan with a roomy interior. What was impressive was the simplicity of the design with its headlights sunk into small tunnels at the front either end of a simple horizontal eight-bar grille with the Rambler name badge on the left and a supplementary air inlet between the grille and substantial bumper that also housed the turn indicators. At the rear it was again very simple with small rectangular tail-lights separated by a four-bar embellishment (fuel filler in the centre) and another substantial bumper that housed the turn indicators. In fact the front and rear bumpers looked to be interchangeable.

Inside there were locally-made bench seats front and rear with good quality padded vinyl upholstery making it a comfortable six-seater with carpets on the floor as virtually the only concession to luxury although there were armrests on all doors, a heater/demister and a cigarette lighter. The dash top was padded, the padding curving down at each end, the actual panel being straight with a pressed-in feature line across the centre. Actual instrumentation was sparse comprising a fan-shaped speedometer flanked by four round 'dials', two each side. In actual fact there was only a fuel gauge and a temperature gauge and a few warning lights; switches for lights and wipers were below along with the key-start, and the automatic transmission selector was on the right of the steering column and not the left where it might have been expected to be. The wipers had a parallel action but were not changed by AMI for right-hand drive so they left a large unswept area in front of the driver's right eye line, they were vacuum operated and the washers were operated by a foot push on the toe board. Luggage space was good but compromised by the placement of the spare wheel on the floor.

Mechanically the American was carry-over six-cylinder Classic, power coming from the same aluminium alloy six-cylinder engine of 3.2-litre capacity and 103kW (138bhp) so performance was quite acceptable at 149km/h (93mph) top speed and 14.9 seconds for the 0–96km/h (0–60mph) dash, economy being 15.8 litres per 100km (18mpg) on test but would be more like 11.8 litres per 100km (24mpg) on a long cruise. Pricing was considered competitive at £1499 for a three-speed manual version and £1659 for the three-speed automatic.

Modern Motor tested the Classic and American against each other in the March 1965 issue. It was heavy weight 147kW (198bhp) V8 versus a lightweight aluminium alloy six-cylinder engine with 103kW (138bhp), 1454kg versus 1230kg (3200lb of automobile versus 2700lb). Both cars had lost their heaters as part of a cost-reduction program (it was available as an extra) and both had the Flash-O-Matic three-speed automatic transmission (based on the Borg Warner Type 35) with two driving ranges – D1 gave all three forward gears, D2 only the two higher gears.

The suspension of both was considered to be on the marshmallow side and allowed a great deal of body roll when cornering, although they said there was now less understeer. On the flipside, the ride was considered to be first-class but the steering garnered more criticism, as did the four-wheel drum braking system which was simply not good enough in their opinion for the near-160km/h (100mph) car that was the Classic V8.

The Rambler American (badged as the 440) continued until late 1968, with a brand new 232cid six-cylinder engine being phased in during 1966, replacing what was a former Nash engine that dated back to 1956. The 232cid engine was a new design with a bore and stroke of 95.25 x 88.9mm for a capacity of 3801cc. It featured a seven-bearing crankshaft and with a two-barrel Holley carburettor and an 8.5:1 compression developed 115kW (155bhp) at 4300rpm and 300Nm (222lb-ft) of torque at 1600rpm. Replaced at the same time were the dreadful vacuum wipers with (at last!) electric wipers.

In that year the final iteration of the Classic was released. From the front it appeared the same apart from a new grille texture but at the rear were new panels because the rear overhang was longer (overall length was now 4953mm (195in) compared with 4826mm (190in) previously) on a wheelbase of 2844mm (112in).

Ramblers won favour with buyers because they were extremely well made by AMI, their assembly and paint quality being on a par with the various Triumph and Toyota cars that went down the same assembly line and through the same paint booth.

During 1967 AMI introduced a completely restyled Rambler, the Rebel 770, a car that gained many plaudits from the media and became popular with government ministers of the time. *Wheels*, for example, opened their road test with the statement "At long last, gentlemen, an American sedan that handles, stops and makes all the proper noises it should." It was even selected over the Falcon GT as a police pursuit car in NSW!

As before, the Rebel was a big compact by US standards sitting on a 2895mm (114in) wheelbase and stretching 4699mm (185in) overall by 1372mm (54in) in height and 1981mm (78in) in width. Kerb weight was a solid 1527kg (3360lb) making it similar in size to the ZA Fairlane. Under the bonnet was AMC's famous 290cid OHV V8 (92.25 x 83.3mm, 4753cc) that produced 168kW (225bhp) at 4700rpm and 406Nm (300lb-ft) at 3200rpm on a 9.0:1 compression using a four-barrel Holley carburettor. Its technical specifications included power-assisted front disc brakes with rotors of 284mm (11.187in) diameter and rear drums of 254mm (10in) diameter with dual circuits, AMC's well respected coil spring front suspension where the coils were mounted on the upper wishbone allied to a live rear axle with four locating links, and coil springs provided the suspension; only power-assisted steering and decent tyres were missing. And there was the usual complaint (justified) about the left-hand drive location of the gear selector and indicator stalk and the sweep of the windscreen wipers.

Against the clock the Rebel returned times of 7.5, 9.8 and 13.2 seconds for the 0–80, 96 and 112km/h (0–50, 60 and 70mph) sprints with 75km/h (47mph) in first gear, 116.8km/h (73mph) in second and 168km/h (105mph) in top gear, economy being just 19–16.5 litres per 100km (15–17mpg)! In conclusion *Wheels* said, "Overall, we liked the car a lot. It is certainly easier to drive quickly than any other American car available on the market, is more comfortably fitted-out and is better put together. If this Rebel is a sample of the new American Motors thinking, then they've got our vote for '68."

The Rebel would continue through until October 1971 with relatively minor updates – better quality tyres from mid-'68 (originally 7.75 x 14 cross-ply, uprated to 8.25 x14 nylons), flush door handles, front marker lights, chrome bead along the fender tops, wide sill moulding and three separate tail-light lenses each side from June 1968. From July 1969, 343cid V8 with 175kW (235bhp), full-length side moulding just below the fender tops, wraparound tail-lights, thin grille bars, reshaped front seat squabs, front anti-roll bar, wider track, power steering as standard along with a smaller diameter steering wheel, And from September 1970 the Rebel had the huge 360cid V8 engine, limited-slip differential, twin ball-joint front suspension, wider 'mouth-type' grille, half-length chrome strip and rear body panels from the Ambassador. This specification would remain to the end. By 1969 the price had risen to $5550 and in 1971 it had risen further to $6088.

In September 1968 AMI released the locally-assembled sporting Javelin two-plus-two coupe to Australia. In the US it was a competitor to the Ford Mustang, Chev Camaro, Pontiac Firebird and Plymouth Barracuda while locally Holden had just released their Monaro that was to some extent chasing the same buyer. It epitomised the long hood–short rear deck style that the Mustang had made both famous and popular over plain-Jane sedan specifications, in this case the humble Rambler American. Its wheelbase was 2768mm (109in), length 4805mm (189.2in) with a body that was 1826mm (71.9in) wide and 1321mm (52in) high and weighed 1559kg (3430lb) at the kerb.

For a US design the Javelin was very clean with no unnecessary embellishment, which was refreshing. At the front was a distinctive twin grille arrangement with the Javelin badge in the left side, single headlights in tunnels each side and a massive chromed bumper with round combination turn/parking lights. Horizontal tail-lights extended across the rear of the coupe and curved around the sides for safety reasons and again there was a big chromed bumper.

Inside was seating for up to four passengers on bucket front seats and rear bench, all upholstered in padded vinyl that AMI used on other models in their range. Appointments were described by the media at the time as being lavish because included in the $7495 retail price were pushbutton radio, heater/demister with a two-speed fan, flow-through ventilation, reclining bucket seats, lap/sash seatbelts, floor carpets plus safety items like a collapsible steering column and illuminated side marker lights. Australian Javelins came equipped with a special handling package that included a heavy-duty front sway bar, firmer springs and dampers and 6 x 14JJ steel rims shod with 205 x 14 radial tyres good for 192km/h (120mph). Shared with the Rebel was the disc front/drum rear braking system (284 x 254mm/11.187 discs, 10in drums) and limited-slip differential.

The dashboard was unusual for a sporty American insofar as it had proper *round* dials in front of the driver – speedometer in the centre, clock to the right and tachometer dial to the left – with two smaller dials above the centre console. Quilted padding covered the dash and the gear selector was in the centre console.

Under the long bonnet was AMC's 343cid 'Typhoon' OHV V8 (103.6 x 83.4mm for 5621cc) that developed 208kW (280bhp) at 4800rpm and 494Nm (365lb-ft) of torque at 3000rpm using a four-barrel Carter carburettor and a 10.2:1 compression. Power went to the rear wheels through a Borg Warner three-speed automatic (no manual was offered) running a 2.87 differential.

Australian Motor Sports ran a full test in its December 1968 issue under the heading of 'Rich Man's Toy' and published figures of 6.9, 9.3 and 11.7 seconds for the 0–80, 96 and 112km/h (0–50, 60 and 70mph) sprints with a top speed of 183.6km/h (114.8mph); fuel consumption was 18 litres per 100km (15.8mpg). Performance was in line with the HK Monaro GTS 327.

As for its handling, author Pat Hayes said, "Within the limits set by its size and its weight, the Javelin handles well. It doesn't wallow at all and although understeer is fairly severe the right amount of power can keep the tail just where it's needed." He was not complimentary about its unwieldy steering but liked the power and consistency of the brakes as well as the comfortable ambience of the interior.

It was more expensive than the Monaro GTS 327 (nearly double the price!) but AMI was able to successfully shift a reasonable number each year until it was discontinued in 1973. More on Rambler in Australia will be found in *Australian Cars of the 70s*.

TOYOTA

AMI and the giant Japanese company Toyota entered into an agreement in April 1963 to assemble selected Toyota passenger cars for the Australian market. The first model selected was the Toyota (sometimes referred to then as a Toyopet) Tiara released in June of that year. Of Toyota's then limited range, this was by far the most suitable having also established a beachhead for the company in the USA. In Australia the Tiara would compete with the Datsun Bluebird, Hillman Minx, Morris Major Elite, Ford Cortina, Vauxhall Victor, Volkswagen Beetle, Fiat 1100, Simca Aronde and Renault R8. It was a crowded field!

The Tiara was a very conventional design because the Japanese engineers were still learning their craft; it was a conventional front engine, rear-wheel drive, four-door, five-passenger compact sedan built on a 2400mm (94.5in) wheelbase and measuring 4458mm (175.5in) in overall length, by 1490mm (58.7in) wide and 1445mm (56.9in) high. Kerb weight was 982kg (2160lb). Under the forward-hinged bonnet was a sturdy all-cast-iron in-line OHV four-cylinder engine with a

three-bearing crank and a bore and stroke of 77 x 78mm for a capacity of 1453cc. It developed 48kW (65bhp) at 4500rpm and drove the rear wheels through a *three*-speed manual transmission with a column shift. The front wheels were suspended by a double wishbone system with longitudinal torsion bars working on the lower wishbone and anchored under the front seat; at the rear was a conventional live axle on semi-elliptic leaf springs. Drum brakes all round did the stopping, the steering was by a worm and sector system and the whole ensemble rode on 5.60 x 13 cross-ply tyres. As I said, *very* conventional.

Its styling broke no new ground being a simple three-box design with a semi-wraparound front screen, slightly recessed headlights at the head of the front fenders, flat side glass and short tail with teardrop-shaped tail-lights. At the front was a broad oval grille with concave vertical grille bars, a winged badge in the centre and large round parking/indicator lights at the ends. Possibly the only interest was in the fact that the bonnet was hinged at the front.

What was a surprise was the neatness and tidiness of the under bonnet layout, which was in direct contrast to the slapdash layout of most of the other cars in its class. For example, the float bowl on the twin-throat carburettor had a glass window for an easy visual check of the fuel level, all pipes were routed around the bay and held in place by neat brackets, the wiring was tidy and again clipped in place giving the engine bay a professional look that stood out at the time.

Inside was a bench seat front and back upholstered in vinyl with rubber mats on the floor, a plain flat dashboard with a horizontal rectangular instrument group comprising a strip speedometer that changed colour from green to red when 80km/h (50mph) was exceeded, a fuel and temperature gauge either side plus some warning lights, one of which told you that the handbrake was on! In 1963 that was a real novelty. On the lower edge of the dash, in the centre, was a row of eight ivory buttons (four each side of the central cigarette lighter), three of which operated the optional heater/demister when fitted.

The showroom price of £915 included reversing lights, two-speed electric windscreen wipers, tinted rear-view mirror, cigarette lighter, automatic choke, internal bonnet lock, an electric power point and a tool kit extensive enough to rebuild the Tiara on the side of the road if you needed to. It was outstanding value for money. A heater/demister was optional as were electric windscreen washers and the car was pre-wired during assembly for both of them. The luggage space was listed at 17cu ft but was hampered by the placement of the spare wheel on the floor, albeit under a neat cover.

Dynamically it was found wanting compared with most of its peers although it did prove to be amazingly reliable and unbreakable where most of its rivals (except perhaps the VW) had very poor reputations for reliability and service backup. Most Tiara owners never touched their toolkit ...

In its January 1964 issue *Wheels* conducted a four-car comparison between the Toyota Tiara, Simca Aronde, Renault R8 and Fiat Riviera. As they said, "Japan, while developing as a car manufacturing country at an extraordinary rate, has had no time or ability to develop a school of styling or engineering design." That was why the Tiara was so conventional although it must be said that neither the Simca nor Fiat could be described as advanced as both were old designs dating from the early '50s. Despite the qualification, the Tiara acquitted itself well – all four had 126km/h (79mph) top speeds and the Tiara's 0–80km/h (0–50mph) acceleration time of 12.7 seconds was the quickest of the group. Only the three-speed gearbox held it back. In conclusion they said, "The Tiara is patently cheaper than the others, and the best equipped, but not the best handling of the four."

AMI offered the Tiara as a sedan at £915, a two-door station wagon at £999 and a half-ton utility for £849. With a relatively small dealer network around the country sales were modest in 1963 but no doubt pleased the people in faraway Nagoya as well as those locally. In May 1964 a slightly revised Tiara was released with the only changes being a new mesh grille with oval-shaped parking lights. Sales of the Tiara continued until November 1964 with the company scoring 5720 sales that comprised the locally assembled Tiara and the imported Corona (that retained for the moment the Tiara's three-speed gearbox) that would soon replace it. By February 1965 the Corona was being assembled locally with the three-speed gearbox, the four-speed being phased in during May production and a two-speed Toyoglide automatic arrived in September. By the end of the year the company's leading product was the Corona.

The Corona generated quite a deal of discussion at the time in relation to its controversial front styling – it is generally remembered as the 'shovel-nosed' Corona and is fondly remembered by former owners. Only the engine was transferred from Tiara to Corona and even that was modified to a bore and stroke of 78mm each for a capacity of 1490cc and 55kW (74bhp) at 5000rpm. Power went to the rear wheels through a four-speed all-synchromesh manual gearbox with the obligatory column shift and while the leaf spring rear suspension and live axle were carried over, up front was a new upper-and-lower wishbone system with coil springs and telescopic dampers; 228mm (9in) diameter drums continued to provide braking and the steering was by a recirculating ball system. Again, all very conventional but from a buyer's point of view that mattered little because the cars were absolutely reliable and cost their owners little in fuel or maintenance. What many owners possibly never realised was that the ordinary looking engine under the bonnet of their car was able to rev to an amazing 7000rpm without destroying itself!

Like the Tiara, the Corona conformed to that small, compact class of car that was emerging as a force in the market place. Built on a floorpan that had a wheelbase of 2420mm (95.3in), it was 4064mm (160in) in overall length, 1549mm (61in) wide, 1422mm (56in) high and weighed 930kg (2040lb). Bench seats were fitted front and rear, the upholstery being a soft pleated vinyl that was part of the local content, which meant that it would easily accommodate dad, mum and two kids plus a modicum of luggage, the boot space again being compromised by the placement of the covered spare wheel. Adult rear passengers were hampered by the small amount of knee room, a problem created by the relatively short wheelbase. In front of the driver was a black-plastic-rimmed steering wheel with a half horn ring that doubled as the indicator switch, and on the dash was a rectangular instrument cluster that housed the fan-shaped speedometer with small round dials at either end for fuel and temperature plus a set of warning lights including one that let you know when the hand brake was on. Black pull-push switches looked after

the operation of the two-speed wipers (pull twice) and electric washers (twist), lights and the ignition, while under the dash was the ashtray with provision for a lighter; in the centre was provision for a radio and clock and there were three horizontal slides for the powerful heater/demister that was a standard fitting. These controls were set in a silver plastic panel with black vinyl padding covering the whole upper dash. Armrests were fitted to the doors.

Wheels carried out a full test of the four-speed Corona and published it in the October 1965 edition. They had previously tested the imported three-speed version and claimed a top speed of 144km/h (90mph); the new model was not quite as fast at 139km/h (87mph) but was quicker through the gears running the 0–80km/h (0–50) and 0–96km/h (0–60mph) dashes in 10.1 and 14.8 seconds respectively. As for its dynamics, they wrote, "For a conventionally suspended car it rides unbelievably well with little pitch, slight roll movement and well-damped vertical movement." The steering they described as "light, smooth pin-sharp and well-tailored to the handling characteristics." On its handling they said, "You can hang the Corona out completely sideways and flick it back into line with a dab of opposite lock." In conclusion they described the Corona as a "fully integrated, well-balanced, well-equipped family sedan" and opined that perhaps there were some object lessons for Western manufacturers. At £979 it was considered to be extremely good value for money.

The Corona was part of a three-pronged marketing strategy by Toyota at the time, the little Publica or 700 as it was known here being below it as an economy car and the Crown above it as the luxury car. Back in 1965 life was so much simpler compared with the ever-expanding niche model marketing that pervades every corner of manufacturing and marketing today.

In late 1963 AMI introduced the fully imported Toyota Crown sedan. It was a very luxuriously equipped family sedan for the time coming with such items as a self-seeker radio with automatic aerial, a powerful heater/demister with a three-speed fan, carpets front and back and in the boot, an expensive-looking brocade upholstery on the front and rear bench seats that each had armrests as did all four doors, reversing lights and an impressive toolkit. The dashboard had overtones of the Ford Zephyr Mark II with the way in which the lower half dropped away to create more knee room for the front-seat passengers. In front of the driver was a broad-but-narrow instrument binnacle that contained a strip speedometer with total and trip odometers, engine oil pressure and temperature gauges to the right of it, and ammeter and fuel contents to the left; below it was the heater/demister slides plus other minor switches.

It was unusual insofar as it was built using a separate chassis with the unitary steel body mounted to it, its suspension was very US GM-like with its coils and wishbones up front and a live axle with links and coil springs at the rear, the braking system comprised cast-iron drums and the recirculating ball steering system had no power assist Under the bonnet was a very conventional in-line four-cylinder engine with a cast-iron block and head, overhead valves, alloy tappet cover, three main-bearing crank and twin-choke downdraft carburettor. Its capacity was 1897cc (88 x 78mm) and it produced 72kW (95bhp) at 5000rpm and 149Nm (110 lb-ft) of torque at 3400rpm and drove the rear wheels through a three-speed manual gearbox (with column shift) that incorporated an automatic overdrive that operated on all three forward gears together with a free wheel unit. For those who found it all too hard or complicated there was a control on the dash that allowed the driver to disconnect the unit thus rendering it a normal three-speed box.

Physically the Crown was comparable to the EJ Holden, standing on a wheelbase of 2667mm (105in) and being 4597mm (181in) in overall length by 1676mm (66in) wide and 1448mm (57in) in height and weighed just under 1272kg (2800lb). Like the Holden it was a comfortable six-seater family car with a huge boot.

Wheels extracted 137.6km/h (86mph) from it for a top speed and it ran the 0–80 and 0–96km/h (0–50 and 60mph) dashes in 11.4 and 16.6 seconds respectively while giving around 11.4 litres per 100km (25mpg)). Its performance was better than an EJ Holden Premier but it did lack a six-cylinder engine, its only negative point. Sales began at £1395 and soon a steady stream of happy owners was taking delivery from their Toyota dealer.

To broaden the Crown's appeal AMI in collaboration with Toyota devised the Crown Special that was released in September 1964. Priced at £1120 for the manual sedan, £1199 for the station wagon and £1025 for the 12cwt utility, they were price-competitive with the Holden and Falcon. The Special retained the 3R 1.9-litre engine in a slightly detuned 64kW (85bhp) form and mated it to a four-speed all-synchromesh manual gearbox using a column gearchange. The biggest change mechanically was the adoption of semi-elliptic leaf springs in place of coil springs for the rear suspension. Even with less power it would run to 132.8km/h (83mph), still competitive.

AMI introduced the Toyota Crown 2000 in March 1966 with little fanfare which was surprising given that it was with this model that the company began assembling Crowns locally. Body-wise it was a continuation of the existing body with a new grille texture and horizontal tail-light units in the rear panel plus a discreet '2000' badge on the boot lid and in the grille. Under the bonnet was the first modern six-cylinder engine from Toyota, the M series, and it would have a very long production life in several guises. It featured a cast-iron cylinder block topped with an aluminium alloy cylinder head featuring a single overhead camshaft driven by a hydraulically tensioned duplex chain that operated on single intake and exhaust valves per cylinder mounted on rocker shafts to give an almost hemispherical combustion

TOYOTA
品川5
19-00

CUSTOM 6

CROWN

chamber. The smoothly curved cast aluminium intake manifold was on the left of the engine (viewed from the driver's seat) with an Aisan twin-choke carburettor while on the right-hand side of the engine was the distributor and spark plugs plus the cast-iron exhaust manifold. The rocker cover was a plain aluminium alloy casting. The new engine fitted comfortably into the existing engine bay.

Cylinder dimensions were 75 x 75mm for a capacity of 1988cc, power output was a competitive 82kW (110bhp) at 5200rpm with 160Nm (118lb-ft) of torque at 3600rpm. Buyers could order the Crown in standard and Deluxe versions with either a three-speed all-synchromesh manual gearbox (with overdrive for the Deluxe) that had a column gearshift or the two-speed Toyoglide automatic also with column shift. *Modern Motor* tested one in the May 1966 issue and said that the new engine would enhance the reputation of the Crown in the battle with Holden and Ford: "Its performance is now between a 149 and 179 Holden", and found the engine so smooth and quiet that they had to keep checking that it was running! The handling characteristics were far better than the local rivals and the only real criticism they could level at the car was its braking – drums all round with very hard linings and no booster meant high pedal pressures. As for actual performance, they achieved a top speed of 149.7km/H (93.6mph), 0–80, 96 and 112km/h (0–50, 60 and 70mph) in 10.5, 14.8 and 20.6 seconds (virtually line-ball with the Corona 1500!), and fuel economy of 10.8 litres per 100km (26.8mpg) over 210 miles of testing.

A year later, March 1967, AMI released the Crown 2300 in the same body that was admittedly beginning to look dated. The extra capacity came from a 10mm longer stroke of the crankshaft (the dimensions were now 75 x 85mm for 2253cc) and this resulted in a boost to 85kW (115bhp) at 5200rpm and torque to 172Nm (127lb-ft). The updated Crown was easily recognised by its flamboyant and obviously American influenced grille; the interior was pretty much unchanged as were the tail-lights.

Australian Motor Sports and Automobiles magazine carried out a full test (July 1967) and were impressed. Regarding its performance they wrote, "Now, the Crown at 137.5 cubic inches can match even the big sixes of Holden and Falcon in power output. Initial acceleration may be a fraction slower, but cruising ability and top gear performance are superior." Against the stopwatch they recorded a maximum speed of 149.4km/h (93.4mph) which made it faster than all but the Valiant that ran to 152km/h (95.1mph) (Holden's top speed was 141.7km/h/88.6mph, Falcon 137km/h/85.7mph) and the classic 0–96km/h (0–60mph) dash took 13.8 seconds for the Crown, 12.5 seconds for the Valiant, 14.6 for the Holden and a slow 16.2 seconds for the Falcon. Whilst it was between $300 and $400 more expensive its list of standard fittings included a push button radio, heater/demister with three-speed fan, full carpeting, full instrumentation, courtesy lights on all doors and reversing lights. Regarding the Crown's finish they commented, "Finish is superb; in this department the Crown really does leave the competition behind." And as regards its dynamic characteristics, they said it handled well on smooth roads and that country roads can be taken in full stride without worrying about the car falling apart. In fact they likened it to the Citroën ID in that respect!

In conclusion they wrote, "This, then, is the Toyota Crown 2300: a comfortable, even luxurious, six-cylinder, six-passenger sedan, economical to run and with long legs. It is, in fact, just the car for a whole lot of Australian families."

AMI and Toyota replaced the original MS40 Crown with the next generation, the MS50 in February 1968. It continued with most of the mechanical specifications – separate chassis, full coil spring suspension system, drum brakes – of the earlier model and was really only a body change. As was Toyota's want in those days, the new Crown featured rather distinctive frontal styling and broad horizontal tail-light units. Up front was a grille with a horizontal theme of finely spaced narrow bars that wrapped around into the leading edge of the front fenders with chrome edging and a narrow open section between the base of the grille and the top edge of the chromed bumper that had the parking/indicator lenses at either end; the unusual feature of the grille was the way in which the four headlights were recessed into it in their lower half and into the fender/bonnet at the top. In the centre was the Crown motif. A strong character line ran full body length a fraction below the waist level

with the faintest suggestion of a Coke bottle hipline by the C-pillar. The cabin area was least changed and at the rear were wide horizontal tail-light units each side of a slightly recessed panel over which luggage had to be lifted. The same panel contained the rear licence plate fixture which hinged down to reveal the lockable fuel tank filler.

Inside were again vinyl upholstered bench seats front and rear with a centre armrest in both, carpets and thick sound deadening material on the floor and a bold new dashboard that featured three large round dials in front of the driver containing speedometer in the middle, clock to the left and minor gauges and warning lights in the one on the right. As with the Corona, the Crown's dash was divided roughly one-third two-thirds with a black padded vinyl top over the whole ensemble. In the left part of the driver's side, in the dash centre, were the slides for the excellent heater/demister/air-conditioning system, the self-seeking push-button radio and ashtray with cigar lighter. Along the lower edge of the panel were switches for ignition, lights and wiper (pull once for slow, twice for high) and washers (twist) and the overdrive unit.

Physically the new Crown was ever-so-slightly larger all round, the wheelbase was 2689mm (105.9in), overall length was 4665mm (183.7in), width 1689mm (66.5in), height 1445mm (56.9in) and kerb weight was 1238kg (2725lb). As before a station wagon version was also available that shared the same dimensions except for its load-carrying capacity, and its weight was 102kg (225lb) heavier. Where the outgoing Crown used a cruciform-type frame the new model adopted a perimeter frame (it was very similar to those being used by the various GM divisions in the US) and wheel size went up to 14in with 5.95 x 14 cross ply tyres and a new three-speed Toyoglide automatic gearbox was available as an option to the standard three-speed manual with overdrive. The 2M engine was unchanged at 2253cc and 85kW (115bhp). It was an engine that Toyota described in their brochures as "the world's most advanced six-cylinder production engine" at a time when Chrysler were saying similar things about their new D engine, aka the Hemi. Interesting.

Despite the fact that the Crown was running fourth in sales to Holden, Ford and Chrysler many people felt that outright power in

CORОLLA
A new look
Toyota Corolla.

TOYOTA
COROLLA 1100

an unsophisticated chassis was not for them. In key areas like seating comfort, interior quietness, ride smoothness on bitumen and rural dirt roads, fuel economy and general running costs the Crown was a clear leader. Against the clock it in reality was no slouch, being able to run to 160km/h (100mph) (manual gearbox, 147km/h/92mph for the automatic) according to *Wheels* magazine and run off the 0–96km/h (0–60mph) dash in 16.2 seconds (manual) or 17.2 seconds (automatic) while returning 12.8–10.8 litres per 100km (22–26mpg).

AMI continued the MS50 into 1971 when it was replaced by the MS60. That, however, is a subject for the next book in the trilogy.

By far the most significant new model for Toyota up to this time arrived in Australia in July 1967, the Corolla. It was a typical story of from tiny acorns mighty oaks will grow. With its cheeky styling and conventional engineering (it was in so many ways a large car successfully and cleverly scaled down) it gave no clue as to its future international success.

In the mid-sixties most of the Japanese manufacturers added cars with 1-litre engines to their model range. Nissan released their Datsun 1000, Subaru their 1000 and Mitsubishi the Colt 1000 all at around the same time. Viewed from the perspective of their vast and rapidly growing home market these cars were a logical step up for buyers from the tiny 360cc K-class cars.

The Corolla was a totally new design, the designers starting from the proverbial clean sheet. It was a two-door sedan built on a wheelbase of 2286mm (90in) with an overall length of 3835mm (151in), width of 1473mm (58in) and height of 1372mm (54in) while the kerb weight was just 702kg (1545 lb). Under the bonnet was the first K series engine, a simple overhead valve design with a cast-iron cylinder block and an aluminium alloy cylinder head. The cylinder dimensions were 75 x 61mm for a capacity of 1077cc; on a 9.0:1 compression with an Aisan twin-throat carburettor the engine produced 45kW (60bhp) at 6000rpm and 82Nm (61lb-ft) torque at 3800rpm. The crankshaft was supported by five main bearings and a short duplex chain drove the high-mounted camshaft that operated the pushrods for the overhead valves. Unusually the engine was tilted at a 20-degree angle in the engine bay.

Like most Japanese cars of the era, the Corolla was rear-wheel drive, power from the engine going through a new four-speed all-synchromesh gearbox to the rear wheels, the gearbox having a long shift lever on the floor. The front suspension was by MacPherson struts with coil springs and lower wishbones (the Corolla was the first Toyota to use this system) with the live rear axle being suspended by semi-elliptic leaf springs with telescopic dampers. Braking was by tiny 203mm (8in) cast-iron drums with 77.3sq in of lining area with no booster (not required) and the steering was by a recirculating ball system. As you can see, Toyota was being very conservative with the Corolla's technical design.

Nevertheless, when the media road-tested the car they raved about its road dynamics, cute styling, ease of driving and economy. *Wheels*, for example, described the styling as being "distinctive and unusual without being revolutionary", and "there was a minimum of fuss in the moulding of the body". They liked the driving position, the support from the front bucket seats and the neat and uncomplicated layout of the dash. For the compact size of the car its interior accommodation was regarded as very good. And its nippiness on the road belied the engine size – its top speed was 134km/h (84mph) and it would sprint from 0–96km/h (0–60mph) in 15.4 seconds which made it almost as quick as the Corona 1500!

An automatic (two-speed Toyoglide) was offered from October 1967 and a two-door station wagon was released in December. The latter was a particularly good seller. AMI priced the sedan at $1698 ($1748 if a heater was ordered), the automatic sedan at $1948 and the wagon at $2048.

Minor changes to the Corolla's grille took place for release in June 1968 and an SL version was added to the range. It had 49kW (66bhp) achieved by gas flowing the cylinder head and fitting a free flow exhaust system. Inside was a new pattern of vinyl upholstery and an 8000rpm VDO tachometer had been added on top of the dashboard. Model identification came from SL badges and the rear boot panel was painted black. Apart from the modified exhaust system, mechanically the Corolla remained the same, not even disc front brakes were offered. AMI claimed a maximum speed of around 144km/h (90mph) and a 0–96km/h (0–60mph) time of 13.3 seconds; it was $200 more expensive.

A Corolla Sprinter SL coupe was added two months later and this had a restyled roofline to emphasise the 'coupe' part of the name, the tail-lights units were slightly larger, chromed wheel trims were fitted and there was a Sprinter badge. Inside was a new three-dial instrument cluster that included a tachometer and a fake wood steering wheel. Under the bonnet was a twin-carburettor version of the 1077cc engine that with a 10.0:1 compression was now producing 54kW (73bhp) at 6600rpm, which pushed the coupe to 153.6km/h (96mph) and ran the 0–96km/h (0–60mph) dash in 13.5 seconds (*Motor Manual,* January 1969). The showroom floor price was $2498.

Lost in all this activity was the fact that the Corona had remained unchanged until September 1966 when a mildly upgraded version appeared. The most obvious change was at the front where the leading edge of the bonnet was lowered, the bumper level raised and the parking/indicator lights relocated under the bumper, the grille had a new texture and the Toyota badge was in the centre of it. At the rear the reversing light lens and reflectors were repositioned within the same (looking) tail-light units. Minor changes were made to the dash – the fuel and temperature dials were now square instead of round and the turning indicator switch was now a lever on the right of the steering column (it used to be the horn ring) and it incorporated a headlight flasher. *Australian Motor Sports* tested one in January 1968 and found the Corona to be a car that was easy to live with that had more than acceptable performance (141km/h (88mph) top speed, 0–96km/h (0–60mph) in 18.7 seconds, 9.5 litres per 100km (30+mpg)) and very competent handling characteristics. It was also very well assembled by AMI with an excellent paint finish.

Little changed until February 1969 when another mildly updated Corona found its way into showrooms around the country. It retained the unusual frontal styling but the pressed aluminium grille had a new texture, the bumpers were reshaped and new narrow full-width tail-lights appeared in the rear panel. Inside mock wood replaced the silver plastic around the instruments that were unchanged, adjustable bucket seats replaced the bench seat in front, a floor gearshift lever replaced the column lever, there was now a steering lock and full flow-through ventilation . Mechanically nothing changed, the 1490cc 55kW (74bhp) engine continued along with the manual and automatic gearboxes and four-wheel drum brakes.

AMI and Toyota ended the sixties in a strong position and were planning further advances into the Australian market for the future. These will be discussed in *Australian Cars of the 70s.*

OFO 303
TEF 201R

Chapter 7

GM VAUXHALL, CHEVROLET AND PONTIAC

Vauxhall was a popular marque in Australia in the sixties with its own dealer network throughout the city and major country centres. The range continued with basically two models – the compact Victor and the family-sized Velox with its luxury Cresta sibling. Both models were assembled in several Holden factories from CKD kits dispatched from Luton in England, the exact factory being denoted by the first letter of the city on the car's body number. For example, a Velox assembled in Adelaide would have a body number beginning with the letter A, one assembled in Sydney would have an S and so on.

The Series III Victor arrived in August 1961, the last update for this body. The almost obligatory new grille appeared, this time with five horizontal bars, the Vauxhall motif in the centre, and a prominent chromed surround that included the parking/indicator lights at each end in their chromed bezels. The bonnet badge was replaced by the name Vauxhall spelt out across the leading edge, there was a larger rear window, lowered roofline, a new boot lid pressing and the Victor name was now on the side spear. Inside there was a completely new dashboard

Under the bonnet the 1.5-litre OHV four-cylinder engine now produced 43kW (55bhp) at 4200rpm through a slight lift in compression and other tuning adjustments. Performance, however, remained unchanged with a top speed of 128km/h (80mph) and a 0–80km/h (0–50mph) time of 14.8 seconds. It was no ball of fire even by the standards of the day.

A completely restyled Victor was released in March 1962 and although it cost almost as much as the Holden Special sedan (£1039 compared with £1110) it was met with enthusiasm by diehard Vauxhall clients. Where the original Victor had been a very extrovert design the new FB Victor was the epitome of British conservatism with a plain, unadorned exterior and a plain-but-simple dashboard. The driver now had two round dials in front that were clearly marked and very easy to read; seating continued to be by benches front and rear. From the exterior, the most notable feature was the prominent swage line running the full body length at waist level; apart from that there was little to comment on from a styling point of view.

The mechanical components were carried over, meaning that the Victor still had an all-synchromesh *three*-speed manual transmission with a column shift (a four-speed manual with floor shift was optional but few were sold), the steering remained a recirculating ball system and the brakes were still by cast-iron drums all round.

Performance was class average at 128km/h (80mph) top speed and times of 12.6 and 18.1 seconds for the 0–80 and 96km/h (0–50 and 60mph) runs, both being hampered by the retention of a three-speed gearbox where all of its rivals had four-speed gearboxes. Not long after it had been released the engine's capacity was expanded to 1594cc by the simple expedient of widening the cylinder bore to 81.6mm and fitting new pistons; nothing else changed apart from an increase in power to 44kW (58.5bhp) at 4600rpm and torque to 114Nm (84lb-ft) at 2400rpm. It proved to be a most uncomplicated car to own and run but GM-H was apparently not all that keen on promoting it. The Victor was to prove to be one of motoring's hidden secrets. The FB body was better protected against rust and so more have survived than its predecessor. Interestingly, the Victor was a true family sedan that was, in fact, very close in size to the original 48/215 Holden. In addition to the four-door sedan Holden assembled small numbers of the Victor station wagon that had a one-piece lift-up rear door supported by gas struts where the Holden still had the old-fashioned horizontally-split tailgate system.

Australian Motor Manual tested a Victor in November 1964, the test car having a four-speed all-synchromesh gearbox with a floor shift. There were a few niggles – the steering was far too low-geared and had a 'spongy' feel, there was some wallowing on the softish suspension and the engine was very noisy when revved hard. What they did like was the roomy interior with its comfortable seating, the large boot, the excellent gearbox and the strong brakes.

To expand their Victor offerings in the UK in particular Vauxhall developed the VX 4/90 and proceeded to chase buyers who were keen drivers and appreciated the niceties of the VX; it was released in England in October 1961 and here in Australia a few months later. Vauxhall engineers did a thorough job of modifying the Victor and, apart from a suspension that remained too soft even though it did feature slightly stiffer springs and dampers, ticked all the right boxes. The engine developed 54kW (71bhp) at 5200rpm through the use of an aluminium alloy eight-port cylinder head running a 9.3:1 compression fed by dual Zenith carburettors and a low restriction exhaust system. Power boosted 266mm (10.5in) front disc brakes were a standard fitting as were 4.5J x 14 steel rims shod with 5.60 x 14 tubeless tyres. As a bonus, the VX 4/90 came with a four-speed all synchromesh manual transmission with a nicely placed floor shift and a higher ratio differential – 3.9:1 against 4.111. Visually the VX 4/90 was distinguished by the extra vertically positioned rear light (it was the brake light) above the existing horizontal units and there was a two-piece chrome flash along the side with a contrasting colour painted within.

Inside, the VX 4/90 owner enjoyed carpets on the floor, bucket seats in front, bench with armrest in the back plus a dashboard with a full set of round Smiths dials – speedometer, tachometer, fuel, temperature, oil pressure and amps – set in an imitation wood feature to keep the driver in tune with his car. As well, a heater/demister with two-speed fan, plus windscreen washers were a standard fitting. GM priced the VX 4/90 at £1330, somewhat more expensive than the Cortina GT that retailed at £1187 and was released two years *after* the VX, a fact that many enthusiasts do not realise.

In September 1962 a mildly revised VX 4/90 was released in which the main change was to the engine's capacity; it was now 1594cc and it developed 61kW (81bhp).

A full test was published by *Wheels* (March 1965) which found the VX 4/90 performed admirably running to 150.4km/h (94mph) and ran the 0–80km/h (0–50mph) sprint in 10.5 seconds; *Modern Motor's* test revealed a top speed of 145km/h (90.78mph) and a 0–80km/h (0–50mph) sprint time of 9.8 seconds. The Cortina GT which was over 136kg (300lb) lighter had, by comparison, a top speed of 147km/h (91.9mph) and a time of 9.7 seconds. Close enough for it not to be a sales issue. What was different was the attitude of Holden which barely promoted the VX, where Ford successfully raced and rallied the GT and won. What the magazines road-testers did say of the VX 4/90 was, "Few cars combine so well good performance, comfort, outstanding brakes and comprehensive equipment in such a tidy package."

By April 1965 the FB Victor was replaced by the FC 101, a model that looked like a slightly smaller HD Holden. All the same styling cues were there even though they had been styled half a world away. Built on the same 2540mm (100in) wheelbase as the previous model, the 101 featured deep, slab body sides with no creases apart from those from the bumpers to the wheel arches front and back; for the first time on a Vauxhall the 101 had curved side glass. Retained from the previous model was the 1594cc four-cylinder engine that was now developing 58kW (76bhp) at 4800rpm mated to a three-speed manual gearbox, a three-speed Borg Warner automatic now being available as an option. There was a VX 4/90 version too but it would appear that this model was imported rather than locally assembled.

Inside the bench seats front and rear were continued making the Victor 101 a nominal six-seater. Where the FB had nice round dials, the

101 reverted to a difficult-to-read fan-shaped speedometer with fuel and temperature gauges set into a broad rectangular binnacle as part of a flat dashboard that had a padded top for safety.

As you can imagine, its performance was line ball with the old FB and road holding suffered slightly because the springs were softened a tad and body lean was increased although the ride was both quieter and smoother – swings and roundabouts! Equipment levels were on a par with an HD Special so nothing to write home about and the showroom price for the Super was £1076 when an HD Special sedan cost £1130. The number of people willing to pay that much money for a four-cylinder sedan with precious little by way of fittings was gradually diminishing plus GM-H was spending fewer and fewer pounds on advertising the Vauxhall brand that it was no surprise that by 1966 the pin was pulled on the Vauxhall side of the business.

The PA Velox was updated to the PA Series II in November 1960 and that brought a raft of changes that included a new one-piece rear window (in place of the three-piece previously), new more sober design of tail-lights and a deeper grille that required a new bonnet pressing. Under the bonnet the engine's capacity had been increased from 2.3 to 2.6 litres (bore and stroke now 82.55 x 82.55mm, 2651cc) which raised the power output to 84kW (113bhp) at 4800rpm and torque to 200Nm (148lb/ft) at 2400rpm. Kerb weight was a reasonable 1196kg (2632lb) so it was no lightweight sedan. The Cresta ran a 3.9:1 rear axle ratio (raised from 4.1:1) and continued with drum brakes even though front discs were an option in England.

Inside was much the same as before except for the completely new dashboard. Gone were the two round dials to be replaced by a flat horizontal speedometer with fuel and temperature gauges plus some warning lights set in a plain rectangular unit. The major interest was in the speedometer itself, known at the time as the "Color-Span" speedo that changed colour from green to amber at 48km/h (30mph) and to red from 96km/h (60mph). Other changes included chrome side mouldings to delineate the duo-tone paintwork, "Magic Mirror" paint finish like that on Holdens and Chevrolets and 14in wheels shod with 5.90 x 14 tyres.

The late David McKay test drove a Cresta which was published in the March 1961 issue of *Modern Motor*; he came away highly impressed making comments like, "I found the driving position better than in most family touring cars … Vision was good all round … The powerful headlights are a real asset in night driving … The ride was pleasantly firm, and the absence of body roll on corners was surprising considering the car's American connections." Against the clock the Cresta recorded a top speed of 152km/h (95mph) and times of 10.4 and 16.0 seconds for the 0–80 and 96km/h (0–50 and 60mph) sprints while returning 14 litres per 100km (20mpg) after all the tests, normal motoring would raise that to 10.8–10 litres per 100km (26–28mpg). A Velox sedan cost £1480, the Cresta £1561 when an FB Holden Special cost £1247 and a Ford Zephyr cost £1384.

The PA gave way to the PB Velox and Cresta in April 1963. Again, the mechanical components were carried over so it was a body change only. In many respects the new PB carried over Victor styling cues with its pronounced ridge running the full length of the body at waist level and small(ish) horizontal tail-light units at the rear either side of a slightly concave section between them. Up front was a bold new grille sporting nine horizontal slats with a narrow Vee-shaped divider and single headlights, and the parking/indicator lights were placed right on the front corner of the fender each side; thin blade-like 'bumpers' featured front and back.

Overall the PB was 69mm (2.75in) longer, 44mm (1.75in) wider and half an inch lower than previously and the wheelbase was increased by 63.5mm (2.5in) to 2730mm (107.5in) to the benefit of rear seat passengers. Inside was a new dashboard that was quite plain in design in comparison with the PA; the instrument cluster was in a rectangular flat binnacle in front of the driver and consisted of a speedometer that was now a wide horizontal unit with dials for fuel and temperature below, and on a strip below were the ignition, lights and wiper switches. Provision for a heater and radio were in the centre.

Lockheed disc front brakes were a standard fitting on both Velox and Cresta, their diameter being 266mm (10.5in) together with 228mm (9in) drums at the rear with a vacuum booster on the system. The only other changes of note concerned the rear axle ratio that was raised to

3.73:1 from 3.90 and the use of parallel action electric wipers in place of the old clap hands system.

Modern Motor published a full road test (July 1963) and was impressed by the build quality, the big sedan's performance (153.6km/h (96mph) top speed, 0–80 and 96km/h (0–50 and 0–60mph) times of 11.2 and 16.8 seconds respectively and 13.5 litres per 100km (21mpg) for the test), the floor-mounted hand brake, and its failsafe handling but expressed the view that GM-H were a bit mean-spirited with the lack of equipment in the car. The floor was covered by rubber mats, there was no heater/demister and no windscreen washers – not good enough in a sedan costing £1482 for the automatic (as tested) or £1356 for a manual. The Cresta version had the Hydramatic automatic gearbox, a heater/demister, floor carpets, windscreen washers, leather-faced seats, roof-mounted clock and some more chrome for an additional £89 – good value. A Holden Premier with just 75bhp and nowhere near the Cresta's performance cost £1420.

The PB Velox and Cresta continued to sell in reasonable numbers although it was apparent that GM-H was losing interest. Assembly of Vauxhalls in Australia ceased in 1966 to the consternation of the loyal dealers (many of whom chose to take on selling a Japanese brand to continue their business) and the many enthusiasts for the marque.

The most interesting news from Vauxhall for the sixties was the introduction of the Viva, a small sedan designed to cater for buyers for whom economy was paramount. Looking for all the world like three boxes on wheels, the Viva was a 'clean sheet' design as it shared nothing with any other Vauxhall. Where BMC had opted for technical sophistication that was let down by abysmal production quality, Vauxhall went for the ultra-conventional to keep manufacturing costs down as Ford had done when developing the 105E Anglia and later the Cortina and Escort.

Built on a wheelbase of 2324mm (91.5in) and with an overall length of 3937mm (155in), width of 1498mm (59in) and height of 1358mm (53.5in), the Viva weighed only 712kg (1568lb) at the kerb. Within those dimensions the Vauxhall engineers managed to create a two-door body with room for four adult passengers and a huge boot that had the tiny 32-litre (7gal) fuel tank tucked away in the left-hand rear fender space and the spare wheel stored upright on the other side (it is easy for the styling guys to do this when they are basically drawing boxes!). Up front was a simple horizontal bar grille flanked either side by the single headlights and tiny parking/indicator lights on each corner, a Vauxhall name badge was in the centre of the grille and a crude (and useless) chromed bumper strip set it all off to give it some aesthetic appeal. At the rear was a similar chrome blade bumper and a simple tail-light unit each side, orange on top for indicators, red below for tail and stop lights.

Under the rear-hinged bonnet (no inside security release, propped open by a rod) was a totally new engine. It was thoroughly conventional in design insofar as it was an overhead valve unit with the valves being angled at 22 degrees from the vertical and operated by pushrods and pressed steel rockers that pivoted on ball studs – there was no rocker shaft as such. Both the cylinder block and head were made from cast-iron. The cylinder dimensions were 74.6 x 60.9mm (bore x stroke) for a capacity of 1057cc and the engine developed 32kW (44bhp) at 5200rpm and 75Nm (56lb-ft) of torque at 3000rpm on a compression ratio of 8.5:1 and using a tiny Solex carburettor, barely class average.

The suspension of the Viva showed a little creativity in an effort to be different and cost-effective. The front was by a transverse leaf spring with upper-and-lower pressed steel wishbones and telescopic dampers while the rear axle was suspended by long semi-elliptic leaf springs with only two leaves each side.

Released in Australia in April 1964, it quickly proved to be popular with buyers despite the lack of equipment and was available in two trim levels – Standard at £839 and Deluxe at £885.

A full road test was published in *Wheels*, June 1964 and despite the poverty equipment levels they found the Viva to be a nice car to drive. The rack and pinion steering, they said, "set new standards for small cars" so smooth and direct was it and light in action, as were the foot pedals; the gearshift needed only light pressure and movement between gears was not much more than a couple of inches. And having many minor functions on a steering column stalk pleased them, too. Handling was regarded as good–average and the ride was a little choppy on anything but a smooth surface. Interior roominess was excellent for four people and the boot was huge for its class.

As for its performance, the Viva ran to a maximum speed of 124.8km/h (78mph) with 40km/h, 70km/h and 102km/h (25mph, 44mph and 64mph) available in the indirect gears, acceleration from rest to 80 and 96km/h (50 and 60mph) took 13.8 and 22.2 seconds making it middle of the class, while for the whole test it returned a remarkable 8.2 litres per 100km (34mpg), over 7 litres per 100km (40mpg) on a long drive so that around 480km (300 miles) was available from the 32-litre (7gal) tank.

Holden assembled the Viva until May 1967 when it was replaced by the altogether more attractive Holden Torana, which was little more than the next generation Vauxhall Viva with new badges and round headlights; its story can be found in Chapter One.

CHEVROLET AND PONTIAC

Chevrolet (and Pontiac) entered the new decade with styling that was only slightly less flamboyant and less controversial. All five divisions of GM in America had pushed the boundaries of styling for the 1959 model year and each pulled back from the brink for 1960. What followed through the sixties was a series of body designs that reflected what many consider to be the high point of American automotive design. Some of the shapes produced were masterpieces. Sadly, from the late sixties it was a gradual downhill slide … almost to oblivion.

For the 1960 model year (May) the Chev's 'seagull fins' were there still but they had been toned down considerably as had the tail-light units. There was new sheet metal front and rear of a passenger compartment that was largely unchanged; from above the grille a prominent ridge extended rearwards and became the much reduced fins at the rear, where there was a neat rectangular rear valance panel with chromed highlight strips that contained four small round tail-lights, two each side. On each side starting on the rear door skin was a chromed piece that looked somewhat like an aeroplane with a long chromed strip running back to the rear.

The interior was still vast with ample room for six passengers on the front and rear bench seat. the broad dashboard was flat with a wide rectangular instrument panel in front of the driver showing only the speed through a fan-shaped speedometer, plus fuel and temperature dials plus some warning lights, of course.

For the first time in Australia the Chevrolet Bel Air was available with the company's famous small block 283cid V8 engine mated to the two-speed Powerglide automatic. Although the V8 had been available in the US for several years, GM-H continued with the six-cylinder engine here for as long as they could on the grounds (excuse?) of cost. With the V8, power rose to 126kW (170bhp) at 4200rpm and torque to 372Nm (275lb-ft) at 2200rpm.

Under the headline of 'Boulevard Bullet' *Modern Motor* published a full test of the Chevrolet Bel Air and while they found some points to criticise – the drum brakes had 199.5sq in of lining area but they struggled to cope with the big and heavy car's performance, the hopelessly low-gear steering that needed 5½ turns lock-to-lock, the suspension allowed a lot of weight transfer side-to-side during cornering, which was disconcerting to passengers, the Powerglide automatic had only two speeds, the placement of the spare wheel on the boot floor with no protective cover, no internal bonnet release and no heater/demister – but there were many good points as well. The storming performance was the big talking point: 166km/h (104mph) top speed with the 80 and 96km/h (50 and 60mph) dashes taking only 8.0 and 10.0 seconds respectively, 64–96km/h (40–60mph) passing acceleration took only 6.0 seconds and the 1730kg (3808lb) heavyweight returned a credible 15.5 litres per 100km (18.7mpg) on test which gave the sedan a touring range of well over 480km (300 miles) from the 74-litre (16.5gal) tank.

Despite the lack of equipment fitted, GM-H charged the princely sum of £2476 for the Bel Air, a price many were prepared to pay.

Every year through to late-1968 Holden assembled the current year model Chevrolet from kits dispatched from Canada so every year Australian motorists had a 'new' Chev to buy. It was all pretty much cosmetic styling changes over existing mechanical components for 1961, 1962 and 1963 while for 1964 the 283cid V8 offered 145kW (195bhp) and for 1965 an Impala Super Sports sedan was introduced with four-door pillarless styling and, hidden underneath, a new perimeter frame chassis. For 1965 Chevrolet introduced Australian motorists to the Coke-bottle styling theme where starting on the rear door the fender line rose and then fell towards the boot line. For most of the period Chevrolet stylists used round tail-lights, usually three per side, and merely varied their shape depending on the style of the car's rear.

For 1966 Chevrolet substituted the 327cid V8 for the 283cid unit and raised power to 172kW (230bhp) and torque to 447Nm (330lb-ft). Despite this, top speed remained at 166km/h (104mph, the final drive gearing was still 3.55:1) and the 0–80 and 96km/h (0–50 and 60mph) times stayed virtually the same but the 64–96km/h (40–60mph) passing time was down to just 4.9 seconds, the product of that mountain of torque.

In 1967 and 1968 there was new sheet metal with added emphasis ('67) on the Coke-bottle hip line and then less ('68) plus the 327cid V8 was rated at 186kW (250bhp) for both years and despite the car's weight and performance braking remained as cast-iron drums when virtually every other manufacturer of high-performance cars had at least disc front brakes – Detroit was a l-o-n-g way behind technologically and did not start to bridge the gap until a decade or so later.

Pontiac for 1960 used a variation of the Chevrolet body but with its own sheet metal front and rear. The passenger section with its six-light style was common to both but the Pontiac had a ridge on each front fender beginning with the leading edge of the bonnet and then another ridge starting behind the rear door shutline and swinging back and across the rear with two small round lights each side.

A new body unique to Pontiac arrived for 1961 in which the two-piece divided grille was prominent, the grille itself sloping back from the bottom edge. While the front windscreen was no longer wraparound, it featured a noticeable curvature up and back to a small 'ledge' over the rear window. At the rear were two groups of three tail-lights each side and along each side of the body were deep strakes pressed into the door skins. The interior featured w-i-d-e bench seats front and back. And the dashboard was massive in size but offering few luxuries. Instruments, such as they were – strip speedometer, fuel and temperature dials plus warning lights – were housed in a very wide-but-shallow binnacle in a recessed section enveloped by crash padding; under that was a flat panel section in which the ignition switch, wipers and (when ordered) the heater/demister and radio were housed.

The seats were upholstered in leather and the floor was carpeted, the electric wipers with washers had two speeds, there was a glove-box light, reversing lights and a cigar lighter but that was the extent of any 'luxury' for 1961.

Power for the Laurentian came from the small block Chevrolet 283cid engine mated to the two-speed Powerglide automatic gearbox and, as with the Chev, power was 126kW (170bhp); braking was by cast-iron drums with 185.6sq in of lining area but the Pontiac weighed 1754kg (3860lb) so they were always working hard even in normal motoring. *Australian Motor Manual* tested a Laurentian and achieved a maximum speed of exactly 160km/h (100mph) with 96km/h (60mph) available in low range, 0–96km/h (0–60mph) taking 12.2 seconds and fuel economy was just 15 litres per 100km (19mpg) giving a range of 480km (300 miles) from the 72-litre (16gal) tank. They described its performance as 'effortless'. At £2753 they thought it to be expensive for what it offered, apart from sheer physical size.

The 1962 was a styling variation of the 1961 but for 1963 Pontiac took steps to better differentiate itself from the slightly less expensive Chevrolet stablemate. The most notable styling difference was at the front where the four headlights were positioned at either end of the divided grille in vertically-stacked pairs. The grille was very restrained in appearance with eight thin bars filling in the space. At the rear the bumper swept up each end into small vertical tail-light units that were on the end of vestigial fins.

Under the bonnet the Chevrolet-sourced V8 engine remained at 283cid (4. 6litres) but new cylinder heads and a higher compression ratio yielded another 18kW (25bhp), up now to 145kW (195bhp) at 4800rpm, and there was now an alternator, three years *after* Chrysler had started the trend! This power went through the Powerglide two-speed automatic to the rear wheels, 120km/h (75mph) being available in low and 158km/h (98.9mph) was registered as the maximum speed in a *Wheels* road test (September 1963).

For 1963 GM-H at last decided to fit a heater/demister as standard on the Pontiac as part of the differentiation program within GM-H to help justify the extra cost of a Pontiac over a Chevrolet. At £2643 buyers would have rightly expect a quality heater/demister and a whole lot of other items but they were to be disappointed. Sheer size *was* the luxury!

For 1964 there was little change at the front apart from three prominent horizontal strips applied to the grille, but at the rear there were new vertical tail-light units recessed into bezels at the end of each rear quarter panel with re-shaped bumper ends to accommodate them, a brushed aluminium panel between the lights had the word 'Parisienne' spelt out, and stuck on the rear panel alongside the tail-light was a separate round indicator light – it was an afterthought to comply with local legal requirements.

New sheet metal arrived for 1965 around a slightly changed passenger compartment. The front fenders peaked over the vertical headlights, the side window glass was curved, there was a prominent body moulding low down on the doors and the tail-lights were horizontal. Inside were new round dials but the rest of the fittings were much the same as the previous year. Two versions were now available – Parisienne with four-door pillared body and 145kW (195bhp), and the Parisienne Sport with a four-door hardtop body and 172kW (230bhp) from the Chevrolet 327cid V8.

Pontiac stylists continued with the same themes for 1966 but with 'pinched' grille sections near the central post and unusual 'dog's ear' folds in the rear quarter panels alongside the horizontal tail-lights with, again, added-on indicator lights. For the following year it was yet another variation on the same theme but this time they used a combination bumper/grille that included the lower headlight, the upper one being housed in the front fender while at the rear were new quarter panels and inverted L-shaped tail-lights. 1968, the last year of locally assembled Pontiacs, saw the return to four horizontal headlights housed within a loop-type bumper with the central dividing post plus prominent side mouldings.

By this time Holden was struggling with sales of its locally assembled Chevrolets and Pontiacs because of cost pressures from the dollar exchange rates which precluded the fitting of many so-called luxury items to help justify the escalating retail price. A home-grown luxury car was in the works – the Brougham – and although it was not as successful as Holden might have wanted, the company was at least able to determine its own pricing policy without worrying about international exchange rates.

revolutionary
1500
Volkswagens

Chapter 8

VOLKSWAGEN

With the Volkswagen Beetle firmly positioned as the biggest selling four-cylinder sedan on the Australian market, the company looked forward to the new decade with confidence. As before, development came from within the car, the exterior design remaining basically unchanged.

During late 1960 a number of small but important changes were made to the Beetle's specification for the 1961 model year. For example, push-button door handles were phased in along with a front stabiliser bar, steering damper, flashing indicators replaced the trafficator arms and there were new tail-lights. Later in the year came the 30kW (40bhp) 1192cc engine and a new all-synchromesh gearbox, a flatter fuel tank (it was an attempt to find more luggage room), padded sun visors, a passenger grab handle and suction-pump windscreen washers. In so many ways enthusiasts look upon the 1961 30kW (40hp) Beetle as an almost new car because it was the car that *really* put VWoA on the local motoring map. So much so that 120 Beetles a day were rolling off the Clayton assembly line.

The 'new' engine was interesting insofar as it shared the exact same cylinder dimensions as previously – 77 x 64mm bore x stroke for a capacity of 1192cc – but there were significant structural differences. In order to improve engine reliability and service life the cylinder barrels were spaced further apart to allow more air to circulate between them; this necessitated a new, stronger magnesium alloy crankcase casting and new forged crankshaft with larger webs and bigger journals, and there was a new camshaft. Engine compression was raised to 7.0:1, there were larger diameter valves with stronger springs, the spark advance was now vacuum-operated only and the choke was now automatic. The only other mechanical change of note was the use of longer rubber cones on the rear suspension.

The Australian economy endured a credit squeeze and recession in 1961–62 which devastated sales – VW sales were down 38 per cent! It took until November 1961 for VWoA to introduce the next raft of changes to appear and again they were minuscule in the bigger picture – an electric fuel gauge (the German VWs had a mechanical gauge) made by the Australian subsidiary of VDO and US-style bumpers. June 1962 saw the announcement of the 1962-and-a-half Beetle that featured the larger three-segment tail-lights, seatbelt anchorage points (but not the belts), spring-loaded front bonnet lift, modified heater with adjustable vents and new seat adjusters, while the doors now had check rods to hold them open and there was a new steering box and sealed-for-life tie rod ends.

At this time VWoA was investing around £2 million annually on locally-sourced tooling – the press shop was pressing all the panels for the Beetle and was now the third largest in the country. In August VWoA announced the Standard model of the Beetle, which retailed at £849, with the Deluxe retailing at £953, a saving of £104. Mechanically the two models were identical but the Standard had no steering damper, silver-painted hubcaps and bumpers, no exterior chrome, no bonnet strip, no exterior mirror and, unimaginably, no Wolfsburg crest. Inside there was no interior light, no fuel gauge, no glove-box lid, no windscreen washers and a driver's side sun visor only. To nobody's real surprise, buyers ignored it and spent the slightly extra amount for the Deluxe.

As Ian Fraser wrote in *Wheels*, October 1962, "By far the best Volkswagen ever, the 1962½ model is smoother, better running and better value than ever before." The standard of paintwork and finish inside and out was superb, and, while the car was well known for its propensity to roll over, this had been reduced by modifications to the suspension geometry. On rough dirt roads, of which there were plenty in the sixties, few other cars could keep up with a well-driven VW such was its suspension's ability to absorb the tough stuff and still provide occupants with a good ride. Performance was pretty much the same as before: around 115km/h (72mph) top (and cruising) speed with 15.2 seconds needed to accelerate to 80km/h (50mph) and a slow 25.9 seconds to 96km/h (60mph).

In a country where the six-cylinder engine was king it was surprising that Australians bought so many VW Beetles – maybe it had something to do with its individuality, its personality or the wonderful backup service?

For years VW in Wolfsburg had been under pressure to produce a successor to the Type 1 Beetle. Numerous prototypes were shown at various times but nothing ever came of those lines of development. However, to broaden the range and attract a slightly wealthier clientele the company developed in collaboration with Porsche the Type 3 sedan and station wagon, albeit based on the same platform as the Type 1. That meant a two-door body of a completely different – more contemporary – design with the same 2400mm (94.5in) wheelbase. Perhaps the greatest novelty of the new Type 3 was the fact that the cooling fan was much smaller in diameter than the big windmill in the VW Beetle and was driven directly off the crankshaft. The whole engine package in the Type 3 was only 406mm (16in) high which enabled the designers to provide two luggage carrying compartments – one in the front and another over the rear engine. The new engine was clearly based on the Beetle's but with a greater capacity, bore and stroke were 83 x 69mm for 1493cc and on a 7.8:1 compression and using a single Solex side draught carburettor it produced 39.5kW (53bhp) at 4000rpm and 114Nm (84lb-ft) of torque at 2000rpm. By comparison with other manufacturers these outputs were very low and conservative.

Like the Beetle, the 1500 was a four-seater, the front passengers seated on very comfortable bucket seats with lock-down catches to prevent them tipping forward under braking. The padded dash had three round binnacles in front of the driver but actual instrumentation remained at speed (middle) with fuel contents and warning lights on

VIC SSE·558

VIC SSE·558

the right and a clock to the left. Push-push switches to the right of the steering column operated the lights and wipers/washer with indicators/ headlight flasher on the left of the column. Three slides in the centre of the dash controlled the heating/demisting system.

VWoA introduced the Type 3 sedan and wagons to Australia in February 1963 with retail prices of £1199 and £1249 respectively. While early stocks were fully imported, by September both models were being assembled on the Clayton line with a substantial local content.

In the March 1963 issue of *Wheels* there was a full test of the new VW 1500, a car that tester Ian Fraser obviously liked. Its maximum speed (and therefore its cruising speed, conditions allowing) was just over 128km/h (80mph), it took 11.8 and 17.6 seconds to accelerate to 80 and 96km/h (50 and 60mph) respectively and still returned more than 9.5 litres per 100km (30mpg). For a VW these were regarded as quite spritely but VW would soon find itself under siege from faster, cheaper and less expensive Japanese cars.

Nevertheless, the VW 1500 had many admirable qualities not the least of which was a high standard of finish and a relaxed, almost disarmingly confident, ability to cover vast distances with ease. As Fraser commented, "Over rough roads the 1500's behaviour is superb and I doubt if there would be another car faster in give and take conditions." In conclusion he wrote, "Whichever way you look at it, the VW 1500 is a particularly pleasing car. The attention to detail and finish are outstanding features. The performance is good without being startling and even driven hard the car will return better than 30mpg."

An important addition to the VW 1500 model range (the Type 3) was the 1500 S, sometimes referred to as the Twin S, that arrived in July 1964 initially as a full import and later locally assembled. At a time when Ford was winning conquest sales with its Cortina GT (also 1500cc) and the Rootes Group was marketing their Humber Vogue Sports, Vauxhall the Victor VX 4/90, Prince Motors their Skyline GT, BMC had the Mini Cooper S and both Datsun and Toyota were importing very small numbers of the Bluebird SSS and Corona 1600 S, it was felt to be important by management at VWoA to compete with a model based on the new Type 3 sedan. Initial stocks were imported but it was soon assimilated on the Clayton assembly line. Its price was £1179, although the imported examples had a price tag of £1325.

Differentiating an S from a standard 1500 sedan was not easy, so few were the differences. The most obvious external sign was a discreet 'S' badge on the rear deck and the front indicator lights were oblong, not

VW 1500...

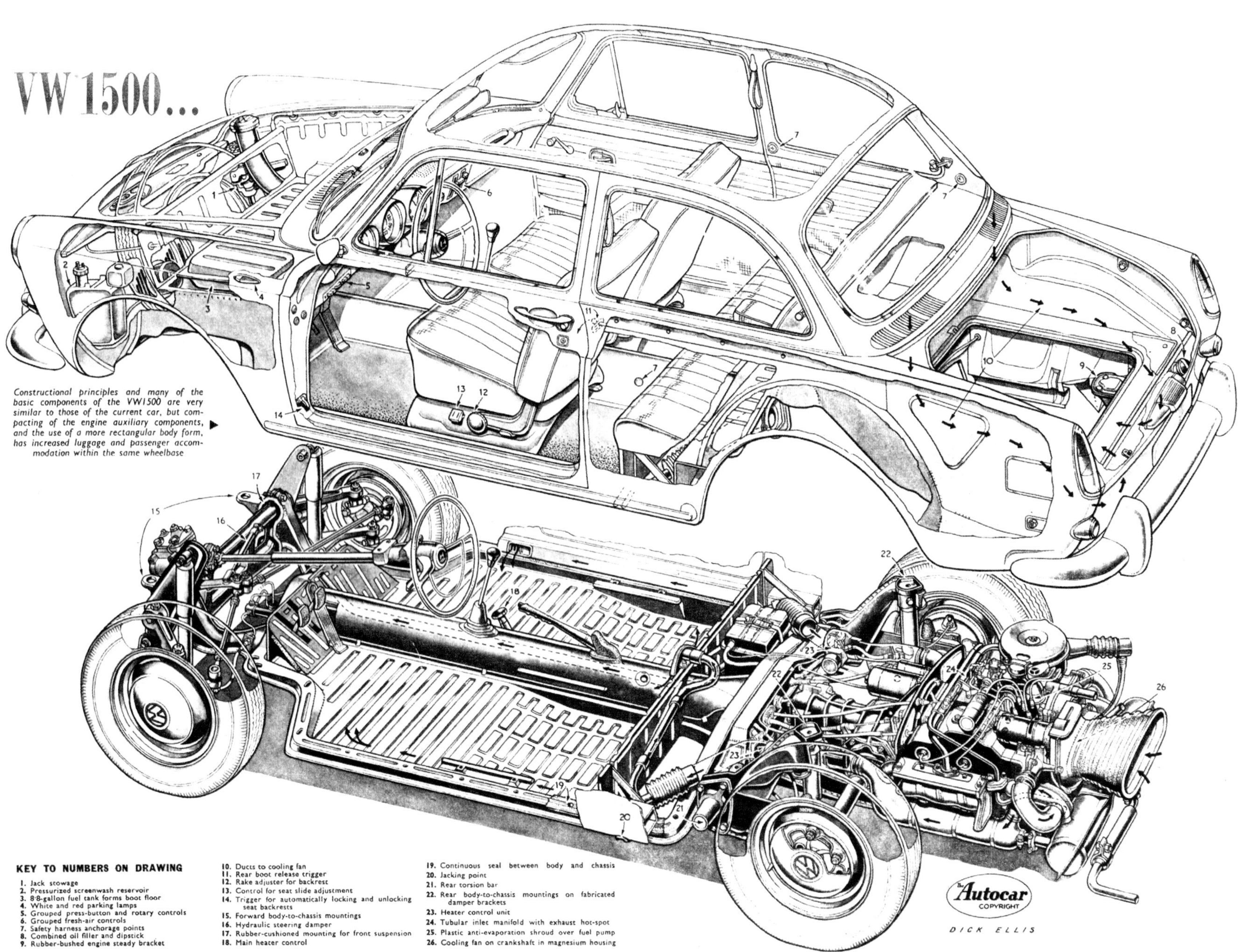

Constructional principles and many of the basic components of the VW1500 are very similar to those of the current car, but compacting of the engine auxiliary components, and the use of a more rectangular body form, has increased luggage and passenger accommodation within the same wheelbase ▶

KEY TO NUMBERS ON DRAWING

1. Jack stowage
2. Pressurized screenwash reservoir
3. 8·8-gallon fuel tank forms boot floor
4. White and red parking lamps
5. Grouped press-button and rotary controls
6. Grouped fresh-air controls
7. Safety harness anchorage points
8. Combined oil filler and dipstick
9. Rubber-bushed engine steady bracket
10. Ducts to cooling fan
11. Rear boot release trigger
12. Rake adjuster for backrest
13. Control for seat slide adjustment
14. Trigger for automatically locking and unlocking seat backrests
15. Forward body-to-chassis mountings
16. Hydraulic steering damper
17. Rubber-cushioned mounting for front suspension
18. Main heater control
19. Continuous seal between body and chassis
20. Jacking point
21. Rear torsion bar
22. Rear body-to-chassis mountings on fabricated damper brackets
23. Heater control unit
24. Tubular inlet manifold with exhaust hot-spot
25. Plastic anti-evaporation shroud over fuel pump
26. Cooling fan on crankshaft in magnesium housing

round. The interior, remarkably enough, did not feature extra gauges as did almost all of the opposition (there was no tachometer, for example, which was a surprising omission in a purportedly sporting sedan) and the seats and other trim remained the same as in the regular 1500. Brakes (drums all round) and tyres also were unchanged. Under the (rear) bonnet, however, some modifications had been made mainly in the form of dual Solex 32PDSIT carburettors, one over each cylinder bank and a marginally higher compression ratio to yield 47kW (63.5bhp) at 4800rpm and 108Nm (80.2lb-ft) of torque at 3000rpm. By way of comparison, the market-leading Ford Cortina boasted 62kW (83.5bhp) at 5200rpm from its 1.5-litre OHV engine.

Australian Motor Manual tested a VW 1500 S and published a top speed of 140.8km/h (88mph) with in-gear maxima of 43/78/115km/h (27/49/72mph), 0–80 and 0–96km/h (0–50 and 60mph) times of 12.8 and 18.2 seconds respectively and reckoned on a fuel consumption of up to 8 litres per 100km (35mpg) under normal usage. These figures were not much different from the standard 1500!

Wheels conducted a four-car comparison between the VW 1500 S, Ford Cortina GT, Humber Vogue Sports and the Fiat 1500 and the VW came last in every performance test conducted. It barely topped 128km/h (80mph) compared with more than 144km/h (90mph) for the other three and was well behind on the standing quarter-mile sprint and its all-drum braking system was criticised. However, it was the best made of the quartet, by far the best on rough roads, and the easiest to drive around town.

For 1965 the VW 1500 continued unchanged with the only change to the 1500 S being the deletion of opening rear side windows and from March 1967 the station wagon and 1500 S adopted the 1584cc engine

VW·1500
VW·1500

from the TS Fastback along with larger rear tail-light units and square rear reflectors.

The 1500 S was not a sales success – too expensive even for VW fanatics, and far too slow – and was replaced in the model range in April 1966 by the (initially) fully imported VW 1600 TS Fastback. Externally the VW stylists had integrated a nice flowing roofline over the original sedan body, but it was not a hatchback as perhaps some might have imagined or even hoped. As part of the styling change the side windows were elongated and there were three sets of air vents in a line along the upper rear fenders that admitted cooling air to the engine compartment.

Under the rear bonnet was an expanded version of the Type 3 engine. It was still air-cooled (of course!) but the cylinder barrels now had a bore of 85.5mm which raised the engine's capacity to 1584cc but actual power output remained at 48kW (65bhp) at 4600rpm, torque was up to 118Nm (87lb-ft) at 2800rpm, a slight improvement over the 1500 S. The Australian 1600 TS differed in several ways from its German cousin: the first was the non-opening rear side windows which would have provided some ventilation for rear-seat passengers on a hot day, drum brakes were fitted all round and not front discs because that would have necessitated five-bolt hubs (instead of four) and VWoA executives decided against it on the grounds of added manufacturing costs, and finally there was no lock on the front-seat backs to prevent them tipping forward in a panic stop. On all three counts the VWoA executives should have had their knuckles rapped.

Australian Motor Sports tested a 1600 TS in June 1966 and was impressed with it apart from the three items mentioned above. Its distinctive style and loping long-distance stride endeared it as did its 136km/h (85mph) top speed – fast for a VW – but its acceleration was classed as mediocre at 12.8 and 18.4 seconds for the dashes to 80 and 96km/h (50 and 60mph), and its instability in side winds was deemed unacceptable. At $2415 it was not inexpensive but was thought to still be value for money for those who wanted something different from their neighbours.

For the rest of the sixties it was a case of changing as little as possible because of the costs of meeting the local content requirements. For 1968 the Type 3 sedan became the VW 1600 by adopting the same engine as the TS and the model names changed – the station wagon became the Squareback, the sedan the Notchback to go with the Fastback. These names were taken from their US cousins.

In May 1969 some significant upgrades came through, like dual braking circuits with discs at the front (at last!) along with an external fuel filler, collapsible steering column, double-jointed rear suspension system, and a three-speed fully automatic gearbox was available as an option.

Beetles for 1964 were practically identical to the '63s but as time went on the Australian-made Beetle became disconnected from its German brother. This came about because of the need to recoup the massive investment made by Wolfsburg in meeting the 95 per cent plan; the reality of this decision was that model year upgrades could not be economically incorporated into the local models. What that meant for local buyers was the use of basically the 1961 body with *some* of the improvements from Germany. We missed out on getting larger windows, uprated windscreen wipers and washers, better heating and demisting and better brakes for several years.

However, for the 1966 model year Australian Beetles received the more powerful 1300cc engine – 77 x 69mm, 1285cc – with 37kW (50bhp), stronger gearbox and wider front brake drums and a '1300' badge, but the old kingpin front suspension remained as did the 6-volt electrics. The engine was essentially the existing 1200 barrels matched with the crankcase and crankshaft of the Type 3 engine. Performance was pretty much the same – 116–122km/h (73–76mph) top speed, 0–96km/h (0–60mph) in 22.8 seconds and, of course, 9.5+ litres per 100km (30+mpg).

Things were the same in 1967 – 1961 body and suspension system – but from May 1968 a near revolution took place with the release of the VW 1500. This blended the Type 1 body with the Type 3 1.5-litre engine to produce the best Beetle ever in the eyes of VW-philes. Not only was there more power – 40kW (53bhp), although it paled compared with 55kW (74bhp) from the Toyota Corona engine, for example – but there were now disc front brakes with separate circuits, an external fuel

The layout of the four-cylinder horizontally-opposed air-cooled engine is the same as for the current unit, but it is much more compact. A gauze filter on the intake side of the pump is the only method of cleaning the oil, which has a cooler, seen to the left of the distributor

filler, 12-volt electrics, stronger bumpers, larger tail-light units and the headlights were now mounted vertically instead of inclined. While the engine shared many components with the Type 3 it did not share the crankshaft-mounted air-cooling fan; true to Beetle folklore the fan remained the large piece of windmill encased in the sheet steel shrouds to blow air over the cylinder barrels.

Volkswagen Australia was fighting to stay in the market and was besieged on all sides by cheaper, more powerful, faster and better-equipped cars like the Toyota Corona, Datsun Bluebird, Mazda 1500, Isuzu Bellett and Prince Skyline not to mention the Ford Cortina and Morris 1100. To this end, in June 1968 VW Australia announced that it would no longer handle the VW business locally. In its place was a new company (in reality the old one renamed) called Motor Producers Limited that would control the Clayton plant and assemble Types 1, 2 and 3 from CKD kits. The new company offered its facilities to other manufacturers in an effort to better utilise the plant's capacity, and Nissan entered into a contract to assemble 15,000 Datsuns annually and soon afterwards Volvo contracted to assemble the 140/240 series at Clayton.

Change would come and that will be discussed in *Australian Cars of the 70s*.

VW·1500

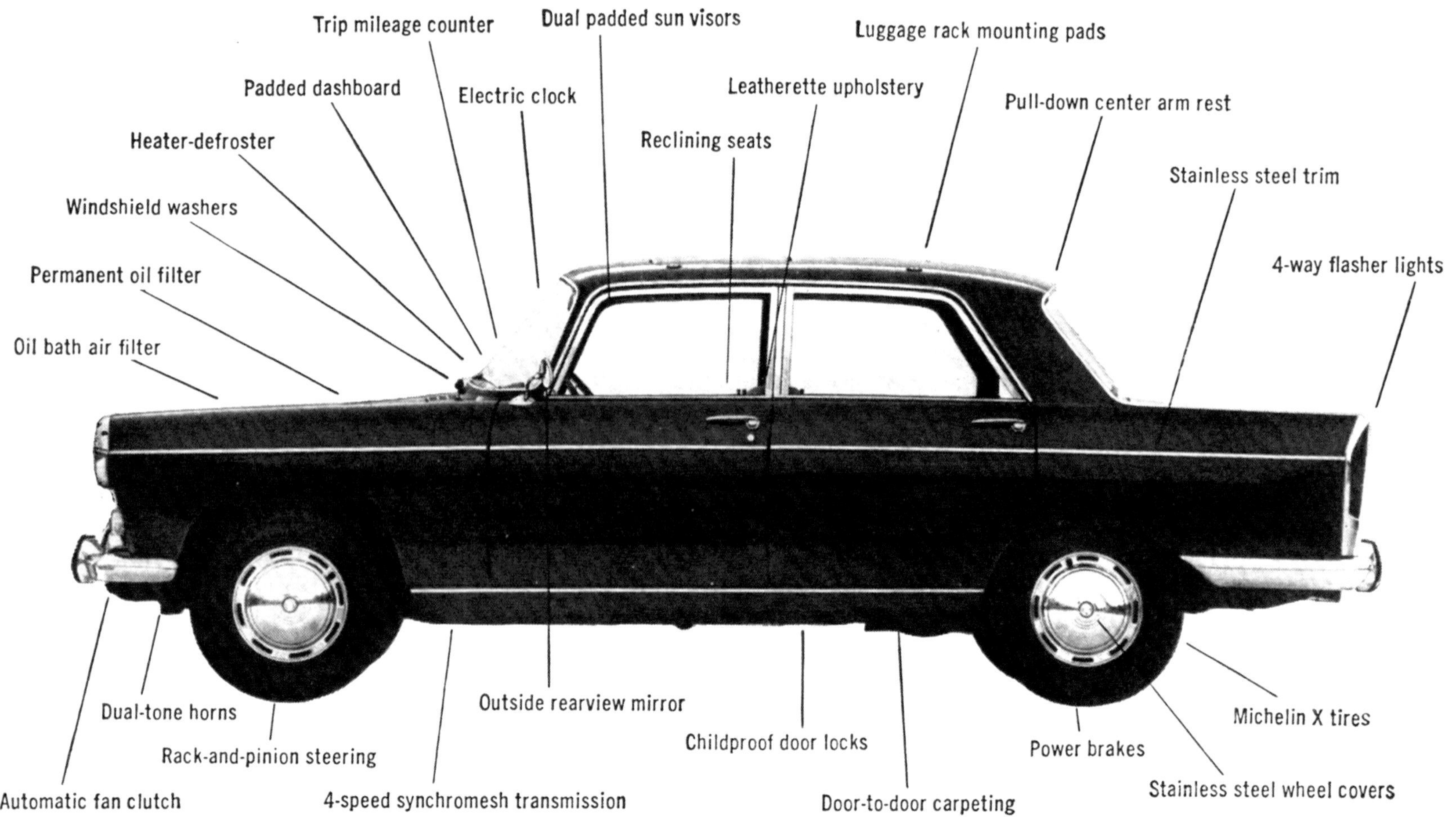
Trip mileage counter
Dual padded sun visors
Luggage rack mounting pads
Padded dashboard
Electric clock
Leatherette upholstery
Pull-down center arm rest
Heater-defroster
Reclining seats
Stainless steel trim
Windshield washers
4-way flasher lights
Permanent oil filter
Oil bath air filter
Outside rearview mirror
Dual-tone horns
Michelin X tires
Childproof door locks
Power brakes
Rack-and-pinion steering
Stainless steel wheel covers
Automatic fan clutch
4-speed synchromesh transmission
Door-to-door carpeting

Chapter 9

THE NICHE MAKERS

By 1960 the urge to create a totally Australian car had subsided somewhat. Mirek Craney had walked away from manufacturing the Ascort and Bill Buckle had ceased making the Buckle GT coupe to concentrate on Goggomobils while Lawrence Hartnett had a small operation going in Brisbane assembling the German Lloyd car. In Adelaide, Harold Lightburn realised a dream he had been nurturing for many years when he announced the Lightburn Zeta, a kind of small utilitarian car that was simple to make and could possibly be made overseas in Third World markets. And despite lofty, over-ambitious plans by Fiat, the assembly operation and agreement with Pressed Metal Corporation in Sydney was ended after less than two years.

CONTINENTAL AND GENERAL

Introduced late in 1961 as a 1962 model was the Peugeot 403B that featured slightly lowered gearing to counter criticism from the media about the car's lack of acceleration, new telescopic dampers replaced the old lever-arm units on the rear suspension, although they remained in use at the front, and the windscreen wiper pattern was changed from a peculiar clap-hands system to the better parallel action. What had not changed was the unusual gearshift pattern. On the exterior, the two chrome side strips were parallel. Like the 203, the 403 was sold in Australia as a sedan with two trim options, a long wheelbase station wagon and as a utility, all of which had a loyal following.

Where the 203 had a 'humpy-back' style reminiscent of various Ford and Chrysler products of the early post-war years, the 403 was a conventional three-box saloon whose styling had been achieved in collaboration with the Italian stylist, Farina, with whom Peugeot had a contract.

Australian Motor Sports carried out a full test in its November 1961 edition and was full of praise for the 403B. As they wrote in their introduction, "The Peugeot first came into the limelight in Australia when the 203 model won the first of the mammoth round-Australia trials. Since then the 403 has been released and this car has won the respect of motorists from all walks of life. The farmer appreciates its long life on tough outback roads, the businessman likes its clean-cut styling and ability to cruise effortlessly at high speeds and the enthusiast has found its roadholding and durability an asset both for racing and trials." As you might have gathered, they liked it! Its maximum speed was 118km/h (74mph) and it ran the 0–96km/h (0–60mph) sprint in 20.0 seconds – not startlingly quick but nevertheless the 403 was brilliantly quick point-to-point like its predecessor. *Modern Motor* also tested the 403B and found it slightly quicker – 127.5km/h (79.7mph) – but also slightly slower – 0–96km/h (0–60mph) in 22.1 seconds. Its price in 1961 was a comparative bargain at £1278.

With the most minor of changes the 403B continued until the end of 1963.

In September 1962 the Peugeot 404 was released with assembly being carried out by Continental and General Distributors. For the first year of 404 production the 403 was continued in parallel such was its popularity. The 404 began life in Australia (as elsewhere) with a 1.6-litre four-cylinder in-line engine that was inclined at an angle of 45 degrees to the right in the engine bay. It was a significant development of the engine from the 403 and shared many of its attributes, like the open-deck cast-iron cylinder block casting with 'wet' cylinder liners, three-bearing forged crankshaft, side camshaft operating cross-over pushrods to give cross-flow porting within a hemispherical combustion chamber, electro-thermatic fan and many other neat features. In the 404 the extra capacity came from cylinder dimensions of 84 x 73mm for 1618cc; initially power was 54kW (72bhp), up from the 403's 48kW (65bhp). This was sufficient to push the 404 to a time of 22.3 seconds for the classic 0–96km/h (0–60mph) sprint and on to a top speed in the region of 139–144km/h (87–90mph), which was outstanding given that its Pininfarina styling had few apparent aerodynamic qualities. As long-time Peugeot enthusiast owners will tell you, it was not the power but the brilliant suspension that allowed the best use of that power to post amazing point-to-point times on long interstate journeys.

Unlike the 403, which featured a transverse leaf independent front suspension, the new 404 was born with Peugeot's first use of the ubiquitous MacPherson strut coil spring front suspension with substantial lower forged links that located the strut while retaining the torque-tube drive to the rear wheels that were suspended by coil springs. Brakes were large diameter 254mm (10in) drums with 142sq in of lining area compared with 228mm (9in) and only 112sq in on the heavier FB-EK Holdens. The 404 was a little larger than the 403, sitting on a wheelbase of 2640mm (104in), was 4420mm (174in) long and weighed a solid 1070kg (2352lb). A companion to the 404 sedan was the station wagon that was built on a longer 2844mm (112in) wheelbase for greater interior room and practicability while the rear suspension featured a pair of coil springs each side. It would prove to be a popular model for many years and quickly gained a faithful following.

Inside were sumptuous bucket seats in front with ample back-and-forth movement, reclining squabs (they could be folded right down to

form a makeshift bed if need be) and a soft vinyl upholstery material over foam rubber cushions and Pirelli webbing. In the back was a wide bench with no wheel arch intrusions, a fold-down centre armrest and the same soft upholstery and supportive webbing. The dashboard was rather plain in appearance but entirely functional; it was straight across the front between the windscreen pillars with a rectangular hooded instrument binnacle in front of the driver that contained a strip speedometer with fuel, temperature and volts dials and a clock underneath, trip and total odometers and some warning lights. The large plastic steering wheel had a full-circle chromed horn ring, big boss with the Peugeot lion, and on the steering column were three levers – the large gearshift lever, indicators/flasher on one side and horn, wipe/wash on the other, and a steering-lock-cum-ignition-switch. A knee pad protected occupants in the event of a crash. Large round, flow-through air vents were located at either side and could be rotated to vary the direction of airflow. It was very 1960s as viewed by one of the world's most conservative but respected automobile manufacturers.

Modern Motor's Bryan Hanrahan tested a 404 in the magazine's February 1963 issue and headed the article with 'One Up For Peugeot'. He described the 404 as a big improvement on the 403, a car that had attracted huge acclaim. With one or two exceptions he enjoyed the interior's roominess and comfort but it was its dynamic road performance that really impressed. The supple all-coil suspension soaked up road surface irregularities with ease and at the same time allowed leech-like cornering with minimal body lean, the rack and pinion steering allowing the driver to place the 404 with pinpoint accuracy. And the big 254mm (10in) diameter brake drums took all the abuse thrown at them. Maximum speed was 132km/h (82.5mph) and the classic 0–96km/h (0–60mph) dash took 21.4 seconds so it was only marginally quicker than the 403, albeit less aerodynamic and slightly heavier with only an extra 5kW (7bhp). At the time of the test the 404's retail price was a highish £1481.

As was the habit with Peugeot in those days, change would come but it was slow and measured and the 404 would have a long and distinguished career all over the world. Peugeot was that kind of company, a little like Mercedes-Benz in Germany. In 1965 the 404 was upgraded with a revised edition of the 1.6-litre engine which received a new five-bearing crankshaft and a host of other seemingly minor modifications that were all aimed at better service life of the car. *Australian Motor Manual* tested the '65 model and found its performance to be slightly better – top speed was 137.6km/h (86mph) and the 0–96km/h (0–60mph) dash took 17.4 seconds while still returning 9.4–8.4 litres per 100km (30–34mpg). In an effort to spice up sales, the price was dropped to £1275.

Two years later, in 1967, the compression was raised to 8.3:1 which raised power to 60kW (80bhp) at 5600rpm and torque to 131Nm (97lb-ft) at 2500rpm. As part of the package came front disc brakes and new-design slotted steel wheels that retained the bolt-on hubcap, while in 1969 an alternator replaced the generator and the dashboard now had padding top and bottom and instrumentation was revised with the dials – clock, speedometer and combination – now all circular. In December 1967 the company introduced a revised gearbox with better ratios and a new conventional gearshift pattern. The suspension had a thicker rear anti-roll bar and the front parking/indicator lens had amber indicators, rectangular reflectors at the rear replaced the previous round ones, the interior trim was revised and the spare wheel was moved to a cradle under the boot floor.

Tested by *Australian Motor Sports* in the May 1969 issue, they noted that while the design was nearly a decade old it still looked classy with the squarish shape bestowing numerous advantages with a high seating position, clear vision, roomy interior and roomy luggage space. Again, the road dynamics came in for considerable praise, especially the low noise level – the 404 had been acknowledged by engineers all over the world as having the lowest levels of road noise, better even than Rolls-Royce. Top speed was 150.7km/h (94.2mph) with 0–80 and 96km/h (0–50 and 60mph) coming up in 10.3 and 15.1 seconds respectively, fuel economy being in the 10–8.4 litres per 100km (28–34mpg) range. At $2575 they rated it one of motoring's all-time bargains.

In the meantime the 404 had been on many markets around the world and had quickly established a reputation for excellence, so much so that the American *Road & Track* magazine included it in their list of the 'world's best seven cars!' Yes, one of the best seven cars in the world – that shows how highly regarded it was. In the harsh glare of competition the 404 had set an enviable benchmark by winning the gruelling East Africa Safari Rally outright in 1966, 1967 and 1968 against all comers. The 1968 event was considered the toughest by far at the time and out of 88 cars that started only nine finished! The winning fuel injected 404 was driven by Bert Shankland with co-driver Chris Rothwell and they lost 572 points in the treacherously muddy conditions.

NSU

Small numbers of the little NSU Prinz were assembled in 1960 and 1961. *Modern Motor* tested a Prinz in its January 1961 issue and came away highly impressed as well as commenting most favourably on the Prinz's success in the 1960 Armstrong 500 race for saloon cars that had been held on the Phillip Island circuit. With former Australian Grand Prix winners Doug Whiteford and Lex Davison and others driving, the NSU's claimed a 1-2-3 class victory. On test the Prinz returned 7 litres per 100km (40mpg) overall, hit a top speed of 120km/h (75mph) and ran the classic 0–96km/h (0–60mph) in 22.0 seconds. The English (*The Motor*) and the Americans (*Road & Track*) also were highly impressed by the car's dynamic character and zip, although both published figures that were fractionally slower than for the Australian car. *Road & Track* said at the end of their report, "Taking everything into consideration, the NSU Prinz is clearly the best designed of all the mini-cars."

Despite good press reviews, sales in Australia were disappointing and the venture was discontinued by late 1961 after the new Prinz 4 had been released in Germany; it came here in small numbers as a full import. As former sale director Mac Chapman said somewhat irreverently about the Prinz, "We used to call them Nothing Stops Us! They were spritely little cars but very noisy and with a very hard ride – good for the race track but not so clever for normal driving – and they were not that reliable. We were not surprised or disappointed when the venture was discontinued." Exactly how many were assembled is not known.

CITROËN

The Citroën ID19 was assembled by Continental and General between 1961 and 1966 during which time it is believed that around 1400 cars were built and sold. Australian-assembled IDs differed in small details from their French cousins by having parallel action wipers (not clap hands), no interior hood lining to the sheet aluminium roof, grey angular dash with Jaeger-made instruments that were later changed to Veglia. It also featured locally-made seat frames and the base unit received extra welds to better cope with the harsh Australian road conditions.

Road tests of Citroëns in Australian car magazines were few and far between but *Wheels* published one in January 1964. As was the way then, they could not help but presage their report by telling their readers just how vastly different a Citroën ID19 was to every other car in Australia, and how expensive they were to maintain. The ID/DS Citroëns were futuristic looking cars with their long shark-like nose for superb aerodynamics, low stance afforded by the unique hydro-pneumatic self-levelling suspension system, inboard front disc brakes and an aged 1911cc OHV four-cylinder engine that developed 56kW (75bhp) at 4500rpm with a Solex carburettor, another 3kW (5bhp) if you ordered a Weber instead. Like the later Renault 16, the ID's engine was behind the gearbox, up against the firewall, with the gearbox out front and the spare wheel located above it.

The locally assembled version was a simplified DS Goddess and soon acquired the local name of Parisienne. For the '64 model year the ID19 gained a new, less complicated and less difficult to use gearchange mechanism (first gear was still not synchronised though). It was a superbly comfortable five-seater that could cruise at high speed no matter what the road surface in total safety. Actual top speed was around 144km/h (90mph) – best one way for *Wheels* was 149km/h (93.2mph) – with acceleration from 0–96km/h (0–60mph) taking 19.9 seconds, not quick. However, Citroën enthusiasts cared little for such figures; they bought the car for its advanced technology and superb driving comfort. At £1697 it was not inexpensive but it did find a certain niche in the market and sold steadily for years.

The year 1964 was a momentous one in the history of Continental and General Distributors because it was in that year that the company bought Canada Cycle and with that they took over the national distribution and assembly of Studebaker cars to add to the Peugeots and Renaults and Citroëns. It meant that assembly of Studebakers was transferred from the old Tottenham factory to West Heidelberg; it also meant that Harden and Johnson in Sydney were dismissed from their Peugeot distribution responsibilities.

The West Heidelberg factory was a hive of activity through the 1960s as the company assembled small numbers of the little NSU Prinz (up to the end of 1961) and the Citroën ID19 (until 1966) in addition to

Peugeot. In 1964 Continental and General began assembling Renaults (R4s and R8s) and in 1966 Renault France bought the company and continued assembling Renaults and Peugeots with all the other brands being discontinued. From that time the company was known as Renault Australia.

RENAULT AUSTRALIA

In July 1960 Renault Australia opened its new headquarters in George Street, Redfern, New South Wales, the new site being their administrative as well as the spare parts repository for the whole of the country and in addition staff technical training was conducted there. As far as the 750 and Dauphine were concerned there were no changes to their specifications but there were two additional models for dealers to sell, both of them fully imported. The first was the Dauphine Gordini which was released in April 1960 powered by an 845cc engine developing 30kW (40bhp) at 5000rpm mated to a four-speed gearbox, with Aerostable rear suspension, rectangular front indicator lights and the fuel filler located in the engine compartment. *Wheels* tested one in April 1961 and returned with a top speed of 126.4km/h (79mph) and a 0–96km/h (0–60mph) time of 17.2 seconds – rather good for such a tiny engine. At the same release also came a startlingly pretty Renault in the form of the Pietro Frua-designed Floride, a two-seater coupe or convertible that used Dauphine Gordini running gear.

From November 1960, for the 1961 model year, the Dauphine underwent a small number of changes from better quality interior trim, nylon door latches to quieten door closing noise, a rear brake pressure limiting valve and Aerostable rear suspension. This consisted of an air-filled cushion in the rear suspension combined with softer coil springs to give a better ride. In February 1961 assembly began of the Dauphine Gordini from CKD packs, these cars featuring ventilated front wheels, round, amber-coloured indicator lenses front and rear, upgraded upholstery, and the price was £1015.

After more than a decade in local production the Renault 750 was replaced by the R4, the first of a completely new generation of front-wheel drive cars from Renault. From June 1962 small numbers of these utilitarian cars were assembled. They were classed as a five-door with their lift-up rear hatch and had a 747cc OHV four-cylinder engine (it was virtually the same unit as in the 750) with a 'sealed for life' cooling system, three-speed manual gearbox with the gearshift lever poking out from the centre of the dashboard. The seats were tubular steel frames with a checked-cloth material over them – they were almost like hammocks – and to add to the load space the rear seat could be easily removed.

In so many ways the R4 was a harbinger of what was to follow and its mechanical layout, too, pointed the way to the future for Renault. The later R5 and R6 were to mimic the layout – gearbox up front with the engine behind, up against the bulkhead – with long torsion bar suspension systems. A comparison test was carried by *Wheels* in September 1962 in which they compared the R4 with the Morris 850 and the Fiat 600D. They were cars competing for buyers with only £800 to spend and as you would expect the R4 was the odd one out – four-doors, lift-up rear hatch, soft suspension to absorb rough roads, station wagon-style body with

ample room for four passengers and their luggage, the large bonnet was hinged behind the bumper bar and tipped forwards, all exterior panels bolted on for easy replacement. But when it came to performance the R4 was third out of three with the slowest top speed (115km/h/72mph) and poorest acceleration (0–80km/h/0–50mph in 18.0 secs), the three-speed gearbox not helping there.

One of the best-selling Renaults of the day was the pert little R8 that arrived on local showroom floors in April 1963. It carried on the tradition of being rear-engined from the Dauphine (which it replaced) and 750 but clothed it in a body that laid claim to a great deal of time in the wind tunnel – Renault boasted of dihedral planes and other technical items that gave it a superior Cd (coefficient of drag). Looking at its very three-box appearance it was perhaps a little hard to swallow but the R8 did boost Renault's presence and sales in Australia significantly. Initially the R8 was assembled by Martin and King in Melbourne (they had been assembling the 750 and Dauphine since June 1958) before the operation was transferred to Continental and General in July 1964 with the local content comprising paint, glass and other minor items.

The R8 introduced buyers to the new 'Sierra' small four-cylinder engine with its cast-iron block and alloy head, 'wet' cylinder liners and five-bearing crankshaft; its bore and stroke were 65 x 72mm for a capacity of 956cc from which was extracted 36kW (48bhp) at 5200rpm and 74Nm (55 lb-ft) of torque at 2500rpm. As before, the engine was overhung at the rear and drove the rear wheels through a four-speed gearbox without synchromesh on first gear and operated by a floor shift lever. A surprise for this class of car was the use of *four*-wheel non-boosted 260mm (10.25in) Lockheed disc brakes – a world-first. The R8 rode on slotted steel wheels shod with 145 x 15 Michelin steel radial tyres, although some cars were fitted with 135 x 15 tyres. As for size, the R8 rode the same 2286mm (90in) wheelbase as the Dauphine but at 3987mm (157in) was 51mm (2in) longer, at 1498mm (59in) in width was actually an inch narrower (although wider inside!) and it stood 1397mm (55in) high. Kerb weight was a light 712kg (1568lb).

Modern Motor published a full test of the new R8 in its June 1963 issue and was full of praise for the little French sedan. They loved the individuality of the design from the wide-opening doors with no wheel-arch cut-outs at the rear, to the clamshell-type front lid that exposed the commodious luggage space and battery, with the spare wheel in a separate compartment behind the front number plate. The square shape meant that there were few compromises inside as far as comfort for four people was concerned. In fact, the seats were a new design using polyurethane foam and soft vinyl upholstery; they really did cosset you, you sat *in* them and not on them as with most other cars at the time. Handling gained praise as did cornering so long as the Michelins were inflated above the factory recommended pressures. There was a small amount of wander in windy conditions but it was less of an issue than with the VW Beetle, for example. The standard heating and fresh air ventilation system (there were large circular vents each end of the dash) came in for high praise, too. Instrumentation was minimalist and was housed in a flat rectangular binnacle in front of the driver; the speedometer was a strip type with a fuel gauge under it plus some warning lights.

Braking, of course, was given a big thumbs up as was the accuracy of the steering; the gearshift was accurate but felt 'woolly' in comparison with the VW and the foot pedals came up through the floor – unusual for a new design at the time. As for its performance, the magazine recorded a top speed of 129.6km/h (81mph), a 0–96km/h (0–60mph) time of 19.4 seconds and an economy of 6.8 litres per 100km (42mpg) in normal driving conditions giving a range of between 400 and 450km (250 and 280 miles) on a tank. At £998 it was very competitively priced.

In its advertising of the R8 Renault made much of the braking system plus the comfort of the new seat design which set new standards in the class. *Wheels* magazine was so impressed that it voted the Renault R8 its inaugural Car of the Year! In the same issue, January 1964, the magazine carried out a four-car comparison between the R8, Fiat 1100, Simca Aronde and Toyota Tiara. Naturally the R8 was the odd one out being rear-engined and with a fully independent suspension system and four-wheel disc brakes. The three European cars were priced just under the magic £1000 barrier but the Toyota was priced at £915 and had the most equipment – a familiar story? All four ran to a fraction under 128km/h (80mph) top speed and the R8 was second quickest in acceleration behind the Tiara that had an engine 500cc larger in capacity. The Renault R8 was generally considered to be the most comfortable and best to drive.

In July 1964 Renault quietly slipped an 1108cc version of the five-bearing engine into the engine bay of the R8 and badged it, appropriately enough, as the R8 1100. The Renault R8 1100 appeared almost indistinguishable from the outside apart from an '1100' badge below the right-hand tail-light and an L-shaped chrome strip on the C-pillar. Extra capacity for the engine had come from wider cylinder bores – now 70mm – that gave 1108cc, raising power to 37kW (50bhp) at 4900rpm and torque to 83Nm (61 lb-ft) at 2500rpm. Accompanying the increased capacity engine there was a new four-speed all-synchromesh gearbox. Performance was basically identical to the original, surprisingly, and the price remained at £998.

From a business point of view, 1964 was a momentous year for Renault because they announced a unique agreement in which they would collaborate with their European rivals, Peugeot, for the assembly and distribution of their cars in Australia. Renault Australia took over the distribution network and at the same time the assembly of cars was transferred from Martin and King at Somerton, Victoria, to Continental and General at West Heidelberg.

A revised R4 came along in late 1962 and cost £839 now with the 845cc engine and all of 24kW (32bhp) at 4700rpm was joined in 1964 by a panel van version for tradies with a price tag of just £799.

Renault Australia imported a small number of R8 Gordini 1100 sedans in July 1965. Available only in French Racing Blue with white racing stripes (it was a roll in the glovebox for dealers or owners to fit later) and a 'Gordini' badge under the right-hand tail-light there was very little to see – the ultimate Q-ship perhaps? Inside the dashboard had circular instruments – large tachometer and speedometer in front of the driver with smaller temperature and fuel contents in the centre. At the press launch only journalists who held a current CAMS licence were allowed to drive it.

Under the rear bonnet Amédée Gordini – known in France as 'Le Sorcier' – had worked some kind of magic. The engine's capacity remained at 1108cc but a new aluminium alloy cross-flow cylinder head sat atop the block. It featured cross-over pushrods (like a Peugeot) so there were four intake ports on the right (driver's side in Australia) and four exhaust ports on the left with the spark plug down the centre at the top of the hemispherical combustion chamber. Two Solex 40PHH carburettors fed the intake and a beautifully fabricated four-branch exhaust manifold was bolted to the other side. On a 10.5:1 compression the engine produced 70kW (95bhp) at 6500rpm and 103Nm (76 lb-ft) of torque at 5500rpm.

Little else was changed apart from harder disc pads with a vacuum booster for the braking system, the suspension was firmed up using higher rate coil springs and twin dampers for each rear wheel, and it had been lowered by 25mm. Imported Gordinis wore Dunlop SP radials.

The R8 Gordini was a little rocket ship on the road. Accompanied by a rorty exhaust just to remind you what you were driving, the car shot to 80km/h (50mph) in 8.9 seconds, on to 96km/h (60mph) in 12.3 seconds, and to 112km/h (70mph) in 16.8 seconds, peaked at 43km/h (27mph) in first gear at 7000rpm, 80km/h (50mph) in second, 126km/h (79mph) in third and 169.6km/h (106mph) in top! *Wheels* summed up its test by writing, "Staggeringly fast, generally inspired handling and all-round performance that will make big car owners sick with envy." Its

9021-NW75

price off the showroom floor was £1315, a tad over £300 more than the standard R8.

August 1966 was another memorable month for the company with the acquisition of the Continental and General business and facility at Doughty Road, West Heidelberg, renaming it Renault Australia with Jacques Thoridnet as managing director. In the same month it introduced the R10, this being an evolutionary development of the R8. The original R8 cabin section and wheelbase was retained but new sheet metal graced the body front and rear of the body. What was improved was the luggage space up front: the R8's luggage space was good for a rear-engined car but the R10 was even better thanks to the 203mm (8in) nose extension. Headlights were round with the parking and indicator lenses integrated and curved around the corner of the front fender. At the rear the tail-light units continued to be rectangular and were placed horizontally, high on the tail panel. Inside the dash had a walnut finish as did the steering wheel spokes and gearshift knob and was a carry-over from the 1966 R8.

Critics have been divided on the merits of the R10's styling, certainly there was no mention of aerodynamic capabilities this time round.

During late 1966 the R4 wagon was discontinued but the R4 van was continued and received a 12-volt electric system – unbelievable! – but the more important event was the beginning of local assembly in April of the R8 Gordini 1300 in batches of 10 units at a time. These cars featured four headlights, laminated windscreen, twin fuel tanks (26 litres in front, 38 litres at the rear), power-assisted braking system, and a 1255cc Gordini-modified engine driving a five-speed all-synchromesh gearbox. The cylinder bore x stroke was now 74.5 x 72mm for 1255cc and with the dual 40DCOE Weber carburettors developed 82kW (110bhp) at 6750rpm and 116Nm (86lb-ft) of torque at 5000rpm. Its performance was stunning for such a small car, its top speed being in the region of 168–172km/h (105–108mph) with the 0–80 and 96km/h (0–50 and 60mph) times being 7.5 and 10.6 seconds. There were many engineers who did not believe the road-test figures because to achieve speeds and times like those meant that there had to be an engine of more than 2 litres under the bonnet. Not so!

Both the initial batches were painted Cannes Blue and to own one you had to have a CAMS license. Two more batches of 10 units were assembled in 1968 painted Moyen Blue and in 1969 the final two batches were assembled and painted Daffodil Yellow. The showroom price was a hefty $2998, big money for a small car in 1967.

From December 1967 a minor styling upgrade of the R10 came as a running change with the headlights now being square with the parking/indicator lights separate and under them, and the tail-lights were placed lower down on the rear panel, flanking the number plate.

In May 1968 *Wheels* published a four-car comparison titled "Four Aces in the Jackpot" in which they compared the Renault 10 with the Toyota Corona, Morris 1100S and Datsun 1600. As was usual, the Renault was the odd one out by having its engine overhung at the rear. All four were aimed at families who needed four doors and had a budget of around $2000. The Datsun was the newest design and was regarded by many in the media as the best thing since sliced bread while the Renault was by far the oldest, the Morris 1100S the most innovative. In terms of performance there was not a lot in it but the Renault was the slowest at 130.8km/h (81.8mph) and almost last in the 0–80km/h (0–50mph) dash at 11.2 seconds but it did have the smallest capacity engine and at 789kg (1736lb) it was the lightest by around 77kg (170lb). The testers were full of praise for the Renault's seats and general levels of comfort inside, although rear-seat legroom could be tight for an adult, but was fine for kids. As for its handling on the Michelin X radials, the testers said, "Once the limit of adhesion is passed the car can become a handful to the novice driver, especially in the wet."

The R10 was priced at $1999 and offered buyers a reasonable level of equipment and the knowledge that they were buying a unique automobile that had gained considerable favour among Australian motorists.

One of the world's truly inspiring cars arrived in Australia, and off the Heidelberg assembly line, in July 1968 – the Renault 16. It was one of those rare cars that came along every now and again; it was a 'clean sheet' design that was based on a new concept of family motoring that had an interior of incredible versatility and a technical specification that showed a degree of cleverness not exhibited by many car manufacturers before or since.

Built on a platform base with the body structure welded to it, the R16 had a wheelbase of 2650mm (104in) on the right and 2717mm (106.9in) on the left, the difference being because the rear suspension comprised parallel transverse torsion bars extending almost the full width of the body and so the wheelbase varied slightly to compensate. Up front were very long longitudinal torsion bars operating on upper and lower wishbones with telescopic dampers. As was typical of French cars then, wheel travel was generous and the suppleness of the suspension allowed considerable body lean when cornering.

Continuing with the model's individuality was the drive-train, which again was not conventional. As Citroën had done with the Traction Avant and continued with the ID/DS, Renault's engineers designed a completely new in-line four-cylinder engine that was behind the gearbox, up against the bulkhead. It featured the use of diecast aluminium alloy castings for the cylinder block (open deck with 'wet' liners) and cylinder head, with the camshaft at the top of the block. In the initial model the engine's bore and stroke were 76 x 81mm for a capacity of 1470cc. On a compression ratio of 8.6:1 and using a single Solex carburettor it developed 47kW (63bhp) at 5000rpm, and 105Nm (78 lb-ft) of torque at 2800rpm, hardly earth-shattering figures but sufficient to provide more than adequate performance.

Positioned in front of the engine was a four-speed all-synchromesh gearbox loosely based on that of the R10 but operated by a column gearshift. Naturally, drive went to the front wheels. Completing the specifications were rack and pinion steering and a non-boosted disc/drum braking system.

The cleverness continued inside the 16 where seven options were available to owners. They were labelled in the brochures as the normal configuration where the seats were in their usual positions and the luggage area (accessed through the lift-up tailgate) was loaded with cases; Holiday-bound, where the rear seat was moved forward by 6in to increase the luggage space; Outsize load, where the rear seat was tipped forward, the backrest was hitched up to hooks and the luggage space doubled in capacity; Going away for the summer where the rear seat and backrest were removed; Taking the baby where the rear seat was pushed fully forward to touch the front seat making a safe (by the standards of 1968!) place for the baby to travel; Rally position where the rear seat-back can be positioned to extend the front seat-back to make a recliner chair; and the Sleeping position where the front seats and the rear squab join to give a comfortable temporary bed for two. It really was quite some car and it did not take Australian buyers long to catch on, making the 16 a very popular car.

A road test appeared in *Wheels* magazine, August 1968, under the headline 'Sweet Sixteen.' It was aimed by Renault Australia at the market populated by the Mazda 1500, Austin 1800, Isuzu Florian and Fiat 125 where it was above the price level of most of the four-cylinder cars on the market and at a point where buyers looked for more than just the price in their decision making. High levels of finish, equipment and comfort were priorities as well as reasonable levels of performance. The combination of a supple suspension system and well-designed seats gave passengers a cosseting ride while the 1.5-litre engine delivered a top speed of 134km/h (84mph) and the ability to dash from 0–96km/h (0–60mph) in 17.6 seconds, and return 8.9–7.5 litres per 100km (32–38mpg) economy. Its party trick was the extremely versatile interior that set it apart from every other car on the market and it was this that ultimately became its unique selling point (USP) on the showroom floor. Its price was just $2495.

Modern Motor tested a 16 in the same month in a test headed by the words "Renault 16: French masterpiece" and they, too, loved it although some of the tiny details were found to be disappointing. They published figures of 139km/h (87mph) top speed, 16.3 seconds for the dash to 96km/h (60mph) and 10.8–8.6 litres per 100km (26–33mpg) fuel economy.

From March 1969 Renault added the 16TS to the range. This was far more than a new badge; it was a thorough re-engineering of the total 16 package. A new alloy crossflow cylinder head with a twin-barrel Weber carburettor along with new cylinder dimensions (77 x 84mm for 1565cc) saw power rise to 65kW (87.5bhp) at 5750rpm, torque to 118Nm (86.8 lb-ft) at 3500rpm. Along with the revitalised engine came a slightly firmer suspension, upgraded brakes, thicker anti-roll bars, wider section Michelin XAS radial tyres, a pair of quartz halogen driving lights up front and a new set of round instruments in front of the driver replacing the rather drab rectangular unit of the standard car. Against the clock the 16TS proved to be a spirited car reaching a top speed of 161.6km/h (101mph) with 48, 80 and 122km/h (30, 50 and 76mph) being available in the indirect gears, the 0–96km/h (0–60mph) time was down to 12.1 seconds and it would still return between 10 and 7.8 litres per 100km (28 and 36mpg) fuel economy.

The 16TS replaced the R8 Gordini as the main weapon of choice for a number of top rally drivers in Australia because it was more readily available and also because the company wanted to prove the durability of the model using a 'production' model rather than one more specialised. Between leaving Ford Australia's competitions department and prior to joining the Holden Dealer Team, Harry Firth cast his magic over the 16TS and developed a superb rally car out of it. Three cars were built and all featured side draught 42DCOE Weber carburettors, extractor exhaust system and suspension modifications. With 86kW (110hp) at its disposal the 16TS had a very successful year and finished second to a highly modified Ford Cortina in the 1969 Australian Rally Championship.

Through the sixties the company participated in limited competition events beginning with the Armstrong 500 at Phillip Island. Four cars were entered – two Renault 750s and two Dauphines. Car 8, a 750 driven by Park/Fleming finished 10th in Class A and 34th overall and was the final car to be classified as a finisher; car 9 crewed by Emmett/Hawkins DNFd; car 11 crewed by Bill Pitt and Leo Geoghegan finished 11th in Class B and 25th overall; car 12, a Dauphine crewed by Des West and Ian Geoghegan was also in Class B and finished 10th in class and 24th overall.

The following year two cars were entered in Class D: car 3 was a Dauphine Gordini for Jim Gullan/Brian Sampson/John Connolly that finished 1st in class and 9th outright, and car 4, also a Gordini, for Bill March/Norm Beechey that finished 2nd in class and 10th outright. In 1963 a solitary Dauphine Gordini was entered for Rex Emmett/John Connolly/Brian Sampson and it finished 1st in class and 6th outright.

Renault 8s, 10s and 16s were privately entered in various Bathurst 500 events but no notable results were achieved.

On the rally side of things, success was quite spectacular in comparison. Mal McPherson and Robin Sharpley in a Renault 8 Gordini 1300 won the 1967 BP Rally outright; second outright was another R8 Gordini 1300 driven by Bruce Collier and Lindsay Adcock while Gerry Crown and Nigel Collier came 7th in a third R8 Gordini. In the 1967 Southern Cross Rally Bruce Collier and Lindsay Adcock finished 1st in Class C.

Driving one of the Harry Firth-modified 16TSs Bob Watson took second place in the 1969 Australian Rally Championship and was the outright winner of the Victorian Rally Championship for that year with Jim McAuliffe as his navigator. Over the border Adrian Callary and Gary Chapman won the 1969 South Australian Rally Championship in a standard 16TS.

CANADA CYCLE AND MOTOR COMPANY LTD

Studebaker was the saviour of Canada Cycle but unfortunately its star was on the wane in America because the corporation was not robust enough, nor did it have the financial resources to compete in a market where, through the actions of Ford and GM, buyers had been educated to only be interested in the 'value' of the trade-in. The company simply did not have the resources to combat the Big Two and gradually lost market share despite having good cars to sell.

The Lark was an instant sales success on its release in Australia in October 1960. Small numbers had been imported before this but once Canada Cycle got the range up and running sales increased substantially as supplies were plentiful and there was a significant reduction in the retail price brought about by a reduction in tariffs. It was regarded as a compact car in the US market, equivalent to the newcomers from Ford (the Falcon) and Chrysler (Valiant) but its basic engineering was a left-over from an earlier era in the US where all cars were made using separate chassis with the monocoque body bolted to it. The new wave compacts featured unitary body construction and many new technologies that Studebaker could not afford. Despite that, the Lark sold well because it was an extremely rugged car with electrifying performance for the day.

Built on a 2743mm (108in) wheelbase and with an overall length of 4572mm (180in) the Lark was slightly bigger than the EK Holden and about the same size as the new Falcon and Valiant; it was, however, significantly heavier at 1350kg (2968lb) at the kerb. Some of the weight had to do with the type of body construction – body-on-chassis – but more had to do with what was under the bonnet where a heavy 259cid (90.4 x 82.6mm, 4247cc) cast-iron V8 engine resided. Running a two-barrel carburettor and an 8.3:1 compression it developed 134kW (180bhp) at 4500rpm and a mountain of torque. It was, in reality, an engine designed by engineers from the old school for a very long and reliable service life.

Power was delivered to the rear wheels through either a three-speed manual or a three-speed automatic gearbox. The front suspension was

by upper-and-lower wishbones with coil springs, hydraulic dampers and an anti-roll bar while the rear was by way of semi-elliptic leaf springs and telescopic dampers on a live axle. Braking was by 254mm (10in) cast-iron drums all round and the steering was a cam and peg system, neither having servo assistance. It rode on 6.40 x 15 tyres at a time when everybody else was running 6.40 x 13s. It was, in effect, a very conservative and conventional car designed and built by a very conservative US company. However, it was ideal for the tough Australian conditions and with prices starting at £1665 it was not long before Canada Cycle's order books were full.

From a styling point of view the Lark was modern and distinctive, its design featuring a prominent ridge at waist level all the way around the body that was picked out by a chrome strip that dipped on the rear doors; at the front was a large, almost square grille with a fine weave pattern flanked at first by single headlights with a supplementary air grille alongside. The later Chrysler Valiant would feature a similar grille. The windscreen was a semi-wraparound and the rear window curved around into the C-pillar, while at the rear were simple single unit multi-function tail-lights set in a plinth each side with a high boot line hiding a commodious boot spoiled only by the spare wheel placement on the floor.

What was noticeable was the comparative lack of equipment inside. The wide bench seats were upholstered in locally-sourced vinyl, the floor had rubber mats and not carpet on it, the foot pedals came up through the floor (could the Lark have been the last car in the world with this feature?) and there was no heater/demister or radio although they were listed as options. The dash was a rather plain affair with a wide binnacle in front of the driver; it contained two large round dials that informed the driver of their road speed on the right, fuel contents and engine temperature in the left. Below them were switches for lights and wipers. A similarly shaped recess in front of the passenger contained the glove box.

Canada Cycle expanded their range beginning in February 1961 by offering the W body (2743mm/108in wheelbase) sedan, Y body Cruiser sedan (2870mm/113in wheelbase), a station wagon (P body) on the 2870mm (113in) wheelbase, and the Hawk two-plus-two coupe

that used the C body. What they did not do was to offer the Lark with the low-powered (75kW/100bhp) ancient six-cylinder engine, instead opting to go V8 only which was a good move, the Larks having a 259cid engine and the Hawk the 289cid version.

Wheels published a full road test in its May 1961 issue and they were impressed with the car, achieving a maximum speed of 162.8km/h (101.8mph) with 76.8 and 128km/h (48 and 80mph) available in first and second gears. It ran the 0–96km/h (0–60mph) sprint in 12.2 seconds and returned 18.8 litres per 100km (15.5mpg) after all tests. In conclusion they wrote, “Its general performance, size and strength should make it a car ideally suited for the variety of conditions that faces the Australian motorist.”

In 1961 a number of police special Larks were assembled, their specification including the 289cid V8 equipped with a four-barrel carburettor, heavy-duty manual three-speed gearbox and clutch, model 44 heavy duty Spicer differential (it was standard in the Hawk and station wagons), finned brake drums and dual exhausts. Both the Victorian and New South Wales forces would run Larks for their highway patrol work.

For the year, around 718 Studebakers were assembled and sold.

The Victorian police force soon had a fleet of Larks that were used for pursuit work. A team of police drivers entered a Lark in the 1961 Armstrong 500 which was held then on Phillip Island, along with another entered by York Motors from Sydney. Although quick, the York Motors car (driven by David McKay and Brian Foley) was beaten into second place outright by Bob Jane and Harry Firth who co-drove a Mercedes-Benz 220 SE; the other Lark (driven by Fred Sutherland and Bill Graetz) came third in class and fourth outright so it was a good showing. Canada Cycle together with the Police Car Club entered a Lark each in 1962 with the Sutherland/Graetz Police car actually being flagged the winner but a recount of lap charts put it back to second place, again. The winning car was again driven by Harry Firth and Bob Jane – a Ford Falcon XL would you believe? The second Lark driven by Don Algie and Kingsley Hibbard finished eighth in Class D.

With the race transferred north to Mount Panorama near Bathurst from 1963, two Larks were entered and driven by Warren Weldon and Bill Needham which finished fourth in Class D some 15 laps behind the

Firth/Jane winning Ford Cortina GT and the other by Jim Wright and Ian Ferguson which did not finish. Two were entered in 1964 – driver pairings were Warren Weldon/Bert Needham and Fred Sutherland/ Allan Mottram – and came home first and second in Class D two and four laps respectively in arrears of the winning Cortina GT of Bob Jane and George Reynolds. In 1965 two Larks were again entered but they finished a long way behind the Cortina GT500. The Lark would see two more years at Bathurst, in 1966 with Warren Weldon and Bill Slattery where they would finish in 38th place and in 1967 (the year of the Falcon GT) they would finish in 11th place. The Lark's swansong was in 1968 when Weldon and Hall drove to finish in eighth place in Class D.

In its brief-but-spectacular racing career the Achilles heel of the Lark was not its power, acceleration or top speed, it was its brakes. They were simply not up to the rigours of long-distance racing particularly at Bathurst.

With the parent company in South Bend, Indiana, experiencing tough times, the styling of the Lark was altered only by new front and rear sheet metal during its tenure on the local market. This meant that for 1962 came a Mercedes-Benz like grille (Studebaker was the Mercedes importer-distributor for the USA) flanked by dual headlights with the indicator lens incorporated in their lower surround, and round tail-lights positioned at waist level with the separate indicator lights just below them. The boot lid was a new pressing and had a much lower lip than previously. From 1962 Canada Cycle rationalised the range and settled on the longer 2870mm (113in) wheelbase for all Larks which took the overall length out to 4775mm (188in). This provided considerably more room inside, particularly for those in the back seat who had vast amounts of legroom to go with already generous head and shoulder room. The showroom price for the manual Lark sedan was £1645, the automatic cost £1799 and now included a heater and windscreen washers (they were extra in the manual) and the wagon cost from £1885. That year the company assembled and sold 1214 units, good business.

For 1963, when 1439 units were assembled (1262 sedans, 152 wagons, 25 Hawks), the styling remained largely unchanged although it now featured a flatter windscreen and repositioned A-pillars. The Lark was now available with either the 259- or 289cid V8. New this year was the Daytona Wagonaire station wagon with the sliding rear roof section, power coming from the 259cid V8 and the Gran Turismo came with 289cid power, three-speed automatic and the option of bucket or bench front seat. New for '63 was a restyled dashboard that featured a prominent binnacle in front of the driver containing three large round dials – speed on the right, decoration/clock in the centre and fuel/temperature gauges in the left one. At either end of the binnacle were slots where the heater/ demister slides would be if fitted, and on the lower edge were four piano-key type switches. A large glove box was in front of the passenger and a grille for the optional radio speaker was on the dash top.

By this time Westminster carpets were standard on the floor, the seats were still of the bench type front and rear, and the foot pedals still came up through the floor.

The 1964 models brought renewed exterior styling with new sheet metal at the front to go with the previous year's revised rear bodywork. This time there was a horizontal grille flanked by dual headlights and small(ish) horizontal tail-lights. An unusual feature of the body styling was the strakes that faced forward from the front wheel arch and rearwards from the rear wheel arch. Small diecast pieces on the rear fenders married the horizontal light units to the flow of the styling lines where on the '63 there had been round lights; in Australia the top lens was for tail/brake lights and the lower lens was amber for indicators/ reversing lights – in the USA both lenses were red. The roof pressing was new because the rear window was now flat like the front windscreen.

Their mechanical specifications and method of construction remained unchanged as did the dashboard and interior.

The Victorian police took delivery of several 'specials' based on the Cruiser, whose specification included 289cid 4V engine with dual exhaust system, four-speed manual gearbox with a floor shifter, finned brake drums, 44 Spicer rear axle and windscreen wipers converted for right-hand drive. They also took delivery of a reasonable number of Commander two-door sedans with the high-performance specifications.

For this year Canada Cycle assembled both the Wagonaire and a conventional Daytona fixed-roof station wagon following owner complaints about dust and water entry with the Wagonaire. It was one of those great ideas whose time had yet to come and sadly for Studebaker they failed to design a sufficiently good sealing system for our market.

By this time Canada Cycle had built up local content to 45 per cent which was quite remarkable. Locally sourced items included the seat frames, upholstery and other interior fabrics, paint colours that were mostly unique to the Australian cars, the radiator top tank was a local item and larger in capacity to suit local conditions, the battery, wheels, tyres as well as the hubcaps were also sourced locally.

In October 1964 the assembly operations were transferred to Continental and General across town in West Heidelberg. In that year just under 1000 units were sold, with production continuing into 1965 (the cars were unchanged) when a further 548 units were sold.

Continental and General continued assembling Studebakers from CKD kits in 1965 and 1966 but they were dispatched from Hamilton, Ontario (in Canada) by this time because Studebaker had transferred its automobile division to that city and closed South Bend, Indiana. It was the last throw of the dice for the company as a car manufacturer. The cars were now powered by the famous small block Chevrolet 283cid V8 engine mated to a Borg Warner three-speed automatic gearbox. On a 9.25:1 compression and with a Rochester two-barrel carburettor it produced 145kW (195bhp) at 4800rpm and 386Nm (285 lb-ft) of torque at 2400rpm and endowed the big sedan (now badged as Cruiser, no longer Lark) with impressive performance. Maximum speed was 160km/h (100mph) with the 0–96km/h (0–60mph) dash taking 12.0 seconds, good for a sedan weighing 1455kg (3200lb). On test by *Australian Motor Manual* it returned 16.8 litres per 100km (17mpg) giving a range of only 400km (250 miles) from the 68-litre (15gal) tank.

Equipment levels had improved dramatically, with a push-button radio, heater/demister, windscreen washers, dashboard padding, door and centre seat armrests, night dipping rear-view mirror, and courtesy light switches on all doors among the long list of items. Curiously, power-assisted steering and boosted disc front brakes were never made available locally although they were available ex-Hamilton and, indeed, from South Bend prior to the move. One has to wonder why.

Interestingly, two Studebakers were entered by the Victorian police in conjunction with Continental and General in the Sandown International Six-Hour touring car race for 1964 with the driver pairings being Fred Sutherland/Allan Mottram and Roger Wood/Warren Weldon; they took first and second respectively in Class A (over 3000cc) and ran without incident.

Studebaker's 'halo' car through the late fifties and into the sixties was the Hawk. In the US it was available as the Silver Hawk or the Golden Hawk depending on what engine was fitted. Between 1960 and 1962 a handful of 'finned' Hawks were assembled before being replaced in Australia by the Studebaker Gran Turismo, the body styling for which had been upgraded by consultant Brooke Stevens. For 1962 it was really a two-door hardtop coupe competing in a niche market for buyers who were seeking something quite different in their motoring lives. The last batch of Gran Turismos was assembled by Canada Cycle in late 1963 and it took until May 1966 to sell them. Today they are collector's cars.

Modern Motor carried out a full road test of a Gran Turismo in its May 1962 edition. Bryan Hanrahan, the tester, loved it. He found it would carry six people (it had a bench front seat) although he did say, "I would have liked to see bucket seats with split, fold-forward squabs." He liked the neat touches like two armrests in the back, coat hooks each side and a single roof interior light. What he especially liked from the driver's perspective was the complete set of Stewart-Warner gauges – tachometer, speedometer, coolant temperature, engine oil pressure, ammeter and fuel contents – all with white graphics on a black background.

On the road the 168kW (225bhp) 289cid V8 provided plenty of performance, from the 171km/h (107mph) top speed, standing quarter mile in 18.7 seconds, 0–96 and 112km/h (0–60 and 70mph) times of 9.9 and 14.0 seconds respectively, 0–160km/h (0–100mph) in 37.6 seconds, and 16.6 litres per 100km (17.2mpg). By the standards of 1962 and for a big two-door hardtop coupe (3000mm (120in) wheelbase, 5182mm (204in) length and 1464kg (3220lb) kerb weight) those figures were sensational. As Hanrahan commented, "This could be a highly rewarding car with a four-speed manual gearbox with a floor lever." He did not like the low-geared steering and felt that there was too much understeer

TWA
LOS ANGELES
SAN FRANCISCO
MADRID
ITALY
ALITALIA

although he found the finned drum brakes to be just fine. At £2397 the Gran Turismo was priced to attract an exclusive clientele.

Intriguingly, throughout this period Studebaker Larks were never offered with front disc brakes (they really needed them!) or power-assisted steering although a Repco after-market unit was retro-fitted by some dealers, Smiths heaters were fitted when ordered for local content reasons in place of the US-sourced unit, power brakes were never an option although a PBR kit could be dealer-fitted. There were a small number of modifications made by Canada Cycle to facilitate easier assembly and included here was repositioning the engine slightly to the left in the engine bay using modified front mounts, which gave more clearance for the steering box and linkage. This space limitation precluded the use of a full-flow oil filter on the right-hand side of the engine and so a bypass system was developed with the filter attached to the oil filler tube at the front top of the engine.

Sadly, Studebaker was unable to maintain the effort and closed its automobile division in Hamilton on 16 March 1966. This meant the end to local assembly of a car that had proven to be strong and reliable in Australian conditions and was a sales success from its introduction here. The fact that its engineering could be regarded as 'old school' was seen as a huge bonus by buyers, particularly those in rural areas where the roads were poor and where towing heavy trailers was the norm.

BUCKLE-GOGGOMOBIL

Production and sales of the Buckle-made Goggomobil sedan and Dart sports car continued through 1960 until ending in November 1961, the company adding the TS400 Coupe to the range in mid-1960. As they had done with the sedan, Buckle imported a single German-bodied TS400 with steel panels and used that as a master to make the moulds for the fibreglass panels for the Australian-made version.

The son of Hans Glas, Andreas Glas, is generally credited with styling the TS400 and for one who was untrained in the art made a good fist of it. The front was dominated by the silver-painted heart-shaped 'grille' with the 'G' badge on the edge of the front panel and under the headlights was the round indicator lens incorporated in a small simulated grille as a styling feature. The sides were completely smooth and unadorned except for a tiny air scoop each side above the rear wheels that fed air into the rear engine compartment. Small two-part, teardrop-shaped tail-lights were positioned at the peak of the rear fenders. There was no front bonnet opening and the two doors were rear-hinged ('suicide' doors) which must make them the last of their kind.

Under the neat body was a platform similar to the Goggo sedan with a wheelbase of 1790mm (70.5in) and an overall length of 2997mm (118in) riding on tiny 10in split rims and 4.80 x 10 tyres. Like its siblings the TS400 was powered by a two-cylinder two-stroke engine of 392cc capacity (67 x 56mm) developing 15kW (20bhp) at 5000rpm. *Australian Motor Manual* published a full road test in its November 1960 issue and found the little coupe would run to just 101.6km/h (63.5mph) with in-gear maxima of 27, 54 and 80km/h (17mph, 34mph and 50mph) from the four-speed constant mesh gearbox. Acceleration from 0–80km/h (0–50mph) took 20.9 seconds, to 96km/h (60mph) took 29.8 seconds and from 32–64km/h (20–40mph) in third gear took 9.5 seconds while fuel consumption worked out at 4.5 litres per 100km (63mpg) giving a range of almost 560km (350 miles). The fit and finish of the fibreglass body was considered to be good, the gearchange was quick once the unusual gate had been mastered (the H was sideways!) and roadholding was good. They did say from the outset, however, that the characteristic two-stroke noise and back-lash may deter buyers and they thought the price too high.

Buckle sold the TS400 for £775 and found sales were steady but not spectacular. The Goggomobil business was progressively wound down beginning in early 1961 and by mid-1962 all stock had been cleared allowing the company to concentrate its business activities on its several other retail franchises.

ZETA

Although some critics viewed the Lightburn Zeta as some kind of automotive joke, managing director Harold Lightburn was very serious about it all. Released in November 1963 with the by-line "Australia's own second family car", it was known as the Zeta Runabout. The trouble for Zeta was that BMC had released its Mini which retailed for not much more money (the Zeta's base price was £595) and was a proper car offering buyers well-proven components (mostly) in a neat package with an extensive national service and spares back-up.

Lightburn had been investigating the idea of manufacturing a small car for most of the fifties. He had visited England before the Suez Crisis and was apparently fascinated by the emergence of a plethora of 'economy' cars brought about by the fuel situation in the country; in fact it was not just England that was affected but most of Europe as well. Tiny, primitive cars appeared seemingly overnight to satisfy the need for British motorists to be mobile no matter what, cars like the Frisky, Noble and Peel from the UK and Isetta, Vespa and Zundapp from Europe and the concept crystallised with engineer Frank Leahy 'styling' the boxy body to be made in fibreglass and bolted onto the separate steel chassis. Key features of the Series I body were the large front grille (the chromed surround came from a Morris Minor 1000) with the ID badge placed in the centre, bonnet air scoop, headlights set in flats at the head of the guards with a character line flowing back and down, the roof fins and Mark II Ford Zephyr tail-lights.

The idea of the body was for it to have a maximum of space within the compact dimensions but the lack of rear access was a major blunder. Everything, luggage and passengers, had to be squeezed around the front seats which tilted or by undoing a couple of bolts could be easily removed. Hardly convenient, though.

Power (hardly the right word) came from a Villiers 3T twin-cylinder two-stroke engine driving the front wheels through an integrated motorcycle-type gearbox with a chain drive to the differential. The gearshift was on the steering column and was a typically motorcycle sequential shift, one up and two, three and four down. Suspension was independent all round by coils and wishbones at the front and a trailing arm rear using rubber in torsion, while the brakes were Girling-sourced drums with dual leading shoes all round.

The Villiers 324cc engine (57 x 63.5mm) produced a measly 12.4kW (16.5bhp) at 5000rpm and a modest 24Nm (18 lb-ft) of torque at 4200rpm and was (just) able to pull the little Zeta to 80km/h (50mph) given enough road and it would take 1 minute and 14.4 seconds to run to 80km/h (50mph) from a standing start. Economy was in the 6.4–5.6 litres per 100km (46–50 mpg) range which meant that a reasonable cruising range was available from the 23-litre (5gal) fuel tank mounted on the bulkhead; a plastic tube 'gauge' on the dash kept the driver informed as to its contents.

A road test appeared in the November 1964 issue of *Wheels* magazine and it was not very complimentary. Once staff had gotten over the 'ugly' styling it was the Zeta's lack of performance that pervaded the article. "Its basic fault is lack of performance. While the factory claims a top speed of 60mph, we could not better 50mph." They went on to say, "The acceleration is dreadfully slow, and the engine's lack of real torque makes steep hills a real problem." To keep up with normal traffic they found they had to drive it flat out all the time. As to its handling they said it understeered constantly and that "its ride was quite firm, becoming hard and bouncy over corrugated dirt, with quite a lot of noise from the suspension." They did, however, appreciate the interior for its versatility although its starkness was obvious. There was no sound proofing in the body so the noise levels from the Villiers engine were torturous and in peak traffic the wet clutch was prone to fade and slip.

The four-speed gearbox did not feature a reverse gear, so if you needed to reverse you had to stop the car, turn the engine off, wait a moment, and then turn the key the other way which reversed the polarity of the starter field winding and the engine spun the other way! Voila, you had four-speeds *backwards*.

Much was made in its promotional material of the Zeta's ruggedness, Lightburn having entered it in the 7000-mile Ampol Trial in 1964

LIGHTBURN
SA 123·684

SA 239·926

RWW·286

coming away with a prize. Another was entered in a dash from Newcastle to Adelaide and made it apparently in one piece.

From June 1965 Lightburn announced a revised Zeta in which the styling had been the focus of attention – it certainly needed some work as the original was visually challenging to say the least. A new grille with a larger area and plain horizontal bars within a chromed border together with a new bonnet moulding tidied up the front, a flatter roof shorn of the ugly 'fins' plus a tidy-up at the rear completed the upgrade. Inside was a new quadrant on the steering column that let the driver know what gear had been selected – the original was guesswork at best.

As few as 343 Zetas were made between 1963 and 1965, a far cry from the 50 cars a week that were to be built when it was announced. Lightburn allegedly lost money on every one of them.

While in the UK during the late fifties on a fact-finding mission Harold Lightburn recruited Gordon Bedson, a man of some talent who at the time was export sales manager for Henry Meadows Limited. Prior to that he had designed and built several sports and racing cars for Cyril Keift. Bedson was involved in the ill-fated Frisky Sprint project and it was because of this that he came to Lightburn and Australia. A colleague, Ken Peckmore, came with him but later returned to England very disillusioned.

Bedson and Peckmore brought a Frisky Sprint prototype with them to Australia and this formed the basis of the future Lightburn Zeta Sports. There was talk at the time of styling by Michelotti but that was media spin. Michelotti had a hand in the design of the original Frisky but the Zeta Sports was a Bedson design, although it must be said there are Frisky cues in its lines. Headlights were on the leading edge of the front with a small flat between them for the licence plate and tiny round lights were placed either side of a mesh opening at the rear. There were no bumpers of any sort so the body would have been very vulnerable in traffic situations.

Under the hood at the rear Bedson mounted a German FMR three-cylinder 500cc two stroke engine mated to a four-speed motorcycle gearbox. The suspension was fully independent by coils and wishbones up front, swing axles with trailing arms and coil springs at the rear while the brakes were Girling drums all round, recirculating ball steering was used and the tyres were 5.20 x 10 which was the same size as the Mini.

The original prototype had tiny drop-down doors but they were dispensed with for production on structural rigidity grounds (and no doubt costs) so the Zeta Sports had a cigar-shaped body (in profile) that looked sleek but was crude. Interior comforts were non-existent; apart from the pair of tiny and thinly padded seats the interior was quite bare, the dash having but one circular dial for speed and there were switches for ignition, lights and wipers.

Modern Motor road-tested a Sports (July 1964) under the by-line "Zeta with Zing". They compared it with the long gone Goggo Dart and at £749 they felt it filled a market niche for those who simply had to have something different. Lightburn claimed a top speed of 120km/h (75mph) and a 0–80km/h (0–50mph) time of 12.0 seconds with fuel consumption of better than 7 litres per 100km (40mpg).

Curiously all 35–40 Zeta Sports were built in 1962 and for some unfathomable reason were stored at the Camden factory for about a year before being announced to the public.

There was a bigger picture where the Zeta was concerned but which received little or no comment at the time. Lightburn was keen to sell a manufacturing package to Third World countries where he felt there could be a market for a car that was simple and inexpensive to build and would not rust. Despite considerable time and effort invested, unfortunately there were no takers.

WILLYS JEEP

Production continued in small numbers at the Salisbury North factory in Brisbane through the sixties, sales being only a fraction of those for Land Rover.

The big news from Jeep in the early sixties was the announcement of the Jeep Wagoneer, the world's first all-wheel drive station wagon. Today's fashionable and trendy SUV vehicles can trace their lineage back to the Wagoneer (not that any of today's marketeers are interested).

By the standards of the time these were big wagons standing on a wheelbase of 2794mm (110in) and stretching 4673mm (184in) overall by 1930mm (76in) wide and 1625mm (64in) high; they were available with rear-wheel drive and in that configuration weighed 1630kg (3585lb) or as all-wheel drive and weighed in at 1720kg (3758lb). Willys Motors (Australia) only assembled the four-wheel drive version for the local market.

Styling was related to the Gladiator trucks but refined in a way that gave it a real sense of style in the day. The bluff front had a square chromed grille flanked by a headlight and an air intake each side and a chromed steel bumper, the body sides being unadorned by chrome (unusual for an American car) and there was a drop-down tailgate with a wind-down window at the rear. Inside were bench seats front and rear, the rear seat could be folded down to expand the luggage space.

In keeping with its Jeep roots, the Wagoneer was built on a substantial separate chassis with the body mounted onto it at a number of points using rubber bushes. The suspension comprised four semi-elliptic leaf springs with tubular dampers attached to heavy duty live axles, the brakes were by cast-iron drums and the steering was a non-assisted recirculating ball system that needed 5½ turns lock-to-lock for a huge turning circle. All mechanical components – engine, gearboxes, steering – were mounted high in the chassis to minimise problems when crossing creeks and such like.

During the decade the factory assembled the CJ3B, CJ6 as well as some trucks and the wagons. The conversion to right-hand drive was carried out at the Salisbury factory and to comply with local content requirements items like the distributor, starter motors, generators, wiper motors and headlights were sourced locally.

In 1966 Willys entered into an agreement with the Ford Motor Company of Australia to use the 170cid Falcon six-cylinder engine to power the CJ6 which until then had been powered by the four-cylinder Hurricane engine. At around the same time the Queensland government added the CJ6 to their contract list and as a result many CJ6 vehicles were purchased by various departments, including the police who used the vehicles in their more remote stations in western Queensland.

By 1968 Willys Motors contracted the manufacture of components for their vehicles to Shute Upton Engineering. This company engineered a derivative of the CJ6 called the Jeep Combat that was a tray-type commercial to compete with the Toyota Land Cruiser; the numbers made were small. Shute Upton also manufactured an early version of a free-wheeling hub for use on 4WD that required a special tool to lock and unlock the hubs. In addition the company manufactured the transfer case for the XW Falcon utilities that were fitted with their 4WD system. The majority of these high-riding four-wheel drive utes were sold in Queensland.

With sales at such a low volume it became uneconomical to continue assembling the Jeeps locally and by the end of 1969 the business was closed.

LAND ROVER

Having gained the Australian Army contract, Land Rover, in collaboration with Pressed Metal Corporation in Sydney, was able to expand the market for its versatile workhorse using the military business as a solid base. At this time Land Rover had only one real competitor in the world – the ubiquitous Jeep which was being manufactured in Toledo, Ohio at the rate of around 65,000 units a year. The likes of Toyota, Nissan, Mitsubishi et al. were still some way off in the future although it must be recognised that Toyota was in Australia through the agency of Thiess Brothers, which imported them to use on the Snowy Mountains Scheme.

The Series II arrived in Australia in early 1959 and retained the two wheelbase lengths (2235mm and 2768mm (88in and 109in)) as well as the rigid semi-elliptic leaf springs and four by four driveline but the wheel tracks were widened by 1½in and the front hubs were re-engineered to reduce the turning circle, by 3 feet in the short wheelbase models and by a massive 5 feet in the long wheelbase models. Styling appeared to be the same but in fact all the exterior panels were subtly different and there were new front indicator lights and new tail-lights. Other changes included a revised dashboard although the dials (Smiths) were still in the middle and there were new seats and the door windows now had actual glass (no longer Perspex) but they still slid to open.

The Series II saw the arrival of the new OHV four-cylinder engine: this was major news from Land Rover. It had a cylinder bore and stroke of 90.47 x 88.9mm for a capacity of 2286cc; the cylinders had dry liner bores similar to the LR diesel engine and on a compression of just 7.0:1 with a tiny Solex carburettor it developed 53kW (70bhp) at 4250rpm and 168Nm (124lb-ft) of torque at 2500rpm.

CKD components for the Series IIA began arriving by mid-1962 by which time Pressed Steel were pressing their own exterior aluminium body panels on tooling developed in-house. With the IIA came a revised diesel engine that shared its dry liner cylinder block and cylinder dimensions with the petrol engine so from its 2286cc capacity and running a 23.0:1 compression it developed 47kW (62bhp) at 4000rpm and 140Nm (103lb-ft) of torque at 1800rpm. This was up from 38kW (51bhp) at 3500rpm and 118Nm (87lb-ft) at 2000rpm for the earlier 2.0-litre diesel.

Between 1962 and 1966 very little seemed to happen where Land Rover was concerned. Sales continued and Pressed Metal continued their assembly processes but late in '66 the company announced the 2794mm (110in) wheelbase forward control vehicle, the added inch coming from the moving of the front axle forward by that amount – one inch. Along with this came a strengthened chassis and heavy duty front and rear axles and initially it was only available with the 2286cc petrol engine because its tare weight was some 400+ kg (900lb) heavier than the normal control unit! Later came the availability of three engine options, the existing 2286cc petrol, 2286cc diesel and a 2625cc six-cylinder petrol. Interestingly, the styling told you immediately it was a Land Rover.

In its February 1963 issue *Australian Motor Manual* published a full test of a Land Rover 88 with canvas top. The author described it as a combination of a light tractor, a conventional car capable of performing the duties of both. Comments were made about the manual gearbox (no synchromesh on first and second gears) as well as the very firm semi-elliptic leaf spring suspension which caused the driver to slow on rough terrain (he must have been a city slicker!) as well as the high pedal pressure on the brakes and heaviness of the steering at slow speeds. The potential versatility of the Landie impressed the tester with the options list including a capstan winch, centre power take-off, rear power take-off with governor, folding seats for extra passengers and so on. The test car nudged 112km/h (70mph) flat out (96km/h (60mph) was the best cruising speed) and took 18.1 seconds to accelerate from rest to 80km/h (50mph) while returning 13.5 litres per 100km (21mpg). At £1404 including tax it was considered good value against the Patrol and Jeep.

In 1967 the regular short- and long-wheelbase Land Rovers became available with the six-cylinder engine in response to world-wide demand for more power and torque. The engine retained the traditional Rover cylinder head layout of an overhead inlet valve and side exhaust valve per cylinder, its cylinder dimensions being 77.8 x 92.1mm for 2625cc and on a low 7.8:1 compression and small Solex carburettor it produced 64kW (83bhp) at 4500rpm and 173Nm (128lb-ft) at 1500rpm. Rover's engine plant had spare capacity by this time because production of the P4 and P5 sedans had ceased. Six-cylinder LRs received larger 279 x 76.2mm (11 x 3in) brake drums and revised gearbox ratios, the differential ratios remaining unchanged.

The next major change for LR came after the amalgamation of the British Motor Corporation (BMC) and the Leyland Group (which included Rover, Land Rover and Triumph) in May 1968. Recognising the new models was easy – the headlights were moved from in the grille outboard to the leading edge of the front fenders in response to increasing legal requirements. The grille was still made of 'wobbly wire' but was now rectangular.

After the amalgamation events at Rover and Land Rover things were never the same. Precious resources were concentrated on the other parts of the new empire and all efforts at Rover were directed towards getting the Range Rover into production, but that is another story altogether for another occasion. The workhorse Land Rovers were left to soldier on in the international market place with little development or improvement in the face of mounting challenges from Japan Inc., which quickly eroded LR's presence in Australia.

NISSAN-DATSUN

Nissan was one of Japan's largest industrial enterprises and was second to Toyota in output within the burgeoning automobile industry of that country. The introduction of Datsun cars (as they were badged then) to Australia came at the 1960 Melbourne Motor Show through the agency of Sir Laurence Hartnett and his company Hartnett Holdings Pty Ltd. It was an example of the Datsun Model P310, which was badged as the Datsun 1200 when ultimately released for sale here. It was quite a different car from the Datsun 1000 that had competed successfully in the 1958 Mobilgas Trial.

After the agreements between Nissan and Hartnett had been signed an order for 10 vehicles was placed for press and promotional work and a further order for 100 vehicles placed. The order encompassed Datsun sedans, station wagons and utilities and they arrived in Melbourne in November 1960. The Japanese were keen to expand quietly into the local market and suggested Hartnett aim for sales of around 2400 vehicles in the first year of operations once distributors and dealers had been established.

The Datsun 1200 sedan was unusual insofar as the unitary body was mounted on a separate chassis; the wheelbase was 2280mm (89.8in), overall length was 3915mm (154in), width 1496mm (58.9in) and height was 1450mm (57in). Weight at the kerb was only 900kg (1890lb). Even though it had four doors, access was restricted by the small size of the car but four people could travel in some comfort seated on vinyl upholstered bench seats front and rear and take a modicum of luggage in the boot.

Under the bonnet was a four-cylinder OHV engine whose design had been influenced by Nissan's years of cooperation with Austin of England. It looked like an Austin engine but was not – it *never* leaked a drop of oil so it could not have been British! With a bore of 73mm and stroke of 71mm it had a capacity of 1189cc, developed 40kW (60bhp) at 5000rpm with the aid of an 8.2:1 compression and a Nikki dual-throat carburettor; torque was 91Nm (67 lb-ft) at 3600rpm. Drive went to the rear wheels through a *three*-speed all-synchromesh gearbox with a column shift lever. Rounding out the technical specifications were drum brakes on all four wheels, recirculating ball steering, coil-and-wishbone front suspension and a live axle on semi-elliptic leaf springs at the rear.

Although not a startling new car insofar as it was not innovative in any way it did prove to be very reliable and was available in two versions – the standard at £993 and the deluxe at £1048 that was something of a bargain because the price included twin exterior rear view mirrors, fog and reversing lights, a heater/demister and a tool kit.

Wheels carried out one of the first full tests of the Bluebird (March 1961) and came away highly impressed. They commented favourably on the quality of the paintwork and careful workmanship that was obvious; so, too, the interior was extremely well made and assembled. On driving it they thought the gearbox was excellent apart from there being only three gears but the synchromesh was unbeatable and the column shift was both light and smooth in its action. They also liked the box-section chassis under the body. As for its handling they said, "On level, straight going the car sat firmly but comfortably with no sign of wind wavering … The combination of weight distribution, direct and light steering and the suspension layout gave the Datsun quite exciting handling qualities."

Against the stopwatch the little Datsun ran to 125.6km/h (78.5mph) for its top speed – 41 and 84km/h (26mph and 53mph) in the indirect gears – and took 12.7 seconds for the 0–80km/h (0–50mph) dash, 20.2 seconds to 96km/h (60mph) and returned more than 9.5 litres per 100km (30mpg).

Datsun sales grew steadily and by 1965 the government was talking of plans for assemblers and manufacturers ranging from Plan A at 95 per cent local content to Plans B1 and B2 for low-volume makers. Nissan studied the small-volume plans and decided that the company would enter the new-for-1964 Datsun Bluebird with its Pininfarina styling for local assembly in collaboration with the Pressed Metal Corporation in Sydney. The agreement was signed in June 1966 with assembly underway by November, the first Datsun Bluebird rolling off the line on the 25th of that month.

The Bluebird, which replaced the 1200 from December 1963, was a

DATSUN
DATSUN

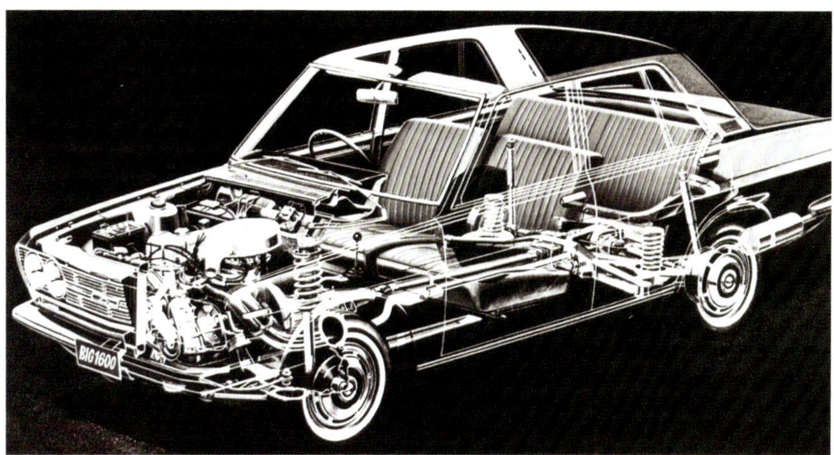
BIG1600

1600
DELUXE

DATSUN

DATSUN

DATSUN

1300

very attractive looking sedan hampered to a certain extent in comparison with the Toyota Tiara 1500 by its slightly smaller engine and body. The wheelbase had been extended to 2380mm (93.8in), length to 4000mm (157.4in), width was now 1490mm (58.7in) (actually 6mm narrower!), height 1430mm (54.8in) and kerb weight for the Deluxe was 960kg (2110lb). The engine's capacity remained at 1189cc with power staying at 40kW (60bhp) at 5200rpm. The rest of its mechanical specifications were largely carried over from the earlier model albeit with minor modifications and, importantly, it now had a full monocoque body.

Its Farina styling, and in particular the roofline, soon earned the car the nickname as the 'banana car' by irreverent members of the media. For a Japanese car of that time its styling was pretty and functional. Up front was a mesh grille with the round 'D' badge in the centre and dual headlights either side, chromed bumpers for protection. A subtle character groove swept from the front to the rear and curved slightly downwards (like a banana) along each side and back around the tail where the horizontal tail-lights were, indicators in orange on the outer edge and the actual tail-light being the large round lens on the inner end. The exterior door handles were neat, chromed lift-up flaps.

As with its predecessor, interior room was fine for four small(ish) adults, a little tight for larger Aussies, and the bench front seat did not go back far enough on the runners for tall drivers. The dash was painted metal (body colour) with a padded black-vinyl-covered upper surface to minimise reflections in the windscreen. In front of the driver was a rectangular-shaped binnacle containing a fan-shaped speedometer with fuel and temperature gauges on either side and some warning lights. Switches for the ignition/starter, lights, wipers/washer were lined up either side of the steering column with the heater/demister slides placed either side of the slot provided for the radio when fitted.

What was obvious to careful observers on the showroom floor was the attention to detailing. Everything fitted precisely inside, the carpets were neatly clipped down, the glove-box lid was an exact fit in the space provided, the doors closed with a soft push. Under the bonnet was a delight for anyone with any mechanical knowledge: the wiring loom was beautifully wrapped and clipped against the side of the engine bay, the spark plug leads were held in neat clips between the distributor and plug, there was a glass float bowl on the front of the carburettor and so on. A salesman did not have to talk hard to persuade a potential buyer into becoming a client.

A new grille appeared on the Bluebird in November 1964 and again in May 1966 when a thoroughly revised Bluebird was released. The engine's capacity had been increased to 1299cc by lengthening the crank stroke to 77.6mm (the bore remained at 73mm) and the power rose slightly to 50kW (67bhp). More importantly, the Bluebird was now available with a four-speed manual gearbox (no synchromesh on first gear) with a neat floor shift. The rest of the car remained the same but the new gearbox did improve the flexibility of driving, acceleration times for the 80 and 96km/h (50 and 60mph) dashes now being 11.9 and 17.6 seconds and the top speed was 129.6km/h (81mph).

In January 1968 Nissan introduced the Datsun 1600 to Australia, a model that has gone on to cult status here and many other international markets. It was the car that literally transformed the fortunes of the company. It was another 'clean sheet' design that shared nothing with any of its predecessors. The media immediately dubbed it "the poor man's BMW", a reference to how close the specifications of the 1600 were to the famous BMW 1600 and 2002.

The completely new all-steel unitary construction body was styled and engineered in-house, and while plain in appearance was simple and attractive with curved door glass and no swivelling vent windows in the front doors. It had a simple pressed aluminium grille with four headlights and horizontal tail-lights as was the norm in 1968. Inside was a plain straight-across dashboard in metal with a plain rectangular instrument unit in front of the driver containing a fan-shaped speedometer, small fuel and temperature gauges and some warning lights, and at either end were round air vents. Either side of the steering column were switches for ignition, lights and wipers/washer that initially had a clap-hands action. In the centre was provision for a heater/demister and radio. Front seat passengers sat on non-adjustable bucket seats while those in the rear sat on a bench seat, all being upholstered in vinyl. Like the little 1000, the body of the 1600 seemed to lack sound-deadening material and so boomed during driving and the engine noise made for noisy travel. While it was touted by the media as the poor man's BMW it was nothing like as refined to drive or travel in – it was poor indeed.

Mechanically the 1600 would prove to be as tough as old nails. The L20 single overhead camshaft engine was the first of a whole new family of engines originally developed in collaboration with Prince Motors, which Nissan merged with in 1966. Prince was in the process of developing a new family of engines and cars to replace the Skyline and Gloria, Nissan brought them to fruition. The 20 of the name perhaps indicated 2.0litre capacity but it had a bore and stroke of 83 x 73mm for 1595cc and developed 72kW (96bhp) at 5600rpm, 136Nm (100 lb-ft) of torque at 3600rpm. The cylinder block was of cast-iron with a five-bearing crankshaft and the overhead cam was chain-driven off the front of the crank. Finger rockers operated two valves per cylinder in a wedge-shaped combustion chamber, the non-cross-flow alloy cylinder head having the inlet and exhaust manifolds on the left side; the engine was inclined by 12 degrees to the right. Drive went to the rear wheels through either a four-speed all-synchromesh manual or three-speed automatic gearbox.

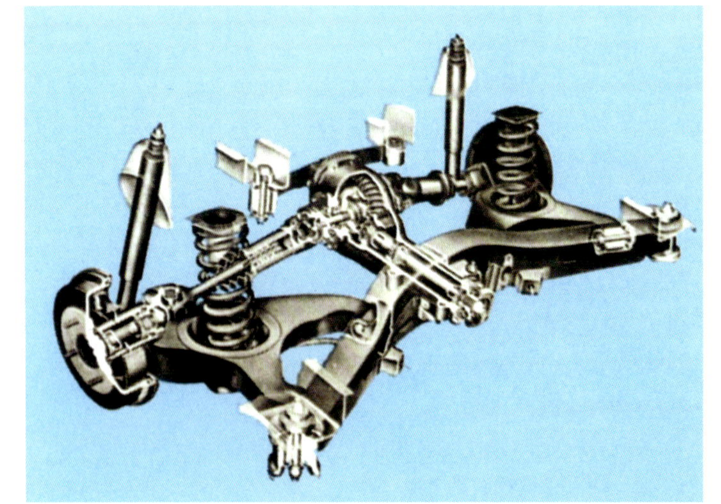

Unusually for a Japanese car from the 1960s, the Datsun 1600 featured a fully independent suspension system, just like a BMW. Up front were MacPherson struts with coil springs, a forged locating arm and an angled drag link to locate the front wheels with a stabiliser bar to minimise body lean. It was simple, effective and relatively inexpensive to manufacture. At the rear was a semi-trailing arm system, again with coil springs and telescopic dampers; the arms were bushed onto a substantial vee-shaped cross member. Each drive shaft featured a universal joint at each end with a ball-splined sliding joint in the middle. Braking was by non-assisted 231mm (9.1in) diameter discs up front with cast-iron 228mm (9in) drums at the rear while the steering was by recirculating ball.

"The introduction of independent rear suspension and a 1.6-litre overhead cam engine has raised the stature of Nissan's medium sized sedan to the point where it is very probably the best car available for the price and represents extremely good value for money," so wrote Peter Robinson in his road test of the new Datsun 1600 in the March 1968 issue of *Australian Motor Sports* magazine. Its delightful handling, slick gearchange and easygoing nature endeared the car to Robinson as did its cabin, which could seat four adults in some comfort, and the fact that it could cruise easily at high speed with decent fuel economy. The maximum speed posted was 153km/h (95.7mph) with the 0–96km/h (0–60mph) dash taking only 12.6 seconds to put the 1600 at the head of the class. And at $2050 it was a bargain even if a heater/demister and radio were extra cost options.

With the release of the 1600, Datsun sales increased dramatically and the head office in Tokyo immediately began exploring ways to increase their volume of production in Australia. Talks were held with Volkswagen whose plant at Clayton was only being partly utilised. An agreement was signed in July 1968 for the 1600 and 1000 to be assembled at Clayton in addition to those units being assembled by Pressed Metal. Around this time VW changed the name of the plant to Motor Producers Limited. The first 1600 rolled off the lines in November 1968, almost two years to the day after the first Bluebird rolled off the PMC line.

Added to the assembly line at Motor Producers Ltd in January 1969 were small numbers of the Datsun 1000 that had been released as an import from March 1967. It was Datsun's competitor to the super-successful Toyota Corolla and like the Bluebird, when compared with the Corona was slightly smaller in size and engine capacity. Unlike the

Bluebird, the 1000 was styled in-house and was plain to the point of boring even when new. Built on a completely new floorpan (the 1000 was another Nissan 'clean sheet' design) with a wheelbase of 2280mm (89.7in), overall length of 3820mm (138.5-ins, 1445mm (width of 57in and height of 1345mm (53in), the whole car weighed just 645kg (1420lb) for the two-door Deluxe and 665kg (1463lb) for the four-door Deluxe.

Under the bonnet was a completely new four-cylinder engine that had a cylinder bore and stroke of 73 x 59mm for a capacity of 988cc that produced 46kW (62bhp) at 6000rpm and 83Nm (61.5 lb-ft) of torque at 4000rpm. Early stock came only with a three-speed all-synchromesh manual gearbox with a column shifter (you must wonder why) although six months later a four-speed all-synchromesh gearbox with a neat floor shifter became available at no extra cost. At the same time a four-door body supplemented the original two-door and a two-door station wagon also became available.

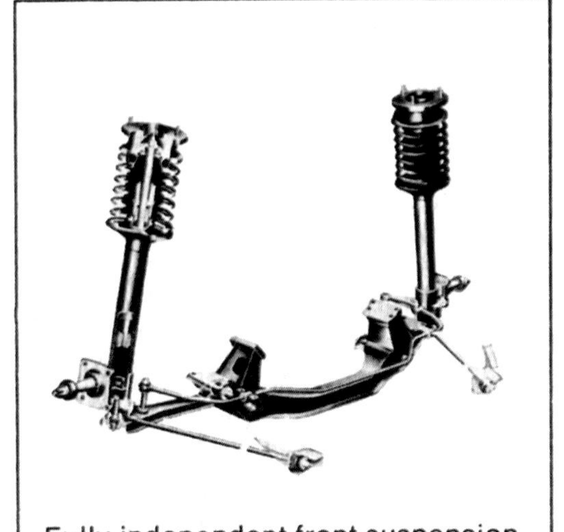

Fully independent front suspension

The front suspension was independent by way of wishbones and a lower transverse leaf spring while at the rear was the usual live axle on semi-elliptic leaf springs with telescopic dampers all round; steering was by a recirculating ball system and braking was by 203mm (8in) diameter cast-iron drums all round with a single circuit. It was rather basic engineering, even for the period.

Inside was a very plain straight-across painted metal dashboard with a padded top (it was wafer thin) and a small rectangular binnacle in front of the driver for the fan-shaped speedo plus fuel and temperature dials and several warning lights with dashboard switches either side of the column for ignition, lights and wiper/washers. Seating was by buckets in front, bench in back with very thin dimpled vinyl upholstery over thin padding. While the car was reliable and simple to drive it nonetheless felt frail and built to a price.

Even though it was an uninspiring design and the body was light in weight and felt 'tinny' the little 1000 was a big sales success in Australia for Datsun. For the 1969 model year an ever-so-slightly modified 1000 appeared with a new texture in the grille and larger-sized tail-lights. Sales just kept on rolling along.

Australian Motor Manual carried out a full test in its January 1969 issue and liked it. After all, it was the Deluxe they tested and it came fitted as standard with a heater/demister with booster fan, carpets, external mirrors, push-button transistor radio and twin sun visors; and like all Japanese cars it had a lockable fuel filler. All for just $1899. Each of the four doors were short so getting in and out required some physical dexterity and movement of the front bucket seats was restricted to allow some legroom for the rear-seat passengers. *AMM* opined that any driver taller than 1.75m (5ft 9in) would be cramped for room at the wheel.

They found the floor gearshift's movements were particularly light and short with unbeatable synchromesh and when pushed up near the 6000rpm limit engine noise became very intrusive. The ride was choppy over rough surfaces because the springs were set up quite firmly to minimise body lean when cornering. They managed a top speed of 131km/h (82mph) with 0–80 and 96km/h (0–50 and 60mph) coming up in 12.8 and 16.9 seconds respectively and fuel consumption worked out at 8.2 litres per 100km (34.6mpg) for the whole test. As a second, or third, family car it worked well.

With the federal government changing the rules regarding low-volume assembly to a more flexible system, Nissan opted to commit to the 60 per cent local content that allowed them to assemble up to 7500 vehicles a year. That decision would have far-reaching consequences for the company over the next two decades. Further discussion of Datsun's fortunes will be found in *Australian Cars of the 70s.*

MODEL SPECIFICATIONS 1960–69

Year	Make	Price £	Engine	Capacity	BHP	Torque lb-ft	Trans	Wheelbase inches	Length inches	Weight lb	Max speed mph	0–50 mph	Economy
1959–62	Austin A40 Farina	915	4-cyl OHV	948cc	34/4750	50/2000	4-sp man	83.5	144	1596lb	67	19.5	33–40
1959–62	Austin A60 Cambridge	1160	4-cyl OHV	1622cc	55/4400	116/1700	4-sp man	99	178	2464lb	78	13.7	28–36
1962–65	Austin Freeway	1130 man 1225 auto	6-cyl OHV	2433cc	80/4350	123/1650	3-sp man, auto	100	178	2576lb	82	12.0	24–30
1965–70	Austin 1800	1165 man $2620 auto	4-cyl OHV	1798cc	84/5300	99/2500	4-sp man	106	164	2520lb	86	12.8	26–32
1958–71	Austin-Healey Sprite	985 ('61) $2198 ('67)	4-cyl OHV	948cc 1098cc 1275cc	42/5000 55/5500 65/6000	52/3300 62/3250 72/3000	4-sp man	80.0	137 136 137	1456lb	87	14.8	39–43
1959–61	Ascort	1998	4-cyl OHV boxer	1192cc (VW)	54/4300	N/A	4-sp man	94.5	162	1624lb	94	11.9	30–36
1960–68	Chevrolet Bel Air	2513	V8 OHV	4638cc	170/4200	275/2200	2-sp auto	119	210.8	3808lb	104	8.5	14–20
1960–63	Chrysler Royal AP3	1910	V8-cyl OHV	5212cc	220/4000	325/2800	3-sp auto	115	200	3584lb	105	8.1	14–20
1962–63	Chrysler Valiant R, S	1299 man 1435 auto	6-cyl OHV	3687cc	145/4000	215/2400	3-sp man, 3-sp auto	106.5	184	2744lb	98	10.5	19–26
1963–67	Chrysler Valiant AP5, AP6, VC	1220 man 1350 auto 1498 Regal	6-cyl, V8 OHV	3687cc 4473cc	145/4000 180/4200	215/2400 260/1600	3-sp man, 3-sp auto	106.5	188	2676lb	100 110	9.8 7.9	20–26 18–24
1968–69	Chrysler Valiant VE, VF Valiant V8	$2628 man $2878 auto $3268 Regal $2828 Pacer	6-cyl OHV V8 OHV	3687cc 4473cc (273) 5192cc (318)	145/4400 160/4600 195/4400 210/4400	215/2400 220/2500 265/2000 320/2400	3-sp man, 3-sp auto	108 108	192.3 194	2650lb 2912lb	100 107	9.8 7.9	20–26 18–22
1969–70	Valiant 2-dr hardtop	$2898 $3838 V8	6/V8 OHV	3687cc (225) 5192cc (318)	160/4500 230/4400	220/2500 340/2400	3-sp man/ auto	111	200	2960lb 3070lb	108 110	9.8 6.5	20–26 18–22
1968–69	VIP by Chrysler	$3650 VEV8 $3598 VF 6 $3998 VF 8	V8-cyl OHV 6/V8	4472cc (273) 3687cc (225) 5192cc (318)	195/4400 160/4500 230/4400	265/2000 220/2500 340/2400	3-sp auto	108 (VE) 112 (VF)	185.5 192.5	2950lb 3210lb	106 104 106	7.2	16–22 18–24 16–22
1964–68	Datsun Bluebird 1200/1300	898 Std 974 Deluxe 1036 S/w	4-cyl OHV	1189cc 1299cc	60/5200 67/5200	70/2800 77/2800	3-sp/4-sp man	93.7	157	2038lb	78 81	13.8 11.7	30–36
1968–72	Datsun 1600	$2050	4-cyl SOHC	1595cc	96/5600	103/36009	4-sp man	95	162	2576lb	96	9.4	28–34
1969	Datsun 1000	$1845 2-dr $1899 4-dr	4-cyl OHV	988cc	62/6000	61/4000	3-, 4-sp man	89	138	1422lb	82	12.2	36–40

Year	Make	Price £	Engine	Capacity	BHP	Torque lb-ft	Trans	Wheelbase inches	Length inches	Weight lb	Max speed mph	0–50 mph	Economy
1960–72	Dodge Phoenix	2595	V8 OHV	5212cc (318) 6274cc (383)	220/4400 330/4400	340/2400 460/2400	3-sp auto	119	210	3472lb	105	7.1	15–22
1960–64	Ford Anglia 105E	872	4-cyl OHV	997cc	39/5000	52.5/2700	4-sp man	90.5	153	1624lb	76	16.6	34–42
1962–66	Ford Cortina Mk I	930/973 1.2 955/998 1.5	4-cyl OHV	1198cc 1498cc	53/4800 65/4600	63/2700 85/2300	4-sp man	98	168	1803lb 1823lb	81 83	15.7 11.8	32–40 28–34
1964–66	Ford Cortina GT Mk I	1223	4-cyl OHV	1498cc	83/5200	97/3600	4-sp man	98	168	1870lb	90	9.9	24–32
1966–70	Ford Cortina GT Mk II	$2530 $2597	4-cyl OHV	1498cc 1599cc	83/5200 93/5400	97/3600 102/3600	4-sp man	98	168	1988lb 2010lb	94 98	9.6 8.2	26–32 26–32
1966–70	Ford Cortina Mk II	$2130	4-cyl OHV	1499cc	65/4750	88/2500	4-sp man; 3-sp auto	98	168	1940lb	78	14.0	28–34
1959–62	Ford Zephyr Mk II	1314 man 1472 auto 1425 wagon	6-cyl OHV	2553cc	85/4400	132/2000	3-sp man, 3-sp auto	107	178.5	2691lb	88	12.1	22–28
1962–65	Ford Zephyr Mk III	1369 man 1501 auto	6-cyl OHV	2553cc	98/4750	135/2000	4-sp man, 3-sp auto	107	180	2688lb	96	8.9	22–28
1960–67	Ford Falcon XK-XM	1141 std 1204 Dx 1323 Dx auto	6-cyl OHV	2365cc (144) 2785cc (170) 3277cc (200)	90/4200 101/4400 121/4400	138/2000 156/2400 185/2400	3-sp man, 2-sp auto	109.5	181	2352lb 2365lb 2591lb	87 92 97	13.4 12.1 8.9	24–30 20–26 19–25
1967–69	Ford Falcon XR-XW	From 2226	6- & V8-cyl OHV	2785cc (170) 3277cc (200) 4735cc (289)	111/4400 121/4400 200/4400	156/2400 185/2400 282/2400	3-sp man, 3-sp auto	111	184	2912lb 2935lb	86 106	13.5 7.4	20–26 15–20
1962–65	Ford Fairlane 500 'Compact'	2069 2192 2223	V8 OHV	3611cc (221) 4258cc (260) 4736cc (289)	145/4500 164/4400 195/4400	216/2200 282/2200	3-sp man, 2-sp auto	115.5	197	3136lb	93	9.8	14–22
1967–69	Ford Fairlane ZA-ZC	$3080 ZA $3880 ZA V8 $3910 ZC	6- & V8 OHV	3277cc (200) 3610cc (221) 4095cc (250) 4736cc (289) 4946cc (302) 5749cc (351)	121/4400 135/4400 200/4400 220/4800 230/4800 290/4800	190/2400 208/2400 282/2400 305/3200 385/3200	3-sp auto	116	196	3215lb 3224lb 4572lb	104.5 99.0 115	8.9 9.5 5.5	16–22 18–22 14–18
1959–62	Ford Fairlane 'Tank'	2345 Custom 2463 500 Ranch Wagon	V8-cyl OHV	5430cc	225/4400	325/2200	2-sp auto	118	208	3594lb	107	9.5	16–22
1964–67	Ford Galaxie 500	2610	V8-cyl OHV	4736cc 6390cc	200/4400 280/4600	282/2400 398/2800	3-sp auto	119	210	3808lb	114	7.5	13–18
1967–70	Ford Falcon GT	XR $3890 XT $4050 XW $4250	V8-cyl OHV	4736cc (289) 4934cc (302) 5751cc (351)	220/4800 230/4800 290/4800	305/3200 310/3800 385/3000	4-sp man/3-sp auto	111	185	3150lb 3136lb 3304lb	121 123 129	6.3 6.3 6.4	17–22 17–22 18–22

Year	Make	Price £	Engine	Capacity	BHP	Torque lb-ft	Trans	Wheelbase inches	Length inches	Weight lb	Max speed mph	0–50 mph	Economy
1969–72	Ford Capri GT	$2950 $3230 V6	4-cyl, V6 OHV	1599cc 2994cc V6	93/5400 144/4750	102/3600 192/3000	4-sp man	100.8	167.8	2016lb 2372lb	99 113	8.6 7.9	30–34 18–22
1958–61	Goggomobil sedan	599	2-cyl 2-str	293cc	15/5000	n/a	4-sp man	71	114	915	60	23.0	55–60
1959–61	Goggomobil Dart	685	2-cyl 2-str	293cc 392cc	15/5000 20/5200	n/a	4-sp man	71	114	865	62	24.0	55–60
1960–62	Goggomobil Coupe	775	2-cyl 2-str	392cc	20/5200	n/a	4-sp man	70.8	119.5	1014	66	15.0	45–52
1962–67	Hillman Super Minx	1109 man 1239 auto	4-cyl OHV	1592	62/4400	86.3/2500	4-sp man, 3-sp auto	101	165	2352	84	15.6	26–32
1963–70	Hillman Imp	799	4-cyl SOHC	875cc	42/5000	66/1600	4-sp man	82	139	1540	80	15.1	36–44
1965–67	Hillman Minx V Gazelle	999 $1998 $2398	4-cyl OHV	1592cc 1725cc 1725cc	56/4100 69.5/4800 85/5500	86/2500 98/2400 106/3500	4-sp man, 3-sp auto	96	164	2296lb	80 83 90	15.3 11.4 11.1	28–35 28–35 26–34
1967–73	Hillman Arrow, Hunter, Hunter GT	$2038 $2188 $2526 GT	4-cyl OHV	1725cc	73/4900 94/5200	99/2700 107/4000	4-sp man, 3-sp auto	98.5	169	2240lb	85 98	11.9 8.3	28–32 28–32
1960–64	Hillman Husky	1042	4-cyl OHV	1390cc	51/4400	72/2200	4-sp man	86	149	2184lb	73	15.8	28–38
1967–69	Holden Torana HB	$1795 $1951	4-cyl OHV,	1159cc	56/5400	67/3000	4-sp man, 3-sp auto	95	162	1750lb	83	12.8	30–36
1969–72	Holden Torana LC	$1820 $2060 $2226 $2576 $2766 GTR	4-cyl OHV, 6-cyl OHV	1159cc 1598cc 2260cc (138) 2638cc (161) 2638cc GTR	56/5400 95/4600 114/4400 125/4800	67/3000 120/1600 157/2000 150/2800	3-, 4-sp man, 3-sp auto	95.8 100	162 173	1848lb 2139lb 2240lb	75 89 92 105	16.5 12.5 11.0 7.5	30–36 26–30 24–30 22–28
1960–63	Holden FB-EK		6-cyl OHV	2262cc	75/4200	120/1400	3-sp man	105	181				
1963–65	Holden EJ-EH	EJ Sp 1110 EH Sp 1111 EH Prem	6-cyl OHV	2262cc 2441cc (149) 2993cc (179)	75/4200 100/4000 115/4000	120/1400 145/2000 175/1600	3-sp man, 3-sp auto	105	179	2492lb 2576lb 2612lb	82 92 98	11.6 9.2 8.9	26–32 22–28 20–26
1965–67	Holden HD-HR HD/HR X2	HD 1130 Sp 1329 Pr HR 1130 Sp 1535 Pr 1327 X2	6-cyl OHV	2441cc/2635cc 2993cc/3023cc 2993cc/3023cc	100/4000 115/4000 145/4600	145/2000 175/1600 184/1600	3-sp man, 2-sp auto	106	181	2608lb 2682lb 2744lb	93 95 97	8.9 8.4 9.2	18–25 18–25 18–24

Year	Make	Price £	Engine	Capacity	BHP	Torque lb-ft	Trans	Wheelbase inches	Length inches	Weight lb	Max speed mph	0–50 mph	Economy
1968–70	Holden HK-HT	$2215 Belm $2359 Kings $2760 Prem	6-cyl OHV V8 OHV	2365cc (161) 3046cc (186) 3046cc (186S) 4142cc (253) 5028cc (307) 5032cc (308)	114/4400 126/4200 145/4600 185/4400 210/4600 240./4800	157/2000 181/1600 184/2200 262/2400 300/2400 315/3000	3-sp man, 2-sp auto	111	185	2814lb 2836lb 2892lb V8 +100lb	86 108	10.9 7.4	20–26 17–22
1968–70	Holden HK-HT Monaro, Brougham	$2575 $3090 GTS $3790 327 $3988 Bro	6-cyl OHV, V8 OHV	2365cc (161) 3046cc (186) 3046cc (186S) 5343cc (327) 5032cc (308)	114/4400 126/4200 145/4600 250/4800 240/4800	157/2000 181/1600 184/2200 325/3200 315/3000	3-, 4-sp man, 2-sp auto	111	185 192	2866lb 2912lb 2940lb 3295lb 3247lb	99 104	8.2 7.9	22–24 14–16
1962–65	Humber Vogue, Sports	1192 man 1319 auto 1285 Sports	4-cyl OHV	1592cc	62/4400 84/5000	86/2400 91/3500	4-sp man/3-sp auto	101	165	2408lb	80 92	15.7 10.7	28–34 26–34
1958–67	Humber Super Snipe Series IV/V	1847 man 1994 auto	6-cyl OHV	2651cc 2951cc	105/5000 125/4700 132/5000	138/2000 161/1800 167/2600	3-sp auto	110	188	3248lb	97 102	11.4 11.2	15–24 15–24
1957–62	Humber Hawk Series I, II	1762	4-cyl OHV	2267cc	78/4400	120/2300	3-sp auto	110	184	3136lb	88	14.1	20–28
	Jeep CJ-7 Sportster Wagoneer	$3076 $5456	4-cyl F 6-cyl 6-cyl OHC V8 OHV	2786cc (170) 3758cc (230) 5343cc (327)	111/4400 140/4000 250/4700	158/2400 210/1750 340/2600	3-sp man + 2-sp 3-sp auto	81 110	131 183	2436lb 3758lb 3850lb	70 90 90	10.5	24 16–22
1960–69	Land Rover	1223 (no tax)	4-cyl OHV petrol 4-cyl OHV diesel 6-cyl OHV petrol	2286cc 2286cc 2625cc	70/4250 62/4000 83/4500	124/2500 103/1800 128/1500	4-sp man	88/109 88/109 88/109	142/175 142/175 142/175	3416lb 3450lb 3582lb	71 65 69	22.1 17.0	20–24 14–20
1963–65	Lightburn Zeta	615 Runab't 749 Sports	2-cyl 2-str	324cc 498cc	16.5/5000 19.5/5000	n/a	4-sp man	74 70	121 127	1120lb 896lb	50 70	1:14.4! 12.0	46–50 30–36
1958–61	Lloyd Hartnett	790	2-cyl SOHC	596cc	28/4800	29/3000	4-sp man	78.5	133	1232lb	63	25.0	40–45
1959–63	Mercedes-Benz 190	2270 Ponton 2390 Fin	4-cyl SOHC	1897cc	84/4800 92/5000	120/2400 125/3000	4-sp man	104 106	176 186	2668lb 2744lb	92 87	12.0 12.2	25–32 22–28

Year	Make	Price £	Engine	Capacity	BHP	Torque lb-ft	Trans	Wheelbase inches	Length inches	Weight lb	Max speed mph	0–50 mph	Economy
1959–63	Mercedes-Benz 220, SE 220 S, SE 'fin'	2886 Ponton 3108 SE 2870 S fin 3335 SE fin	6-cyl SOHC	2195cc	110/5200 120/5000 124/5200 134/5000	152/4100	4-sp man, 4-sp auto	111 108.3	187 192	2920lb 2965lb	103 106 107	11.2 10.6 8.7	22–28 20–28
1963–70	MG B	1365	4-cyl OHV	1798cc	94/5300	110/3000	4-sp man	91	153	2016lb	105	8.3	24–30
1967–72	MG Midget	$2634	4-cyl OHV	1275cc	65/6000	72/3000	4-sp man	80	137	1512lb	85	10.5	34–38
1960–64	Morris Minor 1000	888 2-dr 935 4-d	4-cyl OHV	948cc	37/4800	50/2500	4-sp man	86	148	1650lb 1705lb	74	16.4	36–40
1961–70	Morris 850 Mini Deluxe	775 833	4-cyl OHV	848cc 998cc	34/5500 38/5250	44/2900 52/2700	4-sp man	80	120	1316lb 1428lb	73 78	16.9 14.0	45–50 38–45
1962–70	Mini-Cooper Mini-Cooper S	950 1140	4-cyl OHV	997cc 998cc 1275cc	55/6000 55/5800 75/5800	55/3600 55/3000 80/3000	4-sp man	80	120	1400lb 1450lb	88 98	9.6 7.5	30–38 28–34
1957–62	Morris Major MM Ser II	1025 997	4-cyl OHV	1489cc	50/4200	76/1850	4-sp man	86 92	152 161	2158lb 2218lb	75 76	16.2 14.5	30–38 28–36
1962–64	Morris Major Elite	940	4-cyl OHV	1622cc	58/4250	91/2300	4-sp man	92	161	2128lb	80	13.8	28–34
1964–69	Morris 1100 1100 S	960 $2075	4-cyl OHV	1098cc 1275cc	48/5100 63/5500	60/2500 70/2500	4-sp man	93.5	146	1848lb 1904lb	81 86	14.2 11.6	30–38 30–38
1959–62	Morris Oxford Farina	1160	4-cyl OHV	1622cc	55/4400	116/1700	4-sp man	99	178	2464lb	78	13.7	27–35
1960–62	NSU Prinz	812	2-cyl OHC	583cc	36/5500		4-sp man	78.75	124	1124lb	75	14.6	40–45
1956–64	Peugeot 403	1247	4-cyl OHV	1468cc	65/4750	74/2500	4-sp man	104.5	175	2352lb	85	15.9	28–35
1964–70	Peugeot 404	1450	4-cyl OHV	1618cc	72/5400	94/2400	4-sp man	104	174	2240lb	88	12.8	28–34
1961–68	Pontiac Laurentian	2752	V8 OHV	4638cc	195/4800	285/2400	2-sp auto	119	210	3864lb	102	8.9	16–22
1960–62	Rambler Ambassador	1899 2429	V8 OHV	4798cc 5360cc	198/4700 250/4700	198/2600 340/2600	3-sp auto	112 117	190 199	3024lb 3560lb	105 108	9.0 9.1	16–24 16–20
1961–66	Rambler Classic	2125 1799 1899	6-cyl, V8 OHV	3206cc 4702cc	127/4200 138/4400 198/4700	180/1600 185/1600 280/2600	3-sp auto	108 112	190 190	2940lb 2775lb 3024lb	86 86 103	12.5 11.9 8.6	16–24 20–26 15–22
1964–66	Rambler American	1659	6-cyl OHV	3206cc	138/4500	185/1800	3-sp auto	106	178	2688lb	96	9.7	18–24

Year	Make	Price £	Engine	Capacity	BHP	Torque lb-ft	Trans	Wheelbase inches	Length inches	Weight lb	Max speed mph	0–50 mph	Economy
1967–1972	Rambler Rebel	$4750	V8 OHV	4753cc	225/4700	300/3200	3-sp auto	114	197	3360lb	112	7.5	15–20
1956–1963	Renault Dauphine	986	4-cyl OHV	845cc	30/4250	48/2000	3-sp man	89	155	1500lb	69	18.3	42
1963–69	Renault R8, R10	998 R8 $1996 R10	4-cyl OHV	956c 1108cc	42/5200 50/4900	55/2500 65/2500	4-sp man	89.5	157 165	1568lb 1736lb	82 81	14.8 12.8	32–40 32–38
1967–77	Renault 16	$2540 GL $2885 TS	4-cyl OHV	1470cc 1565cc	63/5000 87/5750	78/2800 88/3500	4-sp man	104/106	166	2304lb 2337lb	87 105	11.4 8.8	26–33 26–32
1958–64	Simca Aronde	999 sedan 1109 wagon	4-cyl OHV	1290cc	52/4900	69/2500	4-sp man	96	165	2016lb	80	13.7	30–36
1959–61	Simca Vedette V8	1799 Imp 1395 CAL	V8-cyl SV	2351cc	84/4800	112/2750	3-sp man	107.5	187	2576lb	93	11.9	20–24
1959–62	Singer Gazelle	1179	4-cyl OHV	1494cc	60/4500		4-sp man	96	163.5	2240lb	82	12.5	25–34
1956–61	Standard Vanguard III	1391std/1430 deluxe	4-cyl OHV	2088cc	68/4200	113/2000	3-sp man	102	172	2688lb	82	15.8	28–34
1961–63	Standard Vanguard Six	1437 man	6-cyl OHV	1998cc	80/4400	107/2500	3-sp man, auto	104	171.5	2940lb	92	11.9	28–32
1960–66	Studebaker Lark, Cruiser	1665 man 17998 auto	V8 OHV	4238cc (259) 4722cc (289)	180/4500 195/4800	260/2800 285/2400	3-sp man, 3-sp auto	108 113	180 188	3024lb 3080lb	98 104	10.1 8.2	18–24 14–20
1960–66	Studebaker Gran Turismo	2397	V8 OHV	4737cc	225/4500	300/2800	3-sp auto	120	204	3220lb	111	7.8	14–20
1963–64	Toyota Tiara	915	4-cyl OHV	1453cc	65/4500	83/3000	3-sp man	94.5	157	2352lb	82	13.7	28–34
1964–70	Toyota Corona	979 $2079	4-cyl OHV	1490cc 1587cc	74/5000 82/5000	85/2600 87/2500	4-sp man	95	159	2016lb	83 93	13.3 9.3	28–35 28–38
1966–70	Toyota Corolla	$1698	4-cyl OHV	1077cc	60/6000	62/3800	4-sp man	90	151	1648lb	85	9.9	32–38
1964–70	Toyota Crown	1369 (4-cyl) $2480 (6-cyl) $3018	4-cyl OHV 6-cyl SOHC	1897cc 1988cc 2253cc	95/5000 110/5200 115/5200	110/3400 117/3600 127/3600	3-sp man; 2-sp auto	105 106	181 183	2650lb 2744lb 2810lb	83 94 94	12.6 11.3 10.3	24–30 24–32 21–30
1964–72	Triumph 2000, 2.5 PI	1535 man 1728 auto $3850 PI M $4120 PI A	6-cyl OHV	1998cc 2495cc PI	90/5000 132/5450	117/2900 153/2000	4-sp man, 3-sp auto	106	174	2576lb 2643lb	95 110	9.8 7.5	25–32 20–26
1959–64	Triumph Herald	935 Herald 952 1200	4-cyl OHV	948cc 1147cc	39/4500 43/4500	51/2750 63/2600	4-sp man	91	153 H	1736lb	70 80	13.1	32–38

Year	Make	Price £	Engine	Capacity	BHP	Torque lb-ft	Trans	Wheelbase inches	Length inches	Weight lb	Max speed mph	0–50 mph	Economy
1962–69	Triumph Spitfire	1070 $2348	4-cyl OHV	1147cc 1296cc	63/5750 75/6000	67/3500 75/4000	4-sp man	83	145	1624lb	92	10.4	30–38
1963–66	Vauxhall Viva	889	4-cyl OHV	1057cc	44/5200	59/2800	4-sp man	91	157	1568lb	80	13.9	36–42
1960–65	Vauxhall Victor 101	1039 1118	4-cyl OHV	1508cc 1594cc	56/4600 69/4800	86/2200 93/2800	3- or 4-sp man	100	173	2128lb	80 84	14.0 13.4	30–34
1961–64	Vauxhall VX4/90	1330 1354	4-cyl OHV	1508cc 1594cc	81/5200 85/5200	91/2800 99/3200	4-sp man	100	173.5	2160lb 2212lb	92 94	10.6 10.5	26–32
1958–61	Vauxhall Velox PA	1393 Velox 1468 Cresta	6-cyl OHV	2262cc	82.5/4400	124/1800	3-sp man, auto	105	178	2520lb	91	11.8	23–28
1962–66	Vauxhall Velox, Cresta PB	1356 man 1482 auto 1571 auto	6-cyl OHV	2651cc	113/4400	148/2400	3-sp man, auto	107	181	2632lb	93	9.7	22–28
1954–59	VW Beetle (Type 1)	899	4-cyl Boxer OHV	1192cc	40/3900	61/2000	4-sp man	94.5	160	1652lb	72	16.2	32–38
1962-	VW 1500, VW 1500 S VW 1600	1099 1299	4-cyl Boxer OHV	1493cc	53/4000 65/4800	78/2000 83/3000	4-sp man	94.5	166	1904lb	83 86	14.0 12.9	30–36 28–34
1962–66	Wolseley 24/80	1225 man 1338 auto	6-cyl OHV	2433cc	80/4350	123/1650	3-sp man, auto	101	178	2576lb	83	13.0	24–30

TRIUMPH HERALD PRODUCTION BY AMI

Year	948 Saloon	948TC Saloon	948TC Coupe	948TC Convertible	1200 Saloon	1200 DL Saloon	1200 Coupe	12/50 Saloon	12/50 Coupe
1959	1758		406						
1960	3920	1174	2439	747					
1961	1065	196	777	205	7				
1962				8	85	953	5		
1963					55	501	130		27
1964						112		202	93
1965								80	24
1966								6	
TOTAL	6743	1370	3622	960	147	1566	135	288	144

PRODUCTION NUMBERS

Make and Model	Production Dates	Number made
Austin Freeway Mark I sedan & wagon	February 1962 – May 1964	13,536
Austin Freeway Mark II sedan & wagon	June 1964 – September 1965	1,500
Wolseley 24/80 Mark I sedan	February 1962 – May 1964	8,486
Wolseley 24/80 Mark II sedan	June 1964 – September 1965	3,310
Morris 1100	February 1964 – June 1969	89,148
Morris 1500 & Nomad	June 1969 – December 1971	27,338
Austin 1800 Mk I & Mk II	December 1965 – November 1970	56,918
Mini Cooper S **Mini Cooper**		7405 (4986 Mk I, 2419 Mk II)
		3888 (2800 with 997cc + 1088 with 998cc engine)
Ford Fairlane FB CKD Canada	July 1962 – November 1962	1632
Ford Fairlane FC CKD Canada	November 1962 – December 1963	1771
Ford Fairlane FD CKD Canada	December 1963 –	1344
Ford Falcon XK	September 1960 – August 1962	68,465
Ford Falcon XL	August 1962 – February 1964	75,765
Ford Falcon XM	February 1964 – May 1965	47,039
Ford Falcon XP	May 1965 – September 1966	70,998
Ford Falcon XR	September 1966 – April 1968	87,270
Ford Falcon XT	April 1968 – July 1969	74,394
Ford Falcon XW	July 1969 – October 1970	99,953
Ford Falcon XR GT	March 1967 – February 1968	600
Ford Falcon XT GT	May 1968	1480/1415?
Ford Falcon XW GT **GT HO**		2287 662
Ford Capri 1600, 1600GT, 3000GT	May 1969 – August 1972	15,122

JEEP PRODUCTION 1958–1968

Model	Units Built
CJ3B, CJ3BL	1000
CJ5, CJ6 4-cyl	1560
6-226 2WD station wagon	6
6-226 4x4 cab/chassis & SW	1133
475 2WD station wagon	236
6-230 2WD station wagon	18
6-230 4WD station wagon	36
6-230 cab/chassis	366
FJ3 Fleetvan	1
FC-150 truck	1
FC-170 truck	126
CJ5 & CJ6 170cid	604
J Series truck	527
M38A1	12

MERCEDES-BENZ PRODUCTION AMI 1959–65

W121 190	90
W121 190b	216
W121 190D	48
W121 190Db	90
W110 190c	222
W110 190c auto	78
W180 220S	354
W111 220Sb	2304
W111 220Sb auto	912
W128 220SE	18
W111 220SEb	810
W111 220SEb auto	1248
Total	6390

HOLDEN FB SPECIAL V FORD XK FALCON V AUSTIN FREEWAY V CHRYSLER R SERIES VALIANT

	HOLDEN FB SPECIAL	FORD XK FALCON	CHRYSLER VALIANT	AUSTIN FREEWAY
Engine bore x stroke	6-cyl 77.8 x 79.4mm	6-cyl 89 x 63.5mm	6-cyl 86.3 x 104.7mm	6-cyl 76.2 x 88.9mm
Capacity	2262cc	2365cc	3688cc	2433cc
Power/rpm	75/4200	90/4200	145/4000	85/4350
Torque/rpm	120/1400	138/2000	215/2400	123/1650
Transmission	3-sp man	3-sp man, 2-sp auto	3-sp man, 3-sp auto	3-sp man, 3-sp auto
Suspension-front	Wishbones, coil springs	Wishbones, coil springs	Wishbones, torsion bars	Wishbones, coil springs
-rear	Live axle, semi-elliptic leaf	Live axle, semi-elliptic leaf	Live axle, semi-elliptic leaf	Live axle, semi-elliptic leaf
Brakes	Drum/drum	Drum/drum	Drum/drum	Drum/drum
Wheelbase	105in	109in	106in	100in
L x W x H	181 x 67 x 60	181 x 68 x 54	184 x 70 x 55	174 x 63 x 58
Weight	2490lb	2352lb	2744lb	2576lb
Tyre size	6.40 x 13	6.00 x 13	5.90 x 14	5.90 x 14
Max speed	84mph	90mph	98mph	82mph
0–60mph	17.9	19.9	14.1	18.6
Economy	28mpg	24–28mpg	19–25mpg	22–28mpg
Price	£1169 Sp sed/£1263 sw	£1256 std/£1318 dx sed	£1299 man/£1435 auto	£1130 man sed
Heater/demister	Option	Option	Option	Standard
Floor material	Rubber mats	Rubber mats	Rubber mats	Rubber mats
Radio	Option	Option	Option	Option
Internal bonnet lock	No	No	No	Yes
Windscreen washers	Option	Option	Option	Yes
Windscreen wipers	Vacuum	Vacuum	Electric	Electric
Reversing lights	No	No	No	Yes

WOLSELEY 24/80 V HOLDEN PREMIER V FORD FALCON FUTURA V CHRYSLER VALIANT REGAL

	WOLSELEY 24/80	HOLDEN EH PREMIER	FORD FALCON XL FUTURA	CHRYSLER AP5 VALIANT REGAL
Engine bore x stroke	6-cyl 76.2 x 88.9mm	6-cyl 90.5 x 76.2mm	6-cyl 88.9 x 74.7mm	6-cyl 86.3 x 104.7mm
Capacity	2433cc	2934cc	2786cc	3688cc
Power/rpm	85/4350	115/4000	101/4400	145/4000
Torque/rpm	123/1650	175/1600	156/2400	215/2400
Transmission	3-sp man, 3-sp auto	3-sp auto	3-sp auto	3-sp auto
Suspension-front	Wishbones, coil springs	Wishbones, coil springs	Wishbones, coil springs	Wishbones, torsion bars
-rear	Live axle, semi-elliptic leaf	Live axle, semi-elliptic leaf	Live axle, semi-elliptic leaf	Live axle, semi-elliptic leaf
Brakes	Drum/drum	Drum/drum	Drum/drum	Drum/drum
Wheelbase	100in	105in	109.5in	106in
L x W x H	174 x 63 x 58	191 x 68 x 58	181 x 70 x 54	186 x 69 x 55
Weight	2595lb	2688lb	2296lb	2860lb
Tyre size	5.90 x 14	6.40 x 13	6.50 x 13	6.50 x 14
Max speed	82mph	89mph	87mph	89mph
0–60mph	18.6 (man) 22.6 (auto)	15.9	15.0	13.5
Economy	22–28mpg	18–24	23–28mpg	18–24mpg
Price	£1280 man/ £1395 auto	£1420 sed/ £1509 sw	£1370 sed	£1498 (sed)/ £1598 sw
Heater/demister	Yes, with fan	Yes, with fan	Option	Yes
Floor carpets	Front and rear	Front and rear	Front and rear	Front and rear
Front seats	Individual, reclining	Individual, reclining	Individual	Bench, armrest
Wood trimming	Yes, burr walnut	No	No	No
Leather upholstery	Yes	No	No	No
Windscreen washers	Yes	Yes	Option	Yes
Internal bonnet lock	Yes	Yes	No	No
Whitewall tyres	No	Yes	Yes	Yes
Child proof locks	Yes	No	No	No
Cigarette lighter	Yes	Yes	No	Yes
Boot light	Yes	Yes	No	Yes
Reversing lights	Yes	Yes	No	Yes

CHRYSLER VALIANT PACER V HOLDEN TORANA GTR V FORD FALCON GT V HOLDEN MONARO HK GTS327

	CHRYSLER VALIANT VF PACER	HOLDEN TORANA LC GTR	FORD FALCON XT GT	HOLDEN MONARO HK GTS327
Engine bore x stroke	6-cyl 86.5 x 105mm	6-cyl 85.7 x 76.2mm	V8 101.6 x 76.2mm	V8 101.6 x 82.55
Capacity	3688cc	2640cc	4934cc	5343cc
Power/rpm	175/4500	125/4800	230/4800	250/4800
Torque/rpm	220/2500	150/2800	310/3800	325/3200
Transmission	3-sp manual, all synchro	4-sp man all synchro	4-sp man, 3-sp auto	4-sp manual
Suspension-front	Wishbones, torsion bars	Wishbones, coil springs	Wishbones, coil springs	Wishbones, coil springs
-rear	Live axle, semi-elliptic leaf	Live axle, 4-links, coil springs	Live axle, semi-elliptic leaf	Live axle, semi-elliptic leaf
Brakes	Disc/drum	Disc/drum	Disc/drum	Disc/drum
Wheelbase	108in	100in	111in	111in
L x W x H	192 x 70 x 57	173 x 63 x 53	185 x 74 x 54	184 x 72 x 54
Weight	2912lb	2240lb	3184lb	2912lb
Tyre size	7.35 x 14	B70H 13	ER70 H 14	D70 x 14
Max speed	107mph	105mph	123mph	115mph
0–60mph	10.5	10.6	8.5	7.8
Economy	20–26mpg	22–28mpg	18–22mpg	15–18mpg
Price	$2798	$2778	$4200	$3790
Heater/demister	Extra	Extra	Yes	Extra
Floor material	Rubber mats	Rubber mats	Carpets	Rubber mats
Front seats	Tombstone buckets	Buckets	Buckets	Buckets
Wood trimming	No	No	No	No
Leather upholstery	No	No	No	No
Windscreen washers	Yes	Yes	Yes	Yes
Windscreen wipers	Electric 2-sp	Electric 2-sp	Electric 2-sp	Electric 2-sp
Internal bonnet lock	Yes	Yes	Yes	Yes
Childproof rear doors	No	No	No	No
Cigarette lighter	Yes	Yes	Yes	Yes
Boot light	No	No	No	No
Reversing lights	Yes	Yes	Yes	Yes
Radio	Extra	Extra	Extra	Extra
Exterior door mirror	No	Yes	No	No
Door courtesy lights	Yes	Yes	Yes	Yes

CHRYSLER VIP V FORD FAIRLANE V HOLDEN BROUGHAM

	FORD FAIRLANE/500	HOLDEN BROUGHAM	CHRYSLER VIP
Engine bore x stroke	6-cyl 93.4 x 79.2mm 200cid V8 101.6 x 72.9 289cid	V8 98.4 x 82.55mm 307cid V8 101.6 x 77.8mm 308cid	V8 92.2 x 84mm 273cid V8 99.3 x 84mm 318cid
Capacity	3268cc (6); 4722cc (V8)	5020cc / 5038cc	4460cc / 5210cc
Power/rpm	121/4400; 200/4400	210/4600; 240/4800	195/4400; 230/4400
Torque/rpm	190/2400; 282/2400	300/2400; 315/3000	265/2000; 340/2400
Transmission	3-sp man/3-sp auto	2-sp Powerglide automatic	3-sp Torqueflite automatic
Suspension-front	Wishbones, coil springs	Wishbones, coil springs	Wishbones, torsion bars
-rear	Live axle, semi-elliptic leaf	Live axle, semi-elliptic leaf	Live axle, semi-elliptic leaf
Brakes	Drum/drum; Disc/drum boost	Disc/drum vac boost	Disc/drum vac boost
Wheelbase	116in	111in	108in VE/ 112in VF
L x W x H	196 x 75 x 55	192 x 71 x 55	192/196 x 70 x 57
Weight	2985lb (6), 3215lb (V8)	3248lb	3248lb
Tyre size	6.95 x 14	7.35 x 14	7.35 x 14
Max speed	95mph/104mph	104mph	108mph
0–60mph	12.2/10.7	10.8	11.7
Economy	14–19mpg	14–18mpg	11–18mpg
Price	$3141 base/$3590 base	$3988	$3998
Air conditioning	Optional	Optional	Optional
Heater/demister	Yes	Yes	Yes
Electric windows	Option	Optional	No
Exterior door mirrors	Yes, driver's side	Yes, driver's side	Yes, driver's side
Prismatic rear view mirror	No	No	Yes
Carpets	Yes	Yes	Yes, interior and boot
Reclining front seats	Yes	Optional	Yes
Interior bonnet lock	Yes	Yes	No
Door courtesy lights	All 4 doors	All 4 doors	All 4 doors
Boot light	No	Yes	Yes
Child proof locks	No	No	No
Audio system	Optional	Optional	Optional
Electric windscreen washers	Yes	Yes	Yes
Windscreen wipers	2-speed, electric	2-speed electric	2-speed electric
Seatbelts	Yes, lap	Yes, lap/sash	Yes, lap/sash

HOLDEN TORANA HB V RIVALS

	Holden Torana HB	Toyota Corolla	Datsun 1200	Mazda 1200	Morris 1100
Engine bore x stroke	77.7 x 61mm	75 x 61mm	73 x 70mm	70 x 76mm	64.56 x 83.72mm
Capacity	1157cc	1077cc	1171cc	1169cc	1098cc
Power/rpm	69/5800	60/6000	69/6000	73/6000	50/5100
Torque/rpm	68/4200	62/3800	70/3600	72/3500	60/2500
Transmission	4-sp man, RWD	4-sp man, RWD	4-sp man, RWD	4-sp man, RWD	4-sp man, FWD
Suspension-front	Wishbones, coils	MacP strut, coils	MacP strut, coils	MacP strut, coils	Hydrolastic
-rear	Live axle, links, coils	Live axle, semi-elliptic leaf	Live axle, semi-elliptic leaf	Live axle, semi-elliptic leaf	Hydrolastic
Brakes	Disc/drum	Drum/drum	Drum/drum	Drum/drum	Disc/drum
Wheelbase	95.8in	90in	90.6in	89in	93.5in
L x W x H	161 x 63 x 53	151 x 58 x 54	151 x 59 x 54	152 x 59 x 55	145 x 60 x 53
Weight	1755lb	1648lb	1576lb	1680lb	1952lb
Tyre size	6.20 x 12	6.00 x 12	6.00 x 12	6.00 x 12	6.20 x 12
Max speed	82mph	86mph	87mph	85mph	77mph
0–60mph	15.6 secs	15.1 secs	16.0	14.7 secs	24.2 secs
Economy	30mpg	35mpg	36mpg	36mpg	33mpg
Price	$2110	$1748	$1999	$1899	$2180

HOLDEN TORANA LC V RIVALS

	Holden Torana LC4	Holden Torana LC6	Ford Cortina 1600	Datsun 1600	Morris 1500
Engine bore x stroke	77.7 x 61mm	85.72 x 76.2mm	80.9 x 70.62mm	83 x 73.3mm	76.2 x 81.28mm
Capacity	1157cc	2630cc	1599cc	1595cc	1485cc
Power/rpm	69/5800	114/4400	75/5000rpm	96/5600	73/5500
Torque/rpm	68/4200	157/2000	97/2500	99.8/3600	81/4000
Transmission	4-sp man, RWD	4-sp man, RWD	4-sp man, RWD	4-sp man, RWD	4-sp man, FWD
Suspension-front	Wishbones, coils	Wishbones, coils	MacP strut, coils	MacP strut, coils	Hydrolastic
-rear	Live axle, links, coil springs	Live axle, links, coil springs	Live axle, semi-elliptic leaf	IRS semi-trailing arms, coil springs	Hydrolastic
Brakes	Disc/drum	Disc/drum	Disc/drum	Disc/drum	Disc/drum
Wheelbase	95.8in	100in	98in	95.3in	93.5in
L x W x H	161 x 63 x 53	172 x 63 x 53	168 x 65 x 54	162 x 61 x 55	146 x 60 x 53
Weight	1770lb	2120lb	2120lb	2016lb	1952lb
Tyre size	6.20 x 12	A78L 13	5.60 x 13	5.60 x 13	6.20 x 12
Max speed	82mph	92mph	90mph	91mph	88mph
0–60mph	15.6 secs	15.3 secs	15.8 secs	13.1 secs	15.4 secs
Economy	30mpg	30mpg	31mpg	32mpg	30mpg
Price	From $1979	From $2283	$2260	$2050	$2150

FORD ZEPHYR MK III V FORD FALCON XL V VAUXHALL CRESTA

	ZEPHYR Mk III	FALCON XL	CRESTA
Engine	6-cylinder in-line, OHV, 2553cc	6-cylinder in-line OHV, 2365cc/2778cc	6-cylinder, in-line, OHV, 2651cc
Bore x stroke	82.55 x 79.5mm	88.9 x 63.5mm/88.9 x 74.6mm	82.55 x 82.55
Power	98bhp at 4750rpm	90bhp at 4200rpm/101 at 4400rpm	113bhp at 4800rpm
Torque	135 lb/ft at 2000rpm	138 lb/ft at 2000rpm/156 lb-ft at 2400	148lb-ft at 2400rpm
Transmission	4-sp all-synchro man; B-W 3-sp auto	3-sp man; 2-sp Fordomatic auto	3-sp man all-synchromesh; 3-sp Hydramatic
Wheelbase	107in	109in	107.5in
Length	180.35in	182in	182in
Width	69in	70in	70in
Height	57.5in	54.5in	56.4in
Weight	2745lb	2448lb	2734lb
Brakes	Disc/drum with boost	Drums all round	Disc/drum with boost
Price	£1369 manual; £1499 automatic	£1125 man; £1282	£1356 Velox/£1571 Cresta
0–60mph	14.9 secs	18.0 secs	19.3 (auto)
Maximum speed	98.7mph	86.2mph	91mph
Windscreen wipers	Electric 2-speed	Vacuum	Electric 2-speed
Windscreen washers	Option	No	Yes
Heater/demister	Option	Option	Yes
Full door upholstery	Yes	No	Yes
Door armrests	Yes	Front only on Deluxe	Yes
Child proof door locks	Yes	No	Yes
Internal bonnet lock	Yes	No	Yes
Radio	Extra	Extra	Extra
Reversing lights	No	No	Yes
Front seats	Bench	Bench	Bench
Floor material	Carpet	Rubber mats	Carpet
Boot light	No	No	No

FORD ANGLIA V RIVALS

	Price £	Engine	Capacity	Trans	Power	Wheelbase	LxWxH Inches	Weight	Max speed mph	0–50mph	Economy
Ford Anglia	951	4-cyl OHV	997cc	4-sp man	39/5000	90in	154x57x56	1642lb	77	15.9	**38–48**
Triumph Herald	970	4-cyl OHV	948cc 1147cc	4-sp man	39/4500 43/4500	91in	153x60x52	1708lb	76	16.1	32–42
VW Beetle	971	4-cyl OHV Boxer	1192cc	4-sp man	40/3600	94.5in	160x60x59	1748lb	73	17.3	39–40
Austin A40 Countryman	925	4-cyl OHV	948cc	4-sp man	34/4750	83in	144x59x56	1718lb	73	18.9	36–46
Fiat 600D	798	4-cyl OHV	767cc	4-sp man	32/4800	78in	127x54x55	1232lb	73	18.1	40–50
Hillman Husky	979	4-cyl OHV	1390cc	4-sp man	43/4000	86in	149x60x62	1988lb	70	16.6	28–38
Skoda Octavia	899 Std 969 Deluxe	4-cyl OHV	1221cc	4-sp man	43/4600	94.5in	160x63x56	2016lb	80	12.8	32–42
Renault Dauphine	964	4-cyl OHV	845cc	3-sp man	38/5000	89in	155x60x57	1456lb	72	18.4	37–47

MORRIS 1100/1100S V RIVALS

	MORRIS 1100/S	**FIAT 1100**	**HILLMAN MINX**	**FORD CORTINA**	**VW Beetle**	**RENAULT R8**
Engine type	In-line four OHV	In-line four OHV	In-line four OHV	In-line four OHV	Flat four OHV	In-line four OHV
Capacity	1098cc/1275cc	1089cc	1592cc	1198cc	1192cc	956cc
Power bhp	50/5100;63/5500	55/5000	56/4100	48/4800	40/3900	48/5200
Torque lb-ft	60/2500;70/2500	53/3500	86/2400	63/2700		55/2500
Wheelbase in	93	92	96	98	94	89
Overall length in	146	154	161	168	160	157
Kerb weight lb	1904lb/1980lb	1975lb	2212lb	1764lb		1568lb
Maximum speed	76.5/87mph	84mph	83mph	78.5mph	70mph	79.4
0–60mph	24.2 secs/16.5	18.8 secs	19.1 secs	22.8 secs	25.0 secs	
Economy	34–42mpg	35–40mpg	28–34mpg	32–40mpg	30–36mpg	36–42mpg
Price	£960/$2075	£989	£999	£973	£971	£998

HILLMAN SUPER MINX V VAUXHALL VICTOR V VW 1500 V RENAULT 16 V HUMBER VOGUE

	HILLMAN SUPER MINX	VAUXHALL VICTOR, VX 4/90	VW 1500, 1500S	RENAULT 16, 16 TS	HUMBER VOGUE SPORTS
Engine type	In-line four OHV	In-line four OHV	Air-cooled 4-cyl boxer OHV	In-line four OHV	In-line four OHV
Capacity	1592cc	1594cc	1493cc	1470cc/1565cc	1592cc
Power bhp	66/4800	69/4000; 82/5200	53/4000; 66/4800	63/5000; 87/5750	84/5000
Torque lb-ft	84/2800	93/2800; 92/2800	78/2000; 82/3000	78/2800; 86/3500	91/3500
Wheelbase in	101in	100in	94in	107/109.5in	101in
Overall length ins	165in	173in	166in	168in	165in
Kerb weight lb	2296lb	2106lb; 2133lb	1910lb; 2072lb	2271lb	2352lb
Maximum speed	78mph	84mph; 92mph	83mph; 80mph	90mph; 101mph	92mph
0–60mph	21.7 secs	20.8; 16.0 secs	17.2; 19.8 secs	Xxx; 12.1 secs [???]	
Economy	24–32	27–34mpg	28–36mpg	26–32mpg	24–32mpg
Price	£1109 man /£1239 auto	£1039 man sed £1330 VX 4/90	£1199; £1299	$2540 / $2885	£1299
Heater/demister	Option	Option	Yes	Yes	Yes
Windscreen wipers	Electric 1-sp	Electric 1-sp	Electric 1-sp	Electric 2-sp	Electric 1-sp
Windscreen washers	No	No	Yes	Yes	Yes
Front seats	Bench	Bench/buckets	Buckets	Buckets	Buckets
Floor material	Rubber mats	Rubber mats	Rubber mats	Carpet	Carpet
Radio	Extra	Extra	Extra	Extra	Extra
Reversing Lights	No	No	No	Yes	Yes
Boot light	No	No	No	Yes	No
Childproof rear door locks	No	No	No	Yes	No
Cigarette lighter	No	No/yes	No	Yes	Yes
Internal bonnet lock	No	No	Yes	Yes	Yes

AUSTIN 1800 V RIVALS

	Austin 1800	Holden EH Special	Ford Falcon XL	Chrysler Valiant	Austin Freeway	Peugeot 404
Engine type	In-line 4, OHV	In-line 6, OHV	In-line 6, OHV	In-line 6, OHV	In-line 6, OHV	In-line 4, OHV
Capacity	1798cc	2934cc (179cid)	2786cc (170cid)	3688cc (245cid)	2433cc	1618cc
Power bhp	84/5300	115/4000	101/4400	145/4000	80/4350	76/5000
Torque lb-ft	99/2100	175/1600	156/2400	215/2800	123/1650	96/2500
Wheelbase in	106	105	109.5	106.5	100	104
O/length in	164	177	182	184	174	174
Kerb weight lb	2520lb	2544lb	2448lb	2604lb	2576lb	2262lb
Maximum speed	84mph	92mph	86mph	99mph	82mph	90mph
0–60mph	17.6 secs	15.9 (auto)	15.3 (auto)	11.5 secs	18.6 secs	17.7 secs
Economy	25–30mpg	22–26	22–26	20–26mpg	22–28mpg	26–34mpg
Price	£1165	£1111	£1125	£1255	£1130	£1275
Brakes	Disc/drum	Drum/drum	Drum/drum	Drum/drum	Drum/drum	Drum/drum
Heater/demister	Yes	Option	Option	Option	Yes	Yes
Windscreen wipers	Electric 1-sp	Electric 2-sp	Vacuum	Electric 2-sp	Electric 1-sp	Electric 2-sp
Windscreen washers	Yes	No	No	Yes	Yes	Yes
Front Seats	Bucket, recline	Bench	Bench	Bench	Bench	Bucket, recline
Floor material	Carpet	Rubber mats	Rubber mats	Rubber mats		
Radio	Extra	Extra	Extra	Extra	Extra	Extra
Reversing lights	No	No	No	Yes	No	Yes
Boot light	Yes	No	No	No	Yes	Yes
Childproof door locks	Yes	No	No	No	Yes	Yes
Internal bonnet lock	Yes	Yes	No	No	Yes	Yes
Cigarette lighter	No	No	No		No	No
Driver's side door mirror	No	No	No	No	No	No

VAUXHALL VIVA AND ITS RIVALS

Make	Price £	Type	Capacity	BHP/rpm	Comp	Torque	Gears/ synchro	Wheelbase	Dimensions L x W x H	Tyres	Weight
Vauxhall Viva	853	2-dr, rwd	1057cc	44/5200	8.5:1	56/3000	4/4	91.5in	155x59x53.5	5.50x12	1624lb
Datsun Bluebird	974	4-dr, rwd	1189cc	60/5000	8.2:1	64/3600	3/3	93.8in	157x 59 x 55	5.60x13	1980lb
Fiat 1100	989	4-dr, rwd	1089cc	55/4800	7.9:1	52/3200	4/3	92in	155x57.5x58.5	5.20x14	1940lb
Ford Cortina	869	2-, 4-dr, rwd	1198cc	53/5000	8.7:1	68/2700	4/4	98in	168x62x54	5.20x13	1744lb
Hillman Imp	799	2-dr, rwd	875cc	42/5000	10.0:1	52/2800	4/4	82in	139x60x54	5.20x10	1512lb
Morris 850	775	2-dr, fwd	848cc	34/5500	8.3:1	44/2900	4/3	80in	120x55x53	5.20x10	1320lb
Morris 1100	960	4-dr, fwd	1098cc	50/5100	8.5:1	60/2500	4/3	93.5in	146x60x56	5.50x12	1904lb
Renault R8	998	4-dr, rwd	956cc	48/5200	8.5:1	55/2500	4/4	89in	157x58x53	5.20x15	1599lb
Toyota Tiara	915	4-dr, rwd	1453cc	65/4500	8.0:1	84/3000	3/3	94in	157x58x56	5.60x13	2165lb
Triumph 12/50	999	2-dr, rwd	1147cc	43/4500	8.0:1	61/2250	4/3	91in	153x60x52	5.20x13	1709lb
Volkswagen 1200	819	2-dr, rwd	1192cc	40/3600	7.0:1	61/2000	4/4	94in	160x60x59	5.60x15	1652lb

SMALL FAMILY CARS COMPARED

	Hillman Minx	Morris Major Elite	VW Beetle 1300	Triumph Herald	Toyota Corona 1500	Datsun Bluebird 1200	Simca Aronde
Engine type	4-cyl OHV	4-cyl OHV	4-cyl air-cooled boxer	4-cyl OHV	4-cyl OHV	4-cyl OHV	4-cyl OHV
Capacity	1592cc	1622cc	1285cc	1147cc	1490cc	1189cc	1290cc
Power bhp	62/4400	55/4250	50/4600	51/5200	74/5000	60/5000	52/4800
Torque lb-ft	86/2500	91/2300	69/2600	63/2600	85/2600	64/3600	69/2500
Wheelbase in	96in	92in	94in	91in	95in	94in	96in
Overall length in	161in	161in	160in	153in	160in	157in	165in
Kerb weight lb	2187lb	2065lb	1820lb	1790lb	2025lb	2038lb	2072lb
Maximum speed	86mph	75mph	74mph	78mph	90mph	78mph	81mph
0–60mph	18.5 sec	22.7 sec	22.2 sec	22.3 sec	14.8 sec	23.0 sec	24.5 sec
Economy	26–34mpg	26–34mpg	30–38mpg	30–38mpg	28–34mpg	32–38mpg	28–36mpg
Price	£999	£940	$1838	£989	£979	£974	£1045
Heater/demister	Extra	Yes	Yes	Extra	Yes, with fan	Yes	Yes
Windscreen wipers	Electric 1sp	Electric 1sp	Electric 1sp	Electric 1sp	Electric 2sp	Electric 2sp	Electric 1sp
Windscreen washers	No	Yes	Yes	No	Yes	Yes	Yes
Reversing lights	No	No	No	No	Yes	Yes	No
Boot light	No	No	No	No	No	No	No
Driver's door mirror	No	No	No	No	No	No	No
Childproof door locks	No	No	No	No	No	No	No
Front seats	Bench	Bench	Bucket	Bucket	Bench	Bench	bench
Floor material	Rubber mats	Rubber mats	Rubber mats	Rubber mats	Rubber mats	Rubber mats	Rubber mats
Internal bonnet lock	No	Yes	No	No	Yes	Yes	No

£1000 FAMILY CAR COMPARISON

From *Wheels* Sep r 1963

Make	Price	Size	Equipment	Power	Performance	Suspension	Brakes
Volkswagen 1200	£953	2 doors 4 seats	Heater/demister, washers	4-cyl OHV boxer,40bhp 61 lb-ft 1192cc	73.4mph 0–50 in 13.2 sec	All independent torsion bars	Drum
Ford Cortina 1200	£948	2 doors 4 seats		4-cyl OHV, 48.5bhp 63 lb-ft 1198cc	77mph 0–50 in 13.9 sec	MacP + coils front, semi-elliptic rear	Drum
Vauxhall Victor	£960	4 doors 5 seats		4-cyl OHV, 56.3bhp 85 lb-ft 1508cc	81mph 0–50 in 17.0 sec	Wishbone + coils front, semi-elliptic rear	Drum
Morris Major Elite	£940	4 doors 5 seats	Heater/demister, washers	4-cyl OHV, 58bhp 91 lb-ft 1622cc	75mph 0–50 in 14.5 sec	Wishbone + torsion bar front, semi-elliptic rear	Drum
Simca Aronde	£999	4 doors 4 seats	Heater/demister, washers, layback front seats	4-cyl OHV, 52bhp 69 lb-ft 1290cc	77mph 0–50 in 14.5 sec	Wishbone + coil front, semi-elliptic rear	Drum
Renault R8	£998	4 doors 4 seats	Heater/demister, washers	4-cyl OHV, 42bhp 55 lb-ft 956cc	75mph 0–50 in 16.1 sec	All independent coil springs	Drum
Fiat 1100	£952	4 doors 4 seats	Heater/demister, washers, layback front seats	4-cyl OHV, 55bhp 55 lb-ft 1089cc	84mph 0–50 in 13.2 sec	Wishbone + coils front, semi-elliptic rear	Drum
Hillman Minx	£999	4 doors 5 seats		4-cyl OHV, 56bhp 86 lb-ft 1592cc	76mph 0–50 in 16.7 sec	Wishbone + coils front, semi-elliptic rear	Drum
Skoda Octavia	£859	2 doors 4 seats	Heater/demister	4-cyl OHV, 47bhp 64 lb-ft 1089cc	84mph 0–50 in 14.7 sec	Wishbone + coils front, transverse leaf rear IRS	Drum
Datsun Bluebird	£946	4 doors 4 seats	Heater/demister, washers, tools	4-cyl OHV, 60bhp 69 lb-ft 1189cc	78mph 0–50 in 12.7 sec	Wishbone + coils front, semi-elliptic rear	Drum
Triumph Herald	£885	2 doors 4 seats	Washers	4-cyl OHV, 43bhp 60 lb-ft 1147cc	77mph 0–50 in 16.1 sec	Wishbone + coils front, transverse leaf rear IRS	Drum
Toyota Tiara	£915	4 doors 5 seats	Washers, tools	4-cyl OHV, 65bhp 86 lb-ft 1453cc	79mph 0–50 in 12.7 sec	Wishbone + torsion bar front, semi-elliptic rear	Drum

REGISTRATION FIGURES FOR AUSTRALIAN-MADE CARS 1960–1969*

*Figures taken from Motor Manual and the Bureau of Statistics by Robert Simpson

Make	**1960**	**1961**	**1962**	**1963**	**1964**	**1965**	**1966**	**1967**	**1968**	**1969**
Austin	10,728	5,470	8,104	5,972	3,632	2,950	10,437	10,920	12,668	11,426
Chevrolet	1,864	1,326	1,533	2,149	2,024	1,544	1,448	1,091	913	499
Chrysler	2,596	1,081	9,408	16,196	28,754	34,866	34,683	38,051	39,229	42,949
Citroën			437	334	208	120	98			
Datsun	11	401	1,250	2,644	4,269	4,866	4,509	9,910	12,717	15,625
De Soto	43									
Dodge	682	573	711	1,020	1,031	1,058				
Ford	38,306	33,704	52,057	52,025	49,865	56,554	57,419	69,092	70,642	81,377
Goggomobil	409	251	57	11	1					
Hillman	10,141	4,482	6,854	6,131	8,733	5,209	4,933	7,959	11,157	14,082
Holden	100,927	86,978	109,563	131,079	130,937	119,502	109,205	109,971	126,766	136,478
Humber	1,455	1,436	1,450	3,174	2,851	3,141	1,118	337	307	45
Lloyd	279	86	77	13	6		2			
Mercedes-Benz	1,479	1,132	1,157	1,226						
MG	605	348	290	466	818	921	1,089	1,316	1,420	1,449
Morris	12,778	12,383	25,999	30,667	36,062	35,593	26,673	26,443	24,220	22,417
NSU	77	151	238	127	107	52	29			
Peugeot	2,274	1,202	1,468	1,171	610	1,177	1,099	1,267	1,469	1,852
Plymouth	62	9		34	18	19	3			
Pontiac	352	435	608	828	898	688	684	729	493	396
Rambler	129	141	460	1,284	1,738	1,764	1,734	1,630	1,018	672
Renault	1,416	997	1,443	1,504	959	924	1,211	2,687	3,636	4,852
Simca	7,747	3,603	4,989	3,724	1,907	364	12	1		
Standard	3,220	1,674	844	466	79					
Studebaker	199	718	1,188	1,414	974	591				
Toyota			5	901	5,720	10,562	14,438	19, 132	25,423	25,666
Triumph	6,930	4,302	1,212	1,282	1,382	1,209				
Vauxhall	6,581	4,699	5,623	6,425	8,418	8,414	5,692	3,101	10	
Volkswagen	24,634	15,118	21,438	24,346	28,882	23,266	16,246	15,604	12,490	10,979
Wolseley	1,877	1,039	3,169	3,978	2,590	1,723	634	13	10	
Zeta				127	120	108	8			
Willys				16	3	7	33	34	50	
TOTAL										

RAMBLER ASSEMBLY – AUSTRALIAN MOTOR INDUSTRIES 1964–1977

Rambler Ambassador:	sedan	1028	
	wagon	256	
Rambler American	sedan	2453	(1964–69)
Rambler Ambassador	sedan	45	(1964–70)
Rambler Classic	sedan	3012	(1964–66)
Rambler Rebel	sedan	2678	(1967–71)
Rambler Matador X	coupe	80	(1974)
Rambler Javelin	coupe	229	(1968–74)
Rambler Hornet	sedan	1825	(1970–75)
AMX	coupe	24	(1969)

Figures provided by Jason Chaplin, AMC/Rambler Club

AMI-TOYOTA PRODUCTION FIGURES

Year	Tiara	Crown	Corona	Corolla	Total
1963	1,082				1,082
1964	596				596
1965	6		4,181		4187
1966		2	7,344		7346
1967		2,897	7,788		10,685
1968		5,336	7,200	2,590	15,126
1969		5,059	7,417	6,052	18,528
Total	1,684	13,294	33,930	8,642	57,550

AUSTIN HEALEY SPRITE/MG MIDGET PRODUCTION*

A-H Sprite Mk I	894	Mk I non O/D	Apr '63 – Jul '68	5059
A-H Sprite Mk II	326	Mk I O/D	Jun '67 – Jul '68	200
A-H Sprite Mk IIA	976	Mk II O/D	Aug '68 – Dec '68	257
A-H Sprite Mk III	600	Mk II O/D	Dec 68 – Aug 70	1519
A-H Sprite Mk IIIA	800	Mk II non O/D	Sep 68 – Aug 70	360
MG Midget Mk I		Mk II Automatic	Sep 68-Aug 70	156
MG Midget Mk II	1184 (Mk I and Mk II)			
TOTAL:	4780	TOTAL		7551

*Figures provided by Craig Watson, publisher *The BMC Experience* magazine

MG B ANNUAL PRODUCTION

1963	444
1964	802
1965	915
1966	1084
1967	1228
1968	1026
1969	1089
TOTAL	6588

RENAULT PRODUCTION

1960	1300
1961	750
1962	1800
1963	1260
1964	650
1965	860
1966	1330
1967	3300
1968	5210
1969	5178

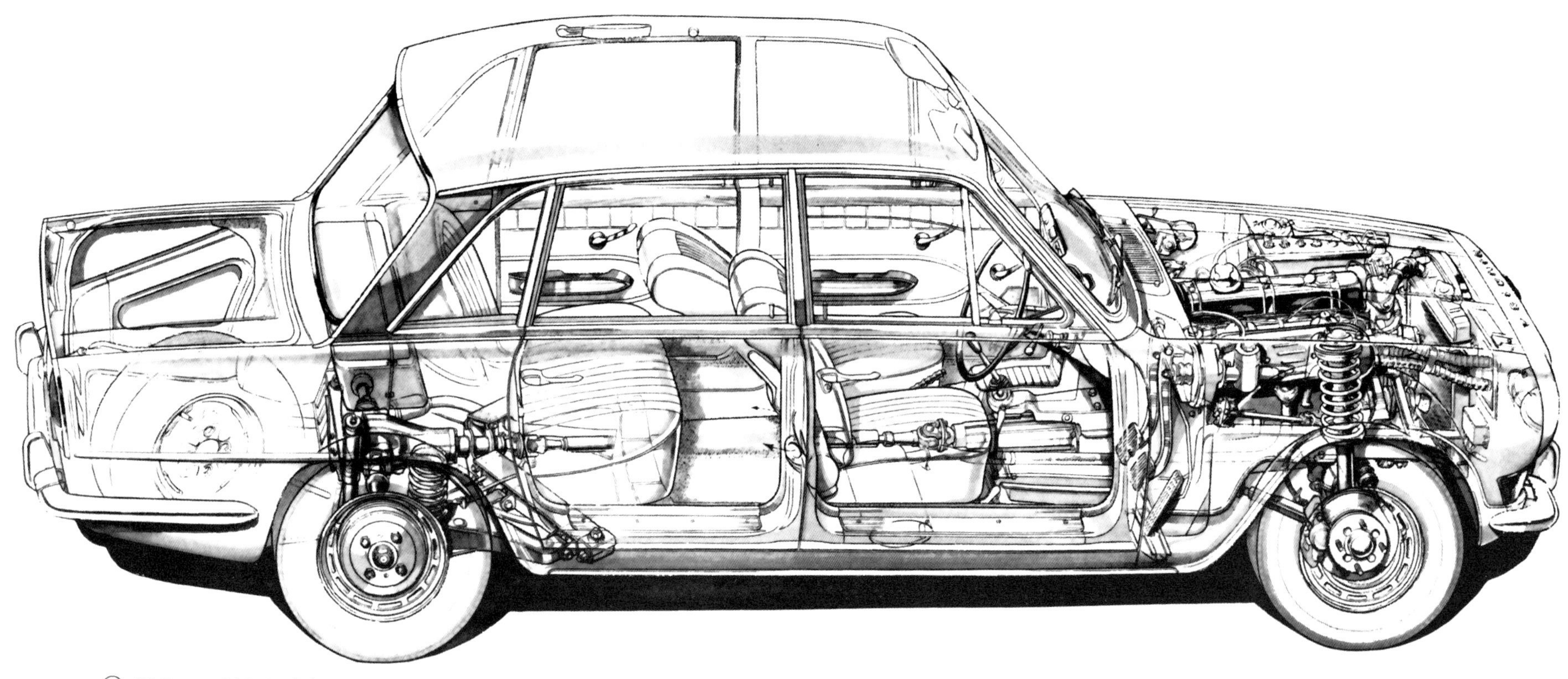

BIBLIOGRAPHY

Motoring magazines from the period: *Wheels, Modern Motor, Motor Manual, The Autocar, The Motor, The BMC Experience*
Australian Car Trials, Bill Tuckey, Golden Press, 1989
Automobiles Australia, Australian Motor Sports Publication, 1960
Automobiles Australia, various, Wylie Publishing, 1960
Cars of the Fifties and Sixties, Michael Sedgwick, Colporteur Press, 1983
Great Ideas in Motion, Gavin Farmer, Ilinga Books, 2010
Jeep, Steve Statham, MBI Publishing Company, 2001
Knowing Australian Volkswagens, Dave Long & Phil Matthews, Bookworks, 1993
Land Rover Series One 1948–1958, Brooklands Books, 1991
Land Rover: Series One to Freelander, Graham Robson, The Crowood Press, 2003
Land Rover: The Early Years, Tony Hutchings, Tony Hutchings Publishing, 1986
Land Rover: The Formative Years 1947–1967, John Smith, Land Rover Series One Club, 2009
The Cars of BMC, Graham Robson, MRP, 1999
The Cars of the Rootes Group, Graham Robson, Mercian Press, 2007
The Heart of the Lion: 50 Years of the Australian Holden, J Wright, Allen & Unwin, 1998
The Holden Heritage, various publications, General Motors-Holden Public Affairs Department
True Blue, 75 Years of Ford in Australia, Bill Tuckey, Focus, 2000
Volkswagen in Australia: The Forgotten Story, Rod & Lloyd Davies, AF Publishing Pty Ltd, 2004
Wheels Across Australia, Pedr Davis, Marque Publishing, 1987

PHOTO CREDITS

Gavin Farmer Library Collection: 8, 9, 13, 17 (top left), 21, 23, 24, 26, 29, 30, 33, 34, 37, 40, 41, 44, 47, 51, 53, 54, 56, 57, 58, 62, 64, 67, 68, 69, 70, 73, 74, 79, 80, 83, 84, 86, 87, 90, 91, 92, 95, 98, 99, 100, 101, 102, 104, 105, 109, 110, 112, 114, 115, 116, 117, 118, 119, 120, 123, 127, 128, 130, 138, 140, 141, 142, 144, 145, 146, 148, 149, 150, 156, 158, 160, 162, 163, 164, 165, 167, 168, 171, 172, 174, 176, 177, 195, 196, 200, 201, 202, 204, 205
Brenton Thomas: 186, 187, 188, 189, 192
Daimler Heritage: 124
Ford Motor Co: 35, 36, 43, 44 (lower right), 49
Holden Ltd: 10, 14, 15, 17, 18, 20, 25
The MOTOR: 88
The AUTOCAR: 116, 170
Regie Renault: 178, 179, 181, 182, 185

ABOUT THE AUTHOR

Gavin Farmer has had a lifetime involvement with motorcars one way or another. He bought his first car magazine – *Modern Motor*, September 1959 – while in high school and this began a collection of magazines, books and model cars that occupy a special place in his life today.

He is one of Australia's leading motoring historians and has regularly contributed to such prestigious publications as *Automobile Quarterly, Collectible Automobiles, The Automobile, Bimmer, Sports Car International* and others around the world. In addition he has written many books relating to the post-war Australian motor industry which can be seen by going to the ILINGA BOOKS website at www.ilingabooks.com.au.

From the 70s through to the 90s he worked in the automobile industry in various roles from manufacturing, sales and public relations before turning his talents to writing. His original professional training was for teaching but he was looking for wider challenges in life. To this end he has been a State Manager for a multi-media educational publisher as well as a company that marketed computerised dispensary systems.

All the while he was adding to his knowledge of automobiles, the industry and the many new technologies. A colleague once described him as a "barefoot engineer!"

A man who is passionate about the automobile and its history, Gavin lives with his wife on a small property in the beautiful Adelaide hills where he enjoys occasional drives in his newly restored and quite rare Subaru FF-1.